D0025076

ROOTS
OF
FAILURE

Recent Titles in
Contributions in Political Science
Series Editor: Bernard K. Johnpoll

Puerto Rican Politics in Urban America
James Jennings and Monte Rivera, editors

Making Campaigns Count: Leadership and Coalition-Building in 1980
Darrell M. West

Congressional Television: A Legislative History
Ronald Garay

Khrushchev's Party Reform: Coalition Building and Institutional Innovation
Barbara Ann Chotiner

Macro-Nationalisms: A History of the Pan-Movements
Louis L. Snyder

Prophets of the Left: American Socialist Thought in the Twentieth Century
Robert Hyfler

Decade of Change: The Remaking of Forest Service Statutory Authority during the 1970s
Dennis C. Le Master

Public Opinion and Foreign Policy: America's China Policy, 1949–1979
Leonard A. Kusnitz

Ethnic Groups, Congress, and American Foreign Policy: The Politics of the Turkish Arms Embargo
Paul Y. Watanabe

Jack London—An American Radical?
Carolyn Johnston

The Myth of Inevitable Progress
Franco Ferrarotti

A Philosophy of Individual Freedom: The Political Thought of F. A. Hayek
Calvin M. Hoy

ROOTS OF FAILURE

United States Policy in the Third World

MELVIN GURTOV
RAY MAGHROORI

CONTRIBUTIONS IN POLITICAL SCIENCE, NUMBER 108

Greenwood Press
WESTPORT, CONNECTICUT
LONDON, ENGLAND

Library of Congress Cataloging in Publication Data

Gurtov, Melvin.
Roots of failure.

(Contributions in political science, ISSN 0147-1066 ; no. 108)
Bibliography: p.
Includes index.
1. Developing countries—Foreign relations—United States. 2. United States—Foreign relations—Developing countries. 3. United States—Foreign relations—1945– . I. Maghroori, Ray. II. Title. III. Series.
D888.U6G87 1985 327.73 84-10718
ISBN 0-313-24561-4 (lib. bdg.)

Library of Congress Catalog Card Number: 84-10718
ISBN: 0-313-24561-4
ISSN: 0147-1066

First published in 1984

Greenwood Press
A division of Congressional Information Service, Inc.
88 Post Road West
Westport, Connecticut 06881

Printed in the United States of America

10 9 8 7 6 5 4 3 2 1

For Leigh Anne
For Joyce Bubello and
Michael M. Maghroori

Contents

Tables

ROOTS OF FAILURE

Introduction

> The political development of great peoples is conditioned and determined by their national experiences, but never by the manipulations of foreign powers in their internal affairs.
>
> —George F. Kennan, *Memoirs: 1925–1950*

Studies of intervention are, unfortunately, as timely as this week's news. As these words are being written, the United States has about 1,500 military advisers in Honduras, Guatemala, and El Salvador; supports some 15,000 Nicaraguan *contras* seeking to overthrow their government; and has deployed a large flotilla of naval warships off the Nicaraguan coast. Under Ronald Reagan's leadership, containment of "international communism" has been restored as the centerpiece of foreign policy. America's "Vietnam syndrome," already under criticism in the Carter administration, was officially buried by Reagan, who called the war a "noble cause." Cold war crusading, with a zeal not seen since the days of John Foster Dulles in the 1950s, is again "in" in Washington.

In the following study the authors examine how ideas, institutions, and instruments of the national security state have shaped U.S. policy in the Third World. And since that policy has always been heavily, even decisively, influenced by perceptions of a Soviet threat, U.S. relations with Moscow also receive attention. We use policy toward Iran, Nicaragua, and Vietnam as recent examples, on three continents, of a foreign-policy failure that is long-standing, deepseated, and threatening to the prospects for humane world order.

Just how persistently the idea of intervention has withstood the test of time was brought home when President Reagan addressed the Congress on U.S. policy toward Central America on April 27, 1983. His speech quoted extensively from the original containment speech of Harry Truman in 1947 before the same body. It featured all the old formulas used by previous Presidents to justify a hard-line foreign policy: falling dominoes, military responses to political problems, the need to salvage America's international credibility, the democratic intentions of U.S. friends, and the unredeeming evil of the socialists. Referring to the concerns of the United States, Reagan stated:

> I do not believe that a majority of the Congress or the country is prepared to stand by passively while the people of Central America are delivered to totalitarianism and we ourselves are left vulnerable to new dangers . . . . If we cannot defend ourselves there, we cannot expect to prevail elsewhere. Our credibility would collapse, our alliances would crumble, and the safety of our homeland would be put at jeopardy. We have a vital interest, a moral duty, and a solemn responsibility.[1]

Six months later, U.S. forces, on the pretext of saving American lives, invaded the tiny Caribbean island of Grenada and installed a friendly government.[2] The implications of the invasion were left to be drawn by the Sandinistas in Nicaragua, who already confront open efforts by the U.S. Central Intelligence Agency to overthrow them. For the United States, the invasion—which removed a brutal group of leftist military officers, not on the invitation of any Grenadans but supposedly at the request of several other Caribbean governments—simultaneously extended the scope of "legitimate" interventions and further eroded the principle of self-determination of peoples. For even in Vietnam, U.S. leaders had always insisted we were there because we were invited by its government.

Abuse of the principle of self-determination, one of the most sacred in the American historical experience, is an underlying theme of the book. Self-determination lies at the core of the Declaration of Independence. Appropriately, revolutionary leaders in Vietnam and elsewhere have quoted from the Declaration to justify their actions. Yet American practice has fallen far behind principle. Self-determination has frequently been used by American policymakers to *justify*, rather than limit or prevent, intervention in other countries' affairs. Here is the marriage of the two dominant schools of thought in American foreign policy, Realism and Idealism, that is noted in the next chapter: The mutual supportiveness of power politics and moralism-legalism—principles that are supposed to be antagonistic to one another. The same Woodrow Wilson who argued for the self-determination of peoples after World War I as one way to "make the world safe for democracy," also supported the Allied intervention against the Bolshevik revolution in 1919. And for the same reason: To project American values and institutions abroad in the belief that the only truly liberated peoples are those who live their lives as we do.

And if it be said that such ideological crusades to remold other societies are common to *all* great powers, there is no dispute here. Significant similarities exist in the bureaucratic behavior, value systems, and ideological dispositions of U.S. and Soviet leaderships. Expansion of national influence is a central objective of both; hence, both have sought to create a world hospitable to their political-economic systems and, with respect to the Third World, to maximize their access to, presence in, and advantages from it. On balance, the authors judge (although not within the confines of the present study) that the United States has been more "successful" than the Soviet Union in achieving this objective. But the study emphasizes the overriding negative costs of such success and therefore the need to develop alternative foreign-policy goals that take human needs and the well-being of the entire planet fully into account.

As these opening remarks suggest, we see politics as the crucial ingredient of foreign policy. The international environment surely affects how and when foreign policy is formulated. But the roots of policymaking, including its failures, are to be found in American society—in the convergence of bureaucratic, economic, and strategic interests around core values and ideas (in a word, an ideology) that direct policy toward particular objectives. In this sense, a critical examination of U.S. policies offers an opportunity to reflect on our own institutions and, in general, the American way of life. The first chapter undertakes these tasks.

In the concluding chapter we join with other writers who have broken new ground in foreign-policy analysis by defining a human interest perspective. "National security," that bedrock of traditional analysis, only makes sense in terms of human security, which requires satisfying the basic material and psychological needs of Third World peoples as much as it requires defending peoples in North America from real threats. We do not wish to diminish feelings of national patriotism; but we believe that in a complex and interdependent world we need to reexamine the traditional notion of "national interest" in the context of new socio-economic imperatives of our time. We need to recognize that good intentions do not necessarily produce desirable outcomes. As Charles Horton Cooley pointed out in 1927, "Too long ago we were taught that good will was the same as goodness. We now see that most evil is done by those who mean well. What we urgently want is knowledge—true perception of the workings of each part on every part in the common life of man."[3] A policy of confrontation with some Third World governments and fragile partnerships with others, we find, undermines national no less than global security. The challenge we pose to American, and other big power decision makers, is to break away from Realism-Idealism dogma and construct the kind of foreign-policy agenda that will bring the national interest in line with the interests of the global community.

NOTES

1. For the text of Reagan's speech see *Los Angeles Times*, April 28, 1983, pt. I, p. 1.

2. Probably the best on-the-spot testimony to dispute the Reagan administration's assertion that American medical students in Grenada were in danger from the Marxist leaders' forces was provided by Peter G. Bourne, whose father was vice-chancellor of the medical school. His article, "Was the U.S. Invasion Necessary?" (*Los Angeles Times*, November 6, 1983, pt. IV, p. 1), puts the lie to other of the administration's pretexts for invading, such as that Grenada was becoming a Cuban military base and an outpost of pro-Soviet Marxism.

3. Charles Horton Cooley, *Life and the Student* (New York: Alfred A. Knopf, 1927), p. 116.

1

The Roots of U.S. Policy

THE GLOBAL CRISIS AND U.S. POLICY

Beyond the headline-dominating talk by U.S. officials of Soviet expansionism, limited nuclear war, and "international terrorism" lurks a fact of far greater global consequence: Within less than twenty years an overwhelming majority of the world's population will be on the borderline of survival. Population growth, limitations on food and energy supplies, and ecological imbalances are profoundly shaping the world's political future. By the year 2000, when an estimated 79 percent of the world's population will be living in the underdeveloped countries, we can expect—barring major changes in the global balance of technological, economic, and ultimately political power—to be living in a far more "dehumanized world in which our mutual vulnerability will impose only one command—survival."[1]

Prevailing notions of national and international security seem strangely out of touch with such globally debilitating trends. Leaders of the superpower states debate nuclear strategies while, by United Nations estimates, nearly 1 billion people in the Third World are chronically malnourished. Worldwide military spending now exceeds $600 billion a year, 80 percent of which is by the NATO and Warsaw Pact countries. Arms purchases from these governments and their semi-private contractors make up an ever-increasing proportion of the other 20 percent, which is spent mostly by Third World governments. The United States, with the Soviet Union close behind, sold well over $25 billion in arms in 1982, more than two-thirds to Third World governments despite their staggering international indebtedness, which is approaching $700 billion.[2] In response to UN appeals for minimum pledges by the developed countries of 0.7 percent of gross national product for Third World development assistance, the United States has been giving less than 0.3 percent, while spending over 6 percent of GNP on the military.

Third World regimes share in the responsibility for these distorted priorities. Many of the same Third World leaders who press for a "new international economic order" to improve terms of trade and external investment respond to the basic needs of their peoples with violent repression, sometimes (as in Guatemala) of genocidal proportions. Instead of adopting self-reliant development plans, these leaders are rapidly developing their own arms industries. They have yielded crucial aspects of their economic sovereignty to the decisions of multinational corporations and international banks and lending agencies, in most of which American interests predominate.

Figures for these developments are disturbing. While Third World GNP has risen about 5 percent a year since 1950, its military spending has gone up about 7 percent a year and its imports of major weapons about 8 percent. Moreover, Third World countries now export some 3 percent of the world's arms, with the leading exporters being U.S. allies: Israel, Brazil, Iran (until 1978), Jordan, and South Africa. Meanwhile, spending by Third World governments on health, education, and public welfare research lags well behind military spending. Throughout the underdeveloped world in the 1970s for example, government spending on health and education was a constant 1.2 percent and 3.3 to 3.7 percent, respectively, of GNP, whereas military spending ranged from 5.5 to 6 percent of GNP.

The increasingly rapid slippage of the quality of life on the planet has been amply documented. For example, in 1980 two major studies showed quite clearly the scope of the global crisis: *North-South*, the Report of the Independent Commission on International Development Issues chaired by Willy Brandt, ex-Chancellor of West Germany,[3] and *The Global 2000 Report to the*

President by Jimmy Carter's Council on Environmental Quality and Department of State.[4] Together, these reports make sobering reading; so much so that their implications, while having attracted some attention in scholarly circles around the world, have been largely ignored by U.S. and other developed-country leaders. For example, the international gathering of government leaders at Cancun, Mexico, in 1981 to discuss the Brandt Report achieved only the thinnest veneer of agreement. The conference served mainly as a vehicle for those present to rehearse their own developmental propaganda. Cancun demonstrated anew that national interests and global community and human interests are as far apart as ever.

As for the United States, the response to Third World indebtedness, systematic human rights violations, and overwhelming impoverishment has been in keeping with postwar tradition. The Third World remains an object of U.S. foreign policy for the extraction of profit, valuable resources, and military vantage points and is not recognized as a partner in the search for a mutually beneficial world order. This is understandable in light of the frequently cited fact that the United States, with about 5 percent of the world's population, consumes over 30 percent of the world's product. Such a voracious appetite creates foreign-policy "imperatives," such as intervention to ensure "stability," and "vital interests," such as secure access to sources of energy, all of which leave little time to spend curing underdevelopment. In the Third World as in the United States itself, U.S. government and business leaders assume that the benefits of concentrated wealth and power will eventually trickle down to the poor and the marginalized.

It is no longer enough to make the world safe for democracy. David Rockefeller, head of Chase Manhattan Bank and founder of the Trilateral Commission to ensure cooperative relationships among the major capitalist leaders, is once said to have declared, "The world must be made safe for interdependence."[5] He meant that nationalism in the Third World and barriers to trade in the "First" World hinder the multinational corporations' pursuit of ever-higher profit margins. That pursuit could not take place without active cooperation from U.S. government policymakers, who see their jobs as including the promotion of private investments and arms sales abroad. After all, as Andrew Young, President Carter's UN ambassador and himself a Trilateralist, once said, the "rightful role [of the United States is] as the senior partner in a worldwide corporation."[6]

From these narrow perspectives, Third World countries clearly cannot be viewed in any but threatening terms. In fact, beginning in the Carter administration, changes in Third World social and economic conditions have been considered almost equally as dangerous as the military threat from the Soviet Union. The nationalization of U.S. investments and marketing services; the cartelization of strategic resources, epitomized by the Organization of Petroleum Exporting Countries (OPEC); the rapid growth of populations (about 2 percent a year); and massive refugee movements—these are among the developments in the Third World that U.S. officials and policy consultants consider to be challenges to the national interest. The stakes, for corporations and bureaucratic leaders, are, after all, high. For example:

About one-quarter of total U.S. direct investment abroad, or roughly $40 billion (in 1978), is in the underdeveloped countries. Oil accounts for about 40 percent of that amount.

Corporate profits are significantly higher from overseas investment than from domestic investment, and from Third World investments than from investments elsewhere.

Over 30 percent of U.S. petroleum is imported from Third World countries.

Necessarily, American jobs (one in twenty, in fact) depend on exports to the Third World—for example, about 800,000 in manufacturing and 350,000 in arms sales—at the same time as multinational corporations, in search of cheap, nonunionized labor, are transferring the labor market from the United States to "safer" climates in the Third World.

U.S. agriculture increasingly produces food for export, much of it (about one of every four acres) to Third World countries that once were self-sufficient in staples. By 1985 the U.S. Department of Agriculture estimates that about 90 percent of U.S. farmland will be devoted to export crops for the world as a whole.

U.S. dependence on metals and minerals is extensive and growing. For example, 82 percent of its tin, 88 percent of columbium, 50 percent of manganese, 75 percent of cobalt, and 75 percent of copper come from Third World countries.

U.S. multinational banks have tied up an extraordinary amount of capital in Third World countries. At the end of 1982, the ten largest banks had an exposure of $43.7 billion, equal to 169 percent of their total equity. Indebtedness to these banks, which is compounded by high interest rates and service payments, prevents them from breaking their dependence for capital, technology, and export production on multinational corporations. Third World countries are thus caught in a "debt trap": They must keep borrowing to pay interest and service on previous debts, but as a result they cannot afford necessary imports and domestic social welfare spending. And so long as these countries are trapped, U.S. hopes for a reversal of its massive merchandise trade deficit (at the end of 1983 U.S. imports exceeded exports by about $65 billion) are nil.

To U.S. officials, the human costs of interdependence with Third World markets and resources—in malnutrition, unemployment, and repression abroad and in inflation, lost jobs, and the concentration of economic power at home—are far outweighed by the "Soviet threat." Secretary of State Cyrus Vance implied as much in a March 1980 speech:

> The United States has a direct stake in the economic vitality of developing countries. They are increasingly important as partners in trade—both as markets and sources of supply. And the political effect of their economic stagnation can have serious consequences for us—with major social disruptions, a reversal of progress towards democratic rule and human rights, and new openings for violence and radicalism.[7]

Consequently, investments backed by U.S. military power are believed useful to enhance stability; military aid, to affirm law and order; food shipments, to reward or punish regimes and create new markets—all with the ultimate aim of outdueling the Russians, who are presumed ready and able to move into every "opening" produced by popular discontent. Not accidentally, the major Third World recipients of U.S. military and economic aid since World War II, such as Egypt, South Korea, Iran, Saudi Arabia, and the Philippines, have been among the most politically repressive and economically inequitable societies.

Such deadly logic is the essence of crackpot realism for it contributes to precisely the authoritarianism and political violence it aims to prevent. It also legitimates interventionism and helps to perpetuate racial and national arrogance. Each of these has reached new heights in the Reagan administration. ("New" heights should be distinguished from "unprecedented" heights, since we will see that officials in every postwar administration have held such views.) Concerning interventions, the President's first special assistant for national security affairs, Richard Allen, boldly announced, "To reject the use of military force in the hemisphere is to go beyond the limits of reasonable action. U.S. military power has always been the basis for development of just and humane foreign policy, and it's something we should be proud of."[8] This astounding statement easily rivals the Brezhnev Doctrine in its presumptions of limited sovereignty for Third World states and a right of intervention for great powers in their internal affairs. It is a variation of the doctrine of "just war," which is usually nothing more than a rationalization of crude imperialism. "Our" interventions are moral, limited, and for the benefit of the people whose society falls within the U.S. sphere of influence. Such self-righteousness is a necessary ingredient of U.S. interference in El Salvador, Guatemala, and Nicaragua just as it is of Soviet interference in Afghanistan and Poland. How else to understand Secretary of State Alexander Haig's anguish about communist-supported "international terrorism" but not about capitalist-supported terrorism? Or Reagan's modest assertion in an April 1981 letter to Brezhnev: "May I say there is absolutely no substance to charges that the United States is guilty of imperialism or attempts to impose its will on other countries by use of force"?[9]

Such arrogance sometimes goes further and incorporates racist assumptions. We see this most clearly in an article Jeane Kirkpatrick wrote for *Commentary* magazine just prior to being appointed ambassador to the United Nations in 1981. There she reiterated the long-standing North American argument that Third World peoples are not ready for democracy, hence their authoritarian governments should not be harshly judged; unless, that is, they happen to be governed by radicals. She stated:

> Because the miseries of traditional life are familiar, they are bearable to ordinary people who, growing up in society, learn to cope, as children born to untouchables in India acquire skills and attitudes necessary for survival in the miserable roles they are destined to fill.[10]

Just as Americans are destined to lead the "free world," people in underdeveloped societies are destined to be miserable and subject to the vagaries of dictatorship. It is the same argument that is directed at the poor and powerless in the United States.

No wonder that the Reagan administration, on taking office, tried to appoint an opponent of human rights legislation (Ernest Lefever) to be an assistant secretary of state for human rights; why it pressed Congress (in most cases successfully) to dismantle human rights legislation; and why, in agreement with Ms. Kirkpatrick's views, it generously extended arms and other aid to repressive regimes from Chile to Pakistan. "We are concerned that open societies sometimes get victimized by the practical consequences of their openness and by the lack of access to information about totalitarian regimes where, it is our conviction, the major abuses to human rights are occurring today," Alexander Haig said in a March 1981 interview.[11] Concretely, he meant that the thousands of deaths and disappearances documented each year in "open societies" such as El Salvador and Argentina are far less interesting to U.S. leaders than are political prisoners in Poland and the Soviet Union.[12]

The magnitude of the global economic and ecological crisis led the Brandt Commission to propose an agenda for major institutional and policy changes. The industrialized nations were called upon to make substantial concessions in their aid programs and trade and investment policies in the course of negotiations for mutual advantage with the Third World. But for the United States, whose policies continue to emphasize the traditional instruments of national self-interest—arms transfers, private investments, and close ties with authoritarian, noncommunist regimes—only the most modest reforms of the international system are acceptable. Politics continues to be "them versus us," as Lyndon Johnson said: "There are three billion people in the world and we have only 200 million of them. We are outnumbered 15 to 1. If might did make right, they would sweep over the United States and take what we have. We have what they want."[13] U.S. policymakers evidently remain committed to the belief that international security is primarily a matter of military advantage, not of social and economic equity. They assume that national-security policies will eventually purchase the kind of security from hunger, terrorism, disease, and unemployment that the Brandt Commission argued cannot be obtained with more weapons. To understand why the values, priorities, interests, and objectives underlying that belief remain constant, we turn to an exploration of the sources of U.S. policy in the Third World.

WELCOME TO "REALISM"

On January 4 and again on January 23, 1980, President Carter addressed the nation on the Soviet occupation of Afghanistan. The speeches were extraordinary, not because (as some people said) they marked a "return" to the cold war—since the cold war never ended—but because the President's images, analyses, and proposals for punishing the Russians were so entirely consistent with a generation of official statements on national security by American leaders. In the second speech, the State of the Union message, Carter treated the Soviet invasion as possibly "posing the most serious threat to the peace since the Second World War." For this the Soviets "must pay a concrete price," which ranged from economic sanctions to boycotting the Moscow Olympic Games. He described Soviet action in falling-domino terms: Afghanistan suddenly had become the gateway to Middle East oil. "This situation," Carter decided, "demands careful thought, steady nerves, and resolute action," for it constituted a "challenge" that would "take national will, diplomatic and political wisdom, economic sacrifice, and, of course, military capability." Like Presidents before him, Carter converted the U.S. response into foreign-policy doctrine. "An attempt by any outside force to gain control of the Persian Gulf region will be regarded as an assault on the vital interests of the United States of America, and such an assault will be repelled by any means necessary, including military force."

Anyone who listened to Carter and who could recall Truman's speech to Congress in 1947 on an alleged international communist threat to Greece and Turkey or Eisenhower's rationale for sending marines into Lebanon in 1958 or Kennedy's warnings to Russia in 1962 over missiles in Cuba or Johnson's justifications for escalation in Vietnam or Nixon's announcement of the invasion of Cambodia in 1970 or Ford's reasoning for using force to recover the *Mayaguez* in 1975—anyone with that background would have had the strong sense of *déjà vu*. In thirty-five years, little of substance had changed in American thinking or behavior. And even if one were to accept the official rationale that Soviet or other communist leaders provoked American actions, one would still have the uncomfortable task of explaining why successive administrations have persisted in believing that communist threats (imagined or real) in the Third World can be effectively contained with counter-threats and military deployments.

Soviet behavior in world affairs since 1945 has aimed at expanding its influence and its margin of security. But the Russians cannot be held solely or even primarily responsible for the character of U.S. foreign policy. U.S. policy has sought to satisfy the economic, political, psychological, and bureaucratic needs of particular groups and persons within the United States as much as it has attempted to contain or to eliminate external threats to the nation's well-being. Indeed, those needs, which are usually hidden in appeals to protect the national interest, have become so compelling that they, rather than any foreign military establishment or ideology, pose the most immediate threats to human security in this country and abroad. This has come about in three principal ways that this chapter explores more fully later on.

First, the national security state—the conglomeration of agencies and institutions (from the President, the CIA, and the military services to the multinational corporations and their supporters in the Democratic and Republican parties) whose interests dictate the direction and content of foreign policy—has developed vast bureaucracies, financial stakes, and technologies that require global military programs to sustain them. The programs embrace military weapons, sales, grants, training, bases, and means of deployment; a "complex" of Pentagon, industrial, academic, media, and congressional interests tied to military research and spending; worldwide banking and investments backed by U.S. security commitments, alliances, and aid programs; and a huge political and intelligence apparatus, working in tandem but sometimes autonomously to monitor, report on, and where necessary interfere in other countries' domestic affairs.

Second, these programs rest on the idea, and indeed could not survive but for the idea, that national security depends on structuring the world along lines that resemble and support "the American way of life." This idea justifies a global foreign policy in which the use of force—or what academics with a flair for code words call "coercive diplomacy"—plays a central role. The logical corollary of the idea is that the health and well-being of North American people depend on effectively policing and eventually pacifying the world, not that their vast resources should mainly be used to protect and expand economic and political rights at home.

Third, the implementation of national-security programs creates insecurity at home and abroad. The very people who are supposed to be protected in fact are those who suffer most. The U.S. government has spent about $2 trillion on foreign aid and military deployments (including wars) since 1945.[14] A great deal of that money has gone to support authoritarian regimes whose conduct flouts elementary principles of human rights to which the U.S. government, alone and as a UN member, is publicly committed. Fascist leaders of highly militarized societies preach "law and order" and "development" with the protection of U.S.-made tanks, U.S.-trained officers and special police, and U.S. security guarantees. The stability these leaders provide is, of course, illusory, as revolutions and coups in Vietnam, South Korea, Angola, Zaire, Guatemala, Nicaragua, and so many other Third World countries have shown.

The insecurity bred by these interventionist policies does not end abroad. Americans pay dearly for them too, as we shall discuss at the end of the chapter. But citizens are told that while the price of national security—of "peace with honor," of "stability and strength"—is indeed high, it must be paid. The cold war has been effectively promoted as an inescapable, unalterable fact of life: Peace is indivisible, conflict is inherent in our species; hence, peace and war are inseparable, like the ebb and flow of the tide. Political leaders (and, of course, not only those in the United States), journalists, and educators, among others, offer this dark perspective as Truth. They insist that what has been in the past will be in the present, which in turn molds the future. We all become hostages to history and other ineluctable forces. Consider Henry Kissinger's statement in his highly influential 1958 study, *Nuclear Weapons and Foreign Policy*:

> The obverse of our reluctance to think in terms of power has been our notion of the nature of peace. We assume that peace is the "normal" pattern of relations among states, that it is equivalent to a consciousness of harmony, that it can be aimed at directly as a goal of policy . . . . *No idea could be more dangerous* . . . . A power can survive only if it is willing to fight for its interpretations of justice and its conception of vital interests.[15]

In fact, this line of thinking has dominated speeches and writings about U.S. foreign policy throughout the century. Its proponents call it Realism. They have included virtually every holder of high office in the national security state since World War II. (There is another mainstream line of thinking, variously called Idealism, Internationalism, or Nationalism, that stands separately from Realism. But Idealism is more a counterpart than an alternative, since it operates on the same premises and goals as Realism, differing only with respect to methods or tactics.) Realism is worth examining in some detail, since it is a paradigm of the philosophy, strategy, and objectives that define the national security state.

The Realist argument springs from the assumption that humankind is basically immoral and power hungry; hence, that world politics is normally characterized by conflict. Each state naturally seeks to maximize its power, and it is therefore idle to expect much of the United Nations, international law, treaties, and appeals to respect human rights. A pragmatic application of the national interest, Realists contend, is the only proper standard for U.S. foreign policy. When, where, and how to pursue that interest are not so easily defined, however. The astute diplomat will decide on the basis of a careful calculation of costs and benefits of particular actions for the national interest. Preserving a balance of power among nations while containing (or eliminating) real threats to U.S. security are central to the Realist's analysis of costs and benefits. The good intentions of other nations, least of all communist ones, must not be assumed. Nor should moral or legal considerations be allowed to determine decisions. There are few natural allies outside Western Europe. The United States must count mainly on itself—and through an adroit combination of balance of power diplomacy, intervention where prospects of success are excellent, aid to regimes that can intelligently use it, and containment of Soviet maneuvers in ways that avoid overreaction, it can preserve its fundamental economic and political interests in a hostile world.

There are many serious problems with this view of the world and of U.S. society. Because Realists assume the worst about people's nature and humankind's possibilities, they urge actions in behalf of the national interest that go a long way toward ensuring continued global tensions and conflict. Their typical national security programs that call for high levels of military spending, preparedness for diverse forms of intervention abroad, major foreign aid packages, and minimal support of international and nongovernmental bodies leave little room for creative diplomacy (breakthroughs in long-unsolved issues such as the Arab-Israeli conflict) or for meaningful reductions of arms. Enough is never enough. Although Realists believe that the nation-state is always out to maximize its own power, nothing they offer seeks to change that circumstance. To the contrary, they accept it as normal and eternal, and give people who see in the nation-state system a root cause of constant war peril no hope of a durable peace.

The national interest as a standard for foreign policy, moreover, is so loose as to be easily manipulated, which, of course, it has been. There have been numerous interventions in behalf of undemocratic, repressive regimes (such as in Korea, Vietnam, and the Congo/Zaire) and several to undermine popular radical nationalist governments (such as in Chile, Cuba, Indonesia, Guatemala, and Iran), all in the name of the national interest. To promote national security, the U.S. government and private interests have aided, traded, invested, courted, and signed military pacts with governments quite happy to agree with Washington about the dangers of international communism—and very little else. Traditionally, American administrations from Truman through Reagan have always placed a higher value on military and investment security than on human rights when determining allies. Such a narrowly self-serving view, which some Realist writers find repugnant, is unfortunately a logical outgrowth of Realism's failure to see how closely connected are the long–term interests of North American peoples and the interests of the rest of humanity.

One reason why the national interest is almost invariably defined in economic and military terms is that the Realists' method of analyzing political choices excludes or minimizes many human factors. The rational, scientific mind yearns to subject political issues to objective measurement. Costs and benefits, risks and opportunities, are assigned weights, added up, and balanced against each other. But while this procedure may work in certain laboratory situations, it carries grave risks when applied to politics. Many costs and benefits, such as those pertaining to human rights and morality, cannot be measured numerically. They are subject to the values of the persons doing the measuring, and to the bureaucratic and historical circumstances in which the analysts find themselves. Costs and benefits for whom, moreover? Just as the "national interest" is often a euphemism for big business or the military, a supposed cost or benefit to "us" often really means to the narrow interest of one segment of one society, the American one. Realist analysis pretends to be scientific and objective when in fact, like any other kind of political analysis, it is heavily value laden: In this case, chauvinistic, elitist, competitive, amoral, violence accepting, fixated on maximizing power, and steeped in pessimism and distrust.

Since it is driven by narrow concern about national power, Realism is capable of inciting the most destructive involvements that may, as in Vietnam, demonstrate both military might and intellectual and moral feebleness. U.S. society, the people of Indochina, and indeed the world community paid dearly for the American Realists' interpretation of historical necessity in Vietnam. Yet only six years after the unification of Vietnam in 1975, Realists were urging that Americans stop being mesmerized by the "Vietnam syndrome" and support a five-year "defense" plan that will cost at least $1.5 trillion. Few people in Congress rose to challenge them.

What would it take to humanize U.S. foreign policy and bring its needs in line with the needs of the world community? Some radicals would say it merely takes the elimination of capitalism and its replacement with socialist means of production and distribution. But recent direct interventions by socialist states—the Soviet Union in Czechoslovakia and Afghanistan, China in Vietnam, and Vietnam in Cambodia—all but destroy the case for socialism, at least in the highly centralized state-bureaucratic forms it has so far taken. The socialist thesis does, however, point to where the problem originates: At home. Contrary to the Realists, foreign and domestic policies are intertwined, the one motivating, reflecting, and reinforcing the other. To answer why Vietnam, why the use of food as a weapon, or why the rapid demise of human rights as a foreign-policy priority, we need to look inward. We do that now by examining three intersecting realms that comprise the domestic arena of foreign policymaking: Ideas, institutions, and weapons.

NATIONAL SECURITY AS IDEOLOGY

"With the splitting of the atom, everything has changed save our mode of thinking," said Albert Einstein. "Thus we drift toward unparalleled destruction."[16] The core ideas that have impelled U.S. foreign policy since 1945 have remained unchanged through eight administrations. No matter whether these were Democratic or Republican leaderships, liberal or conservative, flamboyant "shuttle" diplomats or "quiet dialogue" diplomats. The common denominator of the 500 or so persons who have held high foreign-policymaking posts since World War II is that they have shared basic beliefs about the role the United States played and ought to play in international affairs. This fundamental and enduring consensus, which finds expression in Realism, amounts to an ideology of national interest. Like all ideologies, this one is both a vision of a world order favorable to the interests it reflects and a justification of actions (always "in the national interest") to realize the vision.

The American ideology springs from the dominant political and economic forces and values in U.S. society, which include private property, individualism, the free market (laissez-faire), pluralism, reformism, and civil liberties. A multitude of public, semi-public, and private agencies and institutions established to perform social services purvey these values, one of them being the national-security establishment, which promotes them abroad. These values become more deeply imbedded in the society, as much as a consequence of the strengthened political power of central authority (in government and in the private sector) as of economic success. But in the process, threats to the dominant values seem to grow and become more immediate. Defending them against enemies at home and abroad is put forward, by those groups that have most to lose, as the first requirement of national security. Socialism is the natural and most convenient target of leaders of a "free enterprise" state. U.S. actions in the cold war as diverse as the Marshall Plan for European recovery, alliances and interventions in the Third World, the covert operations of the Central Intelligence Agency and the Federal Bureau of Investigation at home and abroad, the Food for Peace program, the nearly $200 billion of overseas investments by U.S.-based multinational corporations, and the containment and the embracement of China can be fully explained only with reference to the war with socialism. Only in that context do words like stability, peace, equilibrium, national security, defense, and global mission—the stock in trade of corporate leaders in all political systems—have meaning.

The United States emerged from World War II as the world's most powerful state: The only major nation whose home territory had not been laid waste, the only atomic power, and the chief holder of the world's only stable currency. In the years before the Korean War, and despite a rapid demobilization of the armed forces, the United States undertook and completed a total economic restructuring of the capitalist world. This formidable task included the rehabilitation of Western Europe, the integration of West Germany into that region, the rebuilding of

Japan as the U.S. "keystone" in the Pacific, and the creation of new international financial institutions under the Bretton Woods system (the World Bank and the International Monetary Fund), all of which had the aim and the effect of ensuring the dollar's paramountcy in international trade and investment.

These two sources of national power—dollars and the bomb—together account in large part for the "global reach" that the United States possessed unchallenged for so long. It has been difficult for American leaders to accept the decline of one and the neutralization of the other. Rather, their consistent goal has been to maintain an American imperium in the name of the national interest. In their thinking, or ideology, the national interest has three basic axioms that have been discussed elsewhere:[17]

1. America's domestic tranquility depends on security and stability abroad.
2. Security and stability abroad for the forces of freedom depend on America's willingness to carry out the mission and responsibilities entrusted to it.
3. Fulfillment of America's mission and security responsibilities depends on a willingness and ability to intervene in the domestic affairs of other people.

The first axiom has already been noted as a cardinal feature of Realism: The nation's domestic well-being is considered directly tied to the security and stability of regimes and corporations abroad that subscribe to free enterprise values. As President Truman once said: "All freedom is dependent on freedom of enterprise . . . . The whole world should adopt the American system . . . . The American system can survive in America only if it becomes a world system."[18] In the eyes of U.S. policymakers, insecurity and instability abroad spell trouble for the nation's well-being, which explains the persistent knee-jerk reaction in Washington to most every civil war, riot, strike, or other disturbance in a "friendly" country. To them, the causes of such outbursts are not nearly so important as are their consequences for U.S. military and business interests. The first axiom therefore connotes law-and-order policies. So that when a key official such as Alexander Haig in 1981 reiterated the standard U.S. preference for "an environment of security, peaceful change, and the rule of law," he expressed not distaste for violence but support of "anti-communist" repression.[19]

Since the threat to the United States is perceived to be external, global, and continual, and since the United States is the most powerful capitalist state, no wonder that U.S. leaders, as our second axiom suggests, have presumed a national mission of worldwide self-protection. Leadership of the free world, many Presidents and their advisers have said, is a matter of America's destiny. One of Lyndon Johnson's top aides, Walt W. Rostow, urged in the 1960s that we Americans not "renounce our destiny. We are the trustees of the principles of national independence and human freedom all over the globe; and given our history, this is a proud and natural responsibility."[20] Such pronouncements amount to asserting that Americans are uniquely qualified to lead the world and to have others follow. Ours is the path to enlightened political and economic order, for "the world still looks to us for a protecting hand, a mediating influence, a path to follow."[21] Richard Nixon exposed the missionary element in American thinking when, five years before traveling to Beijing, he wrote of China policy:

> Dealing with Red China is something like trying to cope with the more explosive ghetto elements in our own country. In each case a potentially destructive force has to be curbed; in each case an outlaw element has to be brought within the law; in each case dialogues have to be opened; in each case aggression has to be restrained while education proceeds; and, not least, in neither case can we afford to let those now self-exiled from society stay exiled forever.[22]

It is not often that U.S. leaders so starkly reveal their prejudices nor how closely their view of the world parallels their view of American society.

It is but a small leap to the third axiom—that the United States reserves the right to protect its own interests by intervening in the affairs of other societies. Vietnam dramatized this perversion of self-determination; the U.S.-backed overthrow of Salvador Allende in Chile reminded us of the idea's continuity. Henry Kissinger said of Chile: "I don't see why we have to stand back and watch a country go Communist because of the irresponsibility of its own people."[23] He meant that the U.S. government would judge another society's behavior and, like an authoritarian parent, punish, mediate, influence, or stand aside at its pleasure. In the cases of Vietnam and Chile, as well as of the Dominican Republic (1965), Angola (1975), and most recently El Salvador and Grenada, the United States in different ways intervened to stop a revolutionary process, fearing that it would spread, falling-domino fashion, to neighboring countries. One of the greatest dangers of Realist ideology is revealed here: Since U.S. national interests are global and the threats to them are global—"peace is indivisible," as Kissinger often said—what happens in one country must be considered a possibility for another and dealt with accordingly. The popular will is, then, irrelevant. What counts for U.S. leaders is *their* will—to use national power, to be in control of events, and thus to retain international "credibility."

FOREIGN POLICY INCORPORATED

Institutions transmit and debate ideas. In the process, they give policies their shape. In every society, some institutions are more important than others, reflecting the imbalance of real political power. It goes without saying that with plans for the military to absorb about 37 percent of the federal budget by fiscal year 1987, those institutions most directly involved in the defense of the national security state will exert the greatest influence over policymaking. Contrary, therefore, to the concept of pluralism, the critical institutions that shape foreign (and to a great extent, domestic) policy in the United States have not been the Congress, the press, or public opinion. Foreign policymaking has typically not been characterized by democratic accountability, institutional checks and balances, or consultative decision making. The complexity of the policymaking process, involving many personalities, bureaucracies, and levels of activity, official and unofficial, must be distinguished from the hierarchy of interests that governs the process. From above, the forest appears crowded and wild; but at ground level, some trees dominate the landscape.

By now there is a substantial literature (see the bibliography) describing the influence and workings of these powerful institutions: The multinational corporations; the "iron triangle" (discussed in the next section), consisting of the Pentagon, its domestic arms contractors, and supportive members of Congress; certain semi-official research and "think tank" organizations (such as the Trilateral Commission, the Council on Foreign Relations, and the RAND Corporation); and, of course, the executive branch itself. The interflow of personnel among these institutions, the easy access afforded by private economic power to organs of public political power, and the mutual support these institutions and their directors give one another all ensure a continuity of values and ideas in the upper echelons of policymaking. No conspiracy here; rather, what we have is a confluence of interests that meets in Washington. These are people (primarily lawyers, financiers, and industrialists) who speak to one another in a common vocabulary, understand each other's needs and limitations (since often they move in and out of government service), and operate within a common framework of interest. Because their backgrounds, roads to success, and objective interests—profit and market expansion for the giant corporations; increased state and bureaucratic power for the government—are similar, the American elite will generally seek to move foreign (and domestic) policy in a similar direction. The business of the State Department is protecting and promoting American business, as various secretaries of state have said; and the business of business certainly includes disseminating American free enterprise values, stabilizing Third World economies to insulate them from communist-backed violence, and otherwise repaying the U.S. government for its material support.

To be sure, disagreements within policymaking circles abound: No one institution is simply the obedient instrument of the other. What is good for General Motors is not always good for the U.S. government, and vice versa. Nor will General Motors invariably agree with ITT, as was the case in the CIA-backed overthrow of Salvador Allende in Chile. Numerous instances can be cited of policy clashes between the State Department and multinational corporations and among the corporations themselves; but the essential points are (1) that the clashes typically concern immediate interests or foreign-policy tactics, not overall priorities or objectives, and (2) that consensus, not contradiction, is the dominant feature of these inter- and intra-elite relationships.

Likewise with respect to bureaucratic rivalries in the government foreign-policy agencies: Agreements on the ground rules and values that govern U.S. conduct in the world far exceed in importance any disagreements on policy tactics or details in any one part of the world. We would expect to find—and do find—differences of view between, for instance, the State and Defense Departments on the size of a military aid program, within the Pentagon over service budgets, or between the CIA and the State Department on the scope of a covert operation. But it is precisely the narrow range of the disagreements—the exclusion of nonviolent, deescalatory options; the jurisdictional character of the debates; the enforced absence from the policymaking process of moral, legal, and historical considerations; and the persistent pattern of victories for certain kinds of decisions (more military aid, covert operations, and investments abroad) and defeats for other kinds (such as those that would tie aid to improved human rights conditions in Third World partner-regimes)—that clarifies the relatively second order significance of bureaucratic political competition.

It is a question of tactics and style, on one hand, versus strategy and objectives, on the other. One way to see the difference is to consider changes of foreign-policy personnel. Henry Kissinger's replacement by Zbigniew Brzezinski or Cyrus Vance's by Edmund Muskie or Richard Allen's by William Clark mattered much more with respect to bureaucratic style and policy emphasis than to fundamental convictions about U.S. purposes. Kissinger was right to say at a May 1975 news conference that, "if you look at the entire American postwar foreign policy, you will find the changes in the major directions of the foreign policy haven't been all that significant. What is different between various Presidents is the style, the method of doing business."[24] Members of the elite will come and go, but its business will endure. That is true of most any corporation, including the U.S. government.

We have suggested that the reason it is true has mainly to do with shared values and ideology and only secondarily with bureaucratic continuity, similarities of personality, or pluralist give and take. As a result, senior foreign-policy leaders in any period will share basic assumptions and images.[25] Among these are some of special relevance to understanding U.S. policy in the Third World:

Peace is indivisible; hence, threats to the peace, wherever they may occur, must be resisted.

The global balance of power is potentially at risk whenever there is communist-backed violence. A gain for "them" is a loss for "us."

Aggression must not pay.

The best insurance against aggression is military preparedness to meet all kinds of threats, or to negotiate from strength.

Credibility is just as important as actual power. Failure to maintain credibility invites appeasement.

The Third World is the major battleground between the communist and free world forces. "Stability," through capitalist economic development, military strength, and strong central political authority, will keep the Third World from going communist.

Peace is meaningless in the absence of stability. Instability provides opportunities ("power vacuums") for radicalism and prevents social progress.

As a result of these shared beliefs and this interchangeability of top-level personnel between the private and public sectors, we would expect to find that when government officials responsible for foreign policy get together, they behave in fairly predictable ways. And we are not disappointed—whether we are talking about 1945 or 1980, in a Democratic or a Republican administration. Some typical behavior patterns are discussed in the following paragraphs.

Corporate Man. The people who "make it" to the top in government often regard their new post as just another corporate position. They act accordingly. They are fervently loyal to their superiors and "the company." They are also ambitious, fascinated with power, self-certain, nonidealistic, competitive, untrusting, and opportunistic. They must especially be good "team players," prepared—like Vice President Hubert Humphrey and Undersecretary of State Chester Bowles during the Vietnam War—to speak publicly in behalf of policies they privately oppose. Consider the recommendation former Secretary of State Dean Acheson made of Dean Rusk to become Kennedy's secretary of state: "He is loyal, honorable and honest. He has courage. He is cool, intelligent, quite as capable of wrestling with the most complex problems, as well as anybody else. And he is a team player, no prima donna."[26] When Alexander Haig resigned as secretary of state in 1982, the most frequently cited reason was that he had failed to be a good team player; whereas Robert McFarlane's appointment as Reagan's top national-security adviser the next year was based mainly on his ability to be a team player.

The pressures to conform with "the team's" point of view can be intense. Presidents, especially Democratic ones, fear being labeled "soft on communism"; although one recalls Henry Kissinger constantly putting off proposals for a U.S. withdrawal from Vietnam because of an alleged fear of a "right-wing reaction." McCarthyism does not die easily. Always wary of domestic political repercussions from insufficiently tough foreign-policy actions, Presidents "cover their flanks." But such political security helps to steer policy options toward the right. Breakthrough alternatives by creative-minded bureaucrats, such as the initiatives toward China between 1969 and 1972, are few and far between.

And what of those officials and members of the President's team in Congress who become renegades? Some, of course, are fired or forced to resign. Under President Carter, Ambassador Young had to be relieved for consorting with Palestinians; and Cyrus Vance departed with the following backhanded criticism from Carter: "My hope is that with Ed Muskie coming on board as part of our team . . . he will play a somewhat different role than the one Secretary Vance played because of a difference in background and temperament and attitude."[27] Other dissenters are pushed to the President's outer circle, as happened to State Department officers who wanted more serious peace proposals from Lyndon Johnson on Vietnam. Some people get shoved much deeper into bureaucratic Siberia—like Ernest Fitzgerald, who blew the whistle on Lockheed C–5A cost overruns at the Pentagon and soon found himself at a meaningless desk job thanks to President Nixon. (Fitzgerald later sued and won his job back.) Finally, there are those who protest and quit—like members of Kissinger's National Security Council staff following the invasion of Cambodia and two senior officials who resigned from Reagan's Agency for International Development after the United States cast the only vote against a World Health Organization code favoring mothers' milk over Nestlé and other baby formula that is marketed in the Third World. Such protest resignations, however, are relatively rare.

Needless to add, we are also talking about highly skilled, intellectually talented people. Totally confident of their abilities, they often view the task of dealing with foreign governments and their leaders as being no more or less complicated than any other client's business. It's all a matter of getting the job done, negotiating from strength, learning the angles, and adroitly applying leverage at opportune moments. Yet it was Henry Kissinger who, before he became a bureaucratic leader himself, best summed up the weaknesses of such banker-like pragmatism. It "seeks to reduce judgment to methodology and value to knowledge," wrote Kissinger.[28] Foreign policy becomes problem solving and management, leaving little room for building relationships of trust, for empathy, or for long-term global planning.

Groupthink. This word, coined by Irving Janis, a psychologist who has studied foreign-policy decision making, defines the often artificial consensus that develops as groups strive to reach agreement. The artificiality occurs when dissenting views and values are submerged beneath the weight of team play, loyalty, and usually unspoken ideological assumptions. Groupthink is akin to George Orwell's "newspeak" in *1984*. Rarely does a high official break ranks and the rules of the game to challenge the official line and the process by which the line is maintained. Debate over alternative courses of action thus takes place within predefined limits that ensure a quick end to deviant positions. A President's inner circle is properly called "inner," since truly competitive viewpoints are automatically excluded.

Grouptalk. Groupthink takes hold because of shared values.

These are brought out with the help of a common, "loaded" vocabulary. Talk of "moderate" uses of force, "viable" (or "feasible") options, challenges to "our" credibility, and the "responsibilities" of great nations is not neutral. Such language is deliberately designed to deceive or to lull audiences because of its very blandness. Other words are meant to produce a "rally round the flag" and "get behind the chief" effect. Grouptalk often employs macho bravado—tough language that makes international conflict seem like a street fight where everyone's manhood is at stake. When the Cuban missile crisis ended, Dean Rusk proudly described how the Russians and the Americans were "eyeball to eyeball—and the other side blinked."[29] In the world of grouptalk, one speaks not of cooperation and understanding but of facing down the enemy, steady nerves, and resolute will. There is a premium on being hard-nosed.

Lessons Learned. Ernest May, in *"Lessons" of the Past*, has written about U.S. foreign policymakers' consistent misreading of history. Because policymakers made false or misleading analogies with the past, they also made incorrect, often tragic decisions in their own time. Korea and Vietnam, for instance, were considered "test cases" of communist aggression, the test being of American "will." A great deal of blood and treasure was spilled to demonstrate the firmness of that will. Jimmy Carter applied a "test case" to the Soviet invasion of Afghanistan, again raising the spectre of a major cold war confrontation to prove that "aggression will not pay." War in the Persian Gulf did not ensue despite Carter's dire warnings. But draft registration, a Rapid Deployment Force, economic sanctions against the Soviet Union, and an increased military budget were instituted—all decisions that may become part of another historical chapter.

Minimax Solutions. Policymakers like to speak of getting maximum "payoff" from a minimum investment. Their job is to achieve U.S. objectives using options that avoid all-out war and domestic political disaster for their leader. Thus, they search for what *they* call moderate or middle-range alternatives—the inevitable option B between A and C. The problem is that option B invariably is a compromise on the side of violent or militant action: For example, sending 50,000 more troops rather than

100,000 or none at all, as in Vietnam; establishing a naval blockade rather than carrying out an air attack or doing nothing, as in Cuba in 1962; beginning a research program for a new weapon rather than going for immediate deployment or abolishing the program, as with the neutron bomb in 1980. In each case, the middle option is a bureaucratic compromise that everyone (in Washington, that is) can live with.

Devil and Angel. Policymakers habitually attribute the worst characteristics and intentions to "the enemy" and the best to themselves. "They" provoke, "we" respond. "Their" weapons are offensive, "ours" are defensive. "They" are the aggressors, "we" are (in Nixon's words, as he announced the invasion of Cambodia in 1970) the "pitiful, helpless giant." "They" commit terrorism, "we" provide security assistance. Needless to say, each action in accordance with these images confirms them in the minds of the decision makers on both sides. The result is that each side to a conflict sees itself and the other behaving in precisely the same ways—the so-called mirror image phenomenon. And that phenomenon's consequences are compounded by the dehumanizing characterizations leaders make of one another or of other systems, such as Reagan's oral assault on Libya's Kadafi and on the Soviets for having a "morality" that authorizes them to "commit any crime, to lie, to cheat." Policy planning on both sides necessarily adopts worst-case assumptions: The other side probably has aggressive, expansionist intentions, hence "our" side must emphasize military countermeasures. Confrontation becomes self-fulfilling as each side acts out the other's worst fears. Most of the violent cold war confrontations have evolved in this manner. It really is amazing that a nuclear war has not occurred when we consider how universal is the devil-angel mode of perception.

Supermen, Supercountry. To make decisions on behalf of the militarily most powerful society in the world is an awesome responsibility. Ordinary people presumably would feel uneasy about that responsibility, but not American leaders. Believing that their country is and ought to be, number one in world affairs, they welcome opportunities, as they have often put it, to "orchestrate" power. (If they didn't, how could we stay number one?) "Power is there to be used," Zbigniew Brzezinski has said. "It must be used. It is important."[30] But what happens when that power is used irresponsibly—illegally, immorally, disproportionately? This question rarely receives a response from people in power. Except for the President and a few other officials, most foreign-policy advisers and specialists are appointed, not elected. Their ultimate accountability only to the President, the secrecy with which much of their work is conducted, and the extraordinary array of power at their disposal combine to give high officials a sense of invulnerability.

The Weapon of Secrecy. Accountability for an act requires, initially, knowing who committed the act. Foreign-policy bureaucrats have protected against being held responsible for their actions by creating an elaborate classification system. Of course they justify the system by saying it is necessary to safeguard national security; but many people, including one of this book's authors, who has experienced the secrecy system firsthand, know that only a tiny percentage of government documents is classified for reasons of state. Overwhelmingly, classified material keeps American citizens from knowing what is going on and asking embarrassing questions—usually, the public at large and the press; sometimes, members of the Congress as well; less often, other officials (under various "supersecret" classifications, the very names of which, à la *Catch 22*, are supersecret). Secrecy is the great preserver of the arrogance of power.

Personalizing the Game. Senior officials, and Presidents in particular, are notorious for making international conflict a personal contest in which their reputations "before history" are at stake. During the long period of cold war, we find Presidents being moved to action in some part because they believed they had to reestablish their "credibility." Thus, for instance, President Kennedy believed Premier Khrushchev had gotten the better of him at their first summit meeting in mid–1961. Kennedy's subsequent willingness to use force to get Soviet missiles out of Cuba was partly based on his felt need to impress Khrushchev with his toughness. (Another personal motivation, by most recent accounts, was his brother Robert's vendetta to "get Castro.") During the Vietnam War, a common concern of every President was not to be the first to "lose" a war. Jimmy Carter said Premier Brezhnev had lied to him about the reasons for the Soviet invasion of Afghanistan, an action which, according to the President, drastically changed his perception of Soviet foreign policy and led him to conclude that the invasion was part of a worldwide challenge. When Presidents feel deceived, the world has to hold its collective breath.

Taken together, these patterns of perception and action have dire consequences for the conduct of U.S. foreign policy. For this country, they produce rigid formulas of political change, arrogance in assuming responsibility for the fate of others, and a disposition to use force and threats to attain objectives. For unfriendly powers, the patterns mean mistrust of their motives, dehumanization of their leaders, and a strong probability that their intentions will be misperceived and their actions miscalculated. And because of traditional deference to the President in foreign affairs, the press, the public, and their representatives tend to make these patterns of thought and action their own. In such circumstances, the prospects of a direct U.S.-Soviet collision must increase, while those of negotiated agreements or resort to law must decrease. Just as importantly, opportunities are lost for U.S. officials, the press, and others to examine critically their own motives, prejudices, and actions that may have contributed to a crisis. Instituting crisis management, all governments have found, is a marvelous way to evade responsibility for it.

Some examples will help clarify these ideas. The Soviet invasion of Afghanistan led President Carter to impose sanctions as previously noted and to portray the Russians as about to embark on military expansion in the Persian Gulf. The media played its part, reproducing official maps with menacing (red) arrows pointed in the direction of the Gulf and echoing official "reports" that Soviet divisions were poised to invade Iran. When these reports proved groundless, neither the press nor U.S. officials saw fit to explain why they had been issued or even to acknowledge that the State Department had badly misread Soviet intentions. Still more significantly, U.S. officials never publicly examined, nor did the press push them to examine, the possibility that certain U.S. actions preceding the Afghanistan invasion gave Soviet leaders little incentive to hold back: An announced U.S. intention to install several hundred Pershing and cruise missiles in Western Europe; reports of potential U.S.-China military collaboration; and Carter's withdrawal of the SALT II agreements from Senate consideration.

In fact, long before their invasion of Afghanistan, the Russians were perceived in Washington as being totally responsible for a breakdown of detente. In addition to citing as evidence various Soviet actions around the world, the State Department also pointed to the limited international experience and rigid world outlook of the Soviet leadership, the strength of its military bureaucracy, and a lack of resolute counteraction by the United States (the Vietnam syndrome again).[31] Never did a State Department or other U.S. official consider the effects of U.S. actions on Soviet behavior and perceptions, as though various new U.S. missile programs, additions to the U.S. nuclear warhead inventory, military buildups of allies, and flirtations with Soviet enemies (such as the Chinese) surely could not have disturbed anyone in Moscow. When U.S. officials argued before congressional committees that the SALT II treaty with the Soviet Union should nevertheless be ratified, they took pains to point out that trusting the Russians was not necessary for the treaty to be effective! Imagine being a Soviet diplomat and reading such a thing.

WEAPONS AND POLITICS

> We must pay whatever price is required to remain the strongest nation in the world.
>
> —Jimmy Carter, January 21, 1980

> The United States dropped on and around Vietnam the explosive equivalent of one Nagasaki bomb per week for seven and a half years.
>
> —Lovins, Lovins, and Ross[32]

In 1946, General Dwight D. Eisenhower, then chief of staff of the Army, urged that the wartime cooperation between science and business and the military "must be translated into a peacetime counterpart which will not merely familiarize the Army with the progress made in science and industry, but draw into our planning for national security all the civilian resources which can contribute to the defense of the country. Civilian assistance in military planning as well as for the production of weapons" was one of a number of steps Eisenhower believed were necessary.[33] Fifteen years later, Eisenhower, stepping down from the presidency after two terms, reversed his sentiments. He warned of the "grave implications" of vesting so much influence in the military and the arms industry:

> In the councils of government we must guard against the acquisition of unwarranted influence whether sought or unsought, by the military-industrial complex. The potential for the disastrous rise of misplaced power exists and will persist. We must never let the weight of this combination endanger our liberties or democratic processes. We should take nothing for granted.

Eisenhower's farewell address is often quoted; but his initial idea is the one that had the greatest impact.

The Pentagon is the nation's largest property holder (over $300 billion in assets), largest employer (in 1979, about 9 million people relied on the Pentagon for jobs), and biggest spender.[34] It is the cog in a giant wheel—a true complex of institutions. It includes, in addition to the military services,

1. *Government* at all levels: Pentagon spending directly affects jobs, business productivity and profits, taxes, and, therefore, elections and budgets.
2. Major and minor *corporations*: Industry, banks, academia, and research "think tanks" depend to varying degrees on Pentagon contracts and subcontracts, on military protection of overseas investments, and on weapons sales abroad; their executives often sit on each other's boards and dominate the memberships of advisory committees of the military services; they contribute heavily to political action committees and lobbies to ensure the election—and secure the votes—of legislators who support high military spending; and corporate weapons planners regularly take up jobs in military sales and planning with arms contractors.[35]
3. *The media*: Dominated by conglomerates with extensive domestic investments that bring it into close contact with military contractors, the media are quite favorable to Pentagon programs and official perceptions of world affairs.

4. *The Congress*: About three-fourths of its members represent districts with military installations and/or military industries; many of these members have military commissions; and while such connections do not ensure votes favorable to military interests, the probability that such will happen is high, particularly since corporate political spending (via political action committees) can affect a Congressperson's chances of election and reelection.

Militarism—in the sense of deeply held commitments to martial values, ever-increasing spending for weapons, and a willingness to use force and threats to achieve political objectives—is institutionalized in the United States. Additionally, military experience is widely shared in American society. For some it may be startling to learn that about 20 percent of the U.S. population either has had military service or currently works for the military, either in the armed forces, the Pentagon's civilian agencies, or prime military industrial contractors. Implementing nonmilitary alternatives to security becomes all the more difficult in the face of so many personal histories that are tied to the armed forces.

In this section we will examine the implications of the military-industrial complex for three areas of U.S.–Third World relations: Nuclear weapons, nuclear energy and proliferation, and arms transfers. In each case we want to see how ideas and institutions have made nuclear and conventional weapons into the most significant policy instruments in the U.S. arsenal for dealing with international, especially Third World, instability.

Nuclear Weapons

World War II ended with an atomic monopoly for the United States. Ever since, the Soviet Union has had to play catch up, and powerful forces have developed in the United States against the idea that nuclear parity is security enough. Military superiority quickly became central to the waging of cold war against "international communism," as was made abundantly clear in a 1946 memorandum by Clark Clifford (Lyndon Johnson's secretary of defense years later). Clifford's views, said to reflect those of all other top U.S. national-security officials, are quoted by Richard Barnet in *Roots of War*:

> The language of military power is the only language which disciples of power politics [i.e., the Russians] understand. The United States must use that language in order that Soviet leaders will realize that our government is determined to uphold the interest of its citizens and the rights of small nations. Compromise and concessions are considered, by the Soviets, to be evidence of weakness and they are encouraged by our "retreats" to make new and greater demands.[36]

"The United States," Clifford added, "with a military potential composed primarily of highly effective technical weapons, should entertain no proposal for disarmament or limitation of armament as long as the possibility of Soviet aggression exists."[37] Thus, the emerging military-industrial complex would address both ends of the arms equation: Promoting the research and development of weapons to maintain U.S. superiority and resisting proposals for arms reductions. Arms control moved into the realm of public relations, under the title "arms limitations," whereas arms production, under the label "deterrence strategies," received the highest ideological and institutional priority.

Arms control and nuclear information-sharing proposals were early victims of cold war suspicion of the Russians, who of course were not about to become committed to arrangements (such as the Baruch Plan in 1946) that left the U.S. nuclear monopoly intact. Besides, the proposals were sabotaged by the overwhelming power of Pentagon and civilian hard-liners. They saw to it, in 1946 and again in the mid-fifties, for instance, when Eisenhower asked Soviet agreement to "open skies" inspection arrangements, that the Soviets were presented with deals they were certain to refuse. When modest arms control agreements were reached in later years—such as the Nuclear Test Ban in 1963, the Anti-Ballistic Missile Treaty and the Interim Agreement on strategic arms under a SALT I in 1972, and the now-abandoned SALT II (signed in 1979)—bureaucratic politics required that the hard-liners in Washington be compensated with research and production funds for new weapons. Decisions such as these not only ensured a U.S. lead in nuclear warfare capability, they inevitably prompted similar decisions on the Soviet side in order to achieve strategic parity. Arms control agreements have always been one or more critical steps behind the pace set by weapons technology.

The cold war, therefore, has been marked by competitive cycles in which the Russians have striven to close the nuclear-missile gap while the Americans have sought to keep the gap wide, either to maintain strategic superiority or to have enough "bargaining chips" in arms negotiations. Since the end of World War II, the Third World has, with two exceptions (Berlin in 1959 and 1962), been the setting for periodic tests of strength at the peak of these cycles.

One of these nuclear showdowns, the "eyeball to eyeball" confrontation over Soviet missiles in Cuba, was an archetypical cold war event. Portrayed to the American public as a national security crisis—the enemy's nuclear power is only ninety miles from our shores—and hailed subsequently as Kennedy's finest hour, the missile crisis in fact ought never to have occurred. It was a political and psychological test for Kennedy and his Eastern whiz kids, and not—as Kennedy himself would admit, after the danger of nuclear war had passed—a military threat. For in fact the United States then had an enormous advantage over the Soviet Union in long-range bombers and atomic missiles—the Soviet Union had, perhaps, four intercontinental ballistic missiles (ICBMs)—so that a Soviet missile presence in Cuba would not have significantly altered the strategic balance. But Kennedy, while talking publicly about how Premier Khrushchev had betrayed a promise by shipping the missiles, had other reasons for declaring a crisis: The right wing's clamor that he do something about them, with congressional elections just around the corner; concern about a "Castroite" falling-domino effect in Latin America if the United States did not respond forcefully to this Soviet "challenge"; and the President's own need to impress his toughness on the Soviet leadership after appearing to have come out second best in a summit meeting with Khrushchev the year before. And for these reasons, the world was perilously close to a nuclear showdown for a few nerve-shattering days in October 1962.

To possess nuclear superiority was not enough. Each administration also wanted to have a "credible deterrent"—a knockout punch that the Russians would believe the United States would actually use. Hence, Presidents have several times considered using nuclear weapons in Third World "crises." Truman twice considered carrying out a preventive nuclear strike against Soviet and Chinese cities during the Korean War. Eisenhower wrote in his memoirs of his intention to use nuclear weapons if the Panmunjom armistice talks in Korea had dragged on much longer. (Recently published State Department papers document plans for nuclear strikes in North Korea and China.) In the 1958 Taiwan Strait crisis, Eisenhower sent tactical nuclear weapons to Taiwan as a demonstration to China of U.S. "resolve." Kennedy had B–52s in Okinawa readied during the Laos crisis in 1961 for a possible strike against China. And Nixon may have entertained, or actually employed, nuclear threats against the Vietnamese government in the last stages of that war. Presidents would undoubtedly agree with Zbigniew Brzezinski, who wrote in a review of the cold war in 1972 about the "extraordinary salutary effects of nuclear weapons" for achieving a position of strength.[38]

Since the second half of the Carter administration, in fact, U.S. policymakers have shown interest in abandoning deterrence and adopting a nuclear war-fighting strategy. The implications of such a shift for Third World countries, not to mention Western Europe, are very grave. For if the United States continues to develop and to deploy weapons—such as the MX and cruise missiles, the B–1B and "Stealth" bombers, and Trident missiles and submarines—that to the Russians might be intended to initiate an all-out nuclear war against them, or to fight a "limited" nuclear war, the stage is set for the most deadly round of arms competition yet seen. Wayne Biddle, in a study of the U.S. military's push for the MX system, has written that the generals are "paid to be hyper-paranoid" about the Soviet threat.[39] So, presumably, are Soviet generals. Faced with an erosion of deterrence, they essentially have only two choices: Attempt to match every American improvement in weapons technology, a task they have yet to succeed in and which is extremely costly to their troubled economy, or develop their own first-strike capability before the United States tries to disarm their country.

The opportunities for awesome miscalculations are greater than ever before; and the entire world, not to mention outer space, is available as a testing ground for new nuclear-war theories.[40]

Nuclear Energy and Proliferation

Nuclear power and nuclear weapons, often separated in the public's mind, are increasingly coming to be seen as two sides of the same coin. The rise of the nuclear power industry in the United States has been intimately associated with the evolution of nuclear war planning. As technology progresses, possibilities increase for diverting nuclear fuel to making bombs. And the U.S. government, which until the Reagan administration had, although quite inconsistently, restricted the transfer of nuclear fuel and technology to Third World countries, has adopted new policies that may grievously undermine international efforts to prevent the further spread of nuclear weapons.

A brief look back at the origins of the U.S. nuclear power program is in order. The Atomic Energy Act of 1946 had kept nuclear power a preserve of the military. But beginning in the late 1940s, major chemical, construction, and electric utility companies brought pressure on the government to open nuclear power to commercial use. Eisenhower's "Atoms for Peace" speech in December 1953 paved the way for amending the 1946 Act. Nuclear science and technology, so long as they were for "peaceful uses," could now be exported. Although the President seemed inspired by the desire to bring cheap energy to the world, in fact his main motives were to counteract a growing public dread of atomic power, bolster his administration's popularity, and win points over the Russians. These motives fit well with the wishes of the growing nuclear industry.

The Atomic Energy Act was amended in 1954. In 1957 Congress passed the Price-Anderson Act, which drastically limits the liability of public utilities in case of nuclear accidents (such as occurred at Three Mile Island in 1979). Price-Anderson provided critical government subsidization of investments in nuclear power. Without such support, which is only one of several ways in which the U.S. government has underwritten commercial nuclear research and development, it is clear the nuclear energy option would not have been pursued.[41]

Despite all the evidence that nuclear power has failed to match its early claims to provide endless amounts of safe, efficient, low-cost energy, the industry survives and, thanks to the Reagan administration, has a new lease on life. By the same token, despite mounting evidence that energy conservation and investment in renewable energy sources such as solar, wind, and water power are politically and ecologically wise substitutes for nuclear power and petroleum, government support of research and projects in these areas has all but vanished. One major explanation for both phenomena is that a "complex" of interests, with membership that substantially overlaps that of the military-industrial complex, has pushed the nuclear option. As described by John J. Berger, "The complex consists of huge oil companies, leading uranium mining firms, major utilities, enormous financial institutions, large defense contractors, top nuclear equipment manufacturers, vast construction companies, big architect-engineering firms, and all their respective subcontractors and hired industry pressure groups."[42] Here again we find interlocking directorates, market control of energy resources and plant construction, and powerful lobbies that ensure access to the councils of government as well as favorable publicity.

The Nuclear Non-proliferation Treaty of 1968 and the International Atomic Energy Agency (IAEA) of the United Nations were designed to promote civilian nuclear energy programs worldwide under appropriate safeguards to preclude governments from diverting plutonium to use in weapons.[43] But India's nuclear test of 1974 dramatized the ease with which diversion could take place. With the spread of reprocessing technology in the Third World, moreover, the line between civilian and military nuclear facilities is very hard to detect. (A recent case in point: The French-built reactor in Iraq, destroyed by Israeli bombs in June 1981, had been inspected by the IAEA, which determined it was not being used for building bombs. Israel said otherwise.) Three specialists on the issue have written: "Most of the knowledge, much of the equipment, and the general nature of the organizations relevant to making bombs are inherent in civilian nuclear activities, and [as the Acheson-Lilienthal report of March 1946 said] are 'in much of their course interchangeable and interdependent' for peaceful or violent uses."[44]

Despite pressure from both U.S. nuclear firms and energy-poor Third World countries to expand nuclear exports, Presidents Carter and Ford generally restricted the sharing of reprocessing technology. Under the 1978 Nuclear Non-proliferation Act, export controls were tightened. Nuclear trade with any country required its consent to international inspection of its nuclear facilities to ensure the existence of comprehensive safeguards. Carter and Ford also deferred the commercial reprocessing of nuclear fuel, since that increased the risk of theft of weapons-grade plutonium. Under Reagan, both these positions were reversed. Reagan administration officials, while proclaiming their awareness of the risks of nuclear-weapons proliferation and their commitment to the 1968 treaty, strongly supported the nuclear industry's desire to recover its competitive edge over French and German exports. And at the same time that restrictions on nuclear exports to the Third World were relaxed, congressional approval was sought, unsuccessfully, to permit commercial reprocessing, presumably so that the stepped-up U.S. nuclear warhead program will have sufficient enriched plutonium. The contradiction between upholding the treaty and trying to link commercial technology to weapons production is unlikely to be lost on nuclear-minded regimes abroad.

Not that Carter was all that consistent. He overrode a unanimous decision by the Nuclear Regulatory Commission (NRC) to deny India access to U.S. nuclear fuel because of insufficient safeguards. When West Germany decided to sell nuclear technology to Brazil, which, like India, has not signed the Non-proliferation Treaty, Carter rejected congressional urging that he cut off nuclear aid to the Germans. And the same Carter NRC approved the sale of a Westinghouse reactor to the Philippines—a $1.1 billion project put together by the U.S. Export-Import Bank. Yet the Carter administration did act to prevent South Korea and Pakistan from acquiring French reprocessing facilities. And a number of governments signed or ratified the Non-proliferation Treaty during his tenure.

Consistent with its firm backing of the domestic nuclear industry, the Reagan administration actively sought out nuclear customers abroad. Its argument has a strange logic: "In order to influence the development of nuclear energy around the world, in order to ensure that that development is proliferation safe, we must be a leading participant in it."[45] Instead of setting an example for the rest of the world, the Third World in particular, of energy conservation and reliance on renewable sources, the administration proposed to work side by side with the nuclear industry, promoting its exports as vigorously as it promoted any other industry's. The only qualification a government needed to acquire U.S. nuclear fuel or technology was what one official called "nonproliferation merit," a "sense of responsibility [that] is no less than our own."[46] On that basis—which, in light of Reagan's interest in commercial reprocessing, seems weak indeed—the administration approved nuclear exports to Mexico, Egypt, South Africa, and Argentina and was working on new understandings with Brazil and China that might make them eligible. With Pakistan, the administration drew up a large military and economic aid package to compensate for being as yet unable to satisfy that country's nuclear appetite.

As the market for nuclear plants dries up in the United States due to increased costs and health and safety concerns, corporations such as Westinghouse, Bechtel and General Electric look anxiously to the Third World to salvage their investments. It is hardly coincidental that most of their Third World customers for nuclear reactors so far (the Philippines, Brazil, Egypt, South Korea, Mexico, and Taiwan) are among the repressive governments mentioned earlier, and they have more than passing interest in acquiring nuclear bombs. As enrichment technology improves, as more nuclear plants and equipment are made available, as plant inspections become less rigorous, as the myth persists that nuclear power is a substitute for oil (when in fact it can supply only electricity, which accounts for a mere 10 percent of oil's uses worldwide), and as the United States further weakens the concept of nonproliferation by its own practices, the opportunities for bomb production in the Third World are bound to multiply. Whether that comes about by government decision to produce nuclear weapons, by alliance between states anxious to have the bomb, or by theft and terrorism, the world will be that much more unsafe. Israel's attack on the Iraqi facility showed how dangerously unsettling proliferation can be, for now the possession of nuclear power in any form may invite attack.

Arms Transfers

National Security Council Study 68, approved by President Truman just a few months before the Korean War, stated: "Even if there were no Soviet Union we would face the great problem . . . [that] the absence of order among nations is becoming less and less tolerable."[47] Directly imposing order on the Soviet Union proved impossible; but beginning in Korea, U.S. strategists, believing that the Russians were probing and testing American will, adopted containment as the primary method for keeping their influence out of peripheral areas. Thus began the long period, which has not yet ended, in which the Third World—precisely as Mao Zedong had predicted in August 1946—would be the key battleground between socialism and capitalism.

America's "problem" in the Third World has revolved around the issue of order. Democratic rule and capitalist economic development have always been the stated U.S. goals; but these have been qualified with the stipulation that "stability" and "orderly transition" must first be established. Hence, the cozy U.S. relationships with Third World juntas and military establishments—the most reliable instruments for attaining stability and order—and with strong-armed dictators who support or at least tolerate such relationships. One thinks here not only of our three case studies but also of Mobutu in Zaire, Chiang Kai-shek and his son Chiang Ching-kuo in Taiwan, Marcos in the Philippines, and a long list of right-wing regimes in Central America. Nationalist leaders who have rejected dependent ties with the capitalist world, such as Arbenz in Guatemala (1954), Goulart in Brazil (1964), Allende in Chile (1971), Neto in Angola (1975), and the Sandinistas in Nicaragua today often have had to face U.S.-backed military forces in counterrevolutions and coups.

"It is profoundly in our national interest . . . that we support constructive change before such ties erode and the alternatives of radicalism or repression drive out moderate solutions," Secretary of State Vance said in 1979 with reference to the collapse of Somoza's rule in Nicaragua.[48] U.S. officials have typically seen the political choices in revolutionary and prerevolutionary Third World societies in terms of power struggles between moderates, rightists, and communists. In China in the late 1940s, for instance, Truman and his special emissary, General George C. Marshall, searched in vain for Chinese "liberals" who could become a third-force alternative to the communists and the inept Kuomintang. The same vain search characterized U.S. policy throughout the Vietnam War and in Iran as Khomeini's forces began their revolution. Too often, the United States has become saddled with repressive juntas instead. Arthur M. Schlesinger, Jr.'s memoir on the Kennedy years makes the point for us when he reports on how the President evaluated U.S. options in the Dominican Republic after the death of the dictatorial Rafael Trujillo:

> "There are three possibilities," [Kennedy] said, in descending order of preference: a decent democratic regime, a continuation of the Trujillo regime or a Castro regime. We ought to aim at the first, but we really can't renounce the second until we are sure that we can avoid the third.[49]

In being unable to "renounce" the option of continued support of a repressive regime, U.S. officials reveal how they are victimized by their Realism. The possibility that communists also may be nationalists, have popular support for a program of economic and social justice, and be able to work in genuine coalition with other social forces (such as the church, business, students, and even parts of the military) is dismissed out of hand. The assumption is too easily made—most recently in El Salvador under José Napoleon Duarte—that "moderates" have popular support, leadership capability, and independence from the far right and its repressive machinery. And in aligning ultimately with the rightists, U.S. administrations jump out of the frying pan into the fire, supporting anew precisely those elements and methods responsible for the instability Americans dread. It is a trap; and that U.S. leaders keep falling into it is due neither to miscalculation or lack of better choices but rather to their values and ideology, which demand that Third World self-determination be sacrificed to U.S. self-interest.

As with nuclear weapons, so with conventional ones: It has proven extremely difficult for Presidents to push or to be pushed significantly to reduce reliance on arms as the main U.S. instrument for bringing about Third World stability. Table 1 shows the worldwide growth of U.S. weapons sales and services since 1950. Most striking is the emphasis since the Vietnam War on government and private sales of arms instead of direct grants. Overwhelmingly, the weapons are going to the Third World: In 1978, for example, 79 percent, with the Middle East alone accounting for over one-half of all weapons purchases. With so much money at stake (roughly $30 billion in 1984) it is easy to see why arms transfers have created a powerful interest group in Washington. The arms contractors have high profits and hundreds of thousands of jobs to protect; the military professionals have counterparts abroad to satisfy as well as their own jobs to fill; the diplomats have allied governments to keep stable; and the multinational corporations, notably big oil companies, have producers and customers to protect.

In his 1978 State of the Union message, Jimmy Carter had said: "Our stand for peace is suspect if we are also the principal arms merchant of the world." His administration issued new guidelines designed to restrict the volume and calibre of arms sales. Every one of them was seriously compromised. For example, the total dollar volume was to be reduced from one fiscal year to the next; but key exemptions were introduced, such as the omission of commercial arms sales and sales to major U.S. allies (including Israel and the NATO powers), that discredited the administration's claim it had kept arms sales beneath its ceiling. Carter further asserted the United States would not be first to introduce a more advanced weapon system into a Third World region. But that was quickly breached when Iran purchased one-half billion dollars' worth of airborne radar planes,

Table 1
U.S. Deliveries of Military Weapons and Services, 1950–1979 (in Millions of Dollars)

	(in millions of dollars)					
	FMS* Credits	MAP**	Mil. sales financing	Mil. training	Commercial sales	"Excess" items
1950-1959	1,141	20,957	172	631	2,053	
1960-1969	6,718	14,687	1,584	792		
1970-1979	40,472	17,430	18,098	453	6,751***	6,349****
138,288	48,331	53,074	19,854	1,876	8,804	6,349

Sources: U.S. Department of Commerce, Bureau of the Census, Statistical Abstract of the United States for the Year 1980 (Washington, D.C., 1981), Table 601, p. 370; Michael T. Klare, Supplying Repression (Washington, D.C.: Institute for Policy Studies, 1978), pp. 31, 40.

* Foreign Military Sales Program (government-to-government sales).

** Military Assistance Program.

*** Includes estimates for 1977 and 1978; 1979 not included.

**** For 1950-1976 only.

and later when Israel and Saudi Arabia purchased advanced fighter bombers valued at over $4 billion. These and similar "waivers" on national security grounds more than made up, in dollar value, for arms sales lost because of the guidelines.

In the first year of the Reagan administration, moreover, there had been no pretense of adherence to restrictions. New guidelines issued in July 1981 restored the traditional U.S. conviction that arms sales "complement American security commitments" and are "an essential element of [the U.S.] global posture."[50] All future arms sales would be based, Reagan promised, on their net contribution to anticommunist defense and deterrence. Not a word was said about the more probable circumstance that U.S. weapons would be used by Third World regimes for domestic repression. Yet, that was the clear signal sent by Ambassador

Kirkpatrick when she spoke of a "more realistic" Latin American policy. "The Carter administration," she said, "underestimated the fragility of order in [Latin] societies, and overestimated the ease with which authority, once undermined, can be restored."[51] El Salvador soon became America's newest test case.

The lid is now off on total weapons sales, on the introduction of advanced weapons in Third World regions (for example, the sale of F–16s to Venezuela), on the sale of weapons developed solely for export, and on the co-production of weapons with other governments (for example, with Saudi Arabia). As if the overall purpose of Reagan's program was not clear enough, an undersecretary of state, James L. Buckley, clarified its special meaning for developing countries. By working cooperatively with them on arms sales, Buckley said, "in times of crisis, we may be able more effectively to project our own power and thus help deter aggression."[52] No doubt he had in mind the Rapid Deployment Force that was developed under Carter and expanded by Reagan for interventions abroad.

U.S. support of stability-minded authoritarian regimes does have limits, however. Some Third World governments become so heavy-handed in their repression of opponents that they risk encouraging precisely the instability they are supposed to prevent. Such dictators become liabilities. Their brutality is no longer cost effective: It ceases to serve domestic and foreign capitalist interests, and it encourages popular hostility instead of passivity and compliance. As Hipolito Solari Yrigoyen, an exiled former Argentine politician and human-rights activist, has said: "It's much easier for Mr. [David] Rockefeller to do business with a government that says it is in the process of improving than with a government that has an assassin's image."[53] When totalitarian regimes are no longer useful, the U.S. government not only will abandon them; it may work with "reform-minded moderates"—often, the military professionals the United States has trained—to have them overthrown.[54] The point to underscore here is that such a U.S. decision is not primarily motivated by concern about the human rights of the victims of repression, but about the preservation of U.S. economic and strategic interests. If, in traditional power politics, there are only enemies, U.S. foreign policy proves the point.

Military spending, strategies, and weapons systems boggle the minds of most people. No subject so instantly makes people surrender to expert opinion. Strategic concepts are highly esoteric and largely untested, the language of warfare is deliberately elegant and inoffensive, and the numbers involved are staggering beyond imagination. Yet the implications for our daily lives of the national-security establishment are far-reaching. Foreign policy begins at home. We now turn to where it ends, which is in the same place.

THE DOMESTIC COSTS OF GLOBALISM

> Perhaps it is a universal truth that the loss of liberty at home is to be charged to provisions against danger, real or pretended, from abroad.
>
> —James Madison, May 13, 1798

Throughout American history, conservatives and liberals alike have warned about the pernicious consequences of an imperial foreign policy for human rights at home. We reap what we sow. In direct contrast with the first axiom of U.S. foreign-policy ideology, these critics have argued that America's beneficent influence on world politics comes from the example set by adherence to and expansion of political liberties and social and economic justice at home. Neither national security nor the fulfillment of the "blessings of liberty" are achieved through foreign policies that contradict professed democratic values. President Roosevelt, speaking in 1944 with reference to the basic economic and social rights that now are part of the UN covenants on human rights, said: "America's own rightful place in the world depends in large part upon how fully these and similar rights have been carried into practice for our citizens. For unless there is security here at home there cannot be lasting peace in the world."[55]

Roosevelt was aware that foreign policies based on interventionism, a permanent war economy, and monopolistic control of commerce would undermine security for the American people just as surely as they would add to insecurity abroad. The more militarized and centralized a society, he and a few other American leaders (one thinks of Dwight Eisenhower and Senator Robert Taft) seemed to be saying, the less real security it would have. A nation cannot preserve liberty and equality while engaged in support of governments that flout elementary principles of human rights. Attitudes and values, moreover, become as important as practices: Policies that proceed from a sense of omnipotence, arrogance, and insensitivity to other societies' histories and cultures must emerge from, and be reflected in, domestic politics that reflect those same attitudes and values. Since the Vietnam War numerous commentators have drawn the lesson that major powers cannot for long effectively manipulate the political processes of Third World (or any other) societies. To that lesson should be added another: A major power which makes the attempt will suffer greatly for it.

It is appropriate at this point to specify how U.S. policies in the Third World have undermined the human rights of Americans and in the process, have even undermined the long-term interests of those powerful economic and bureaucratic groups in whose short-term interests these policies have typically been undertaken. As we see it, the following are among the most important linkages between foreign policy and domestic affairs.

Living costs and work opportunities for Americans are adversely affected by excessive military spending. In the first place, such spending is highly inflationary. The greatly increased supply of government money for weapons does not produce goods or services for which there is social demand. Because of the highly technical nature of most military research and production, moreover, thousands fewer jobs are created by every $1 billion of military spending than would be created by a comparable amount spent on (for example) education, health services, housing, or public transportation. Worker productivity also suffers: One reason the United States has lost its industrial leadership to Europe and Japan is that large firms have relied over the years on Pentagon contracts and have become used to wasteful practices and cost overruns. Investments to modernize facilities have been put off; now it may be too late to recover.

Working people bear the main financial burden of profligate government spending on the military. This occurs in both direct and disguised ways. Directly, about 32 percent of federal taxes on individual incomes (nearly $5,000 a year for an average family of four) will go for defense in the early 1980s. Indirectly, individuals pay more in rising interest rates stemming from high federal deficits, inflation, and interest paid on the federal debt, all of which result in significant part from excessive military spending. The impact on individuals is far greater than on multinational corporations and Pentagon contractors. Corporations can take advantage of numerous laws favorable to them, such as tax write-offs for research, publicity, and lobbying; credits against taxes paid abroad; deferral of taxes on overseas profits; government bailouts, and insurance of investors against nationalization of foreign assets. Corporate taxes as a percentage of federal receipts under Reagan have dropped to an all-time low of 5.9 percent. All this lost tax revenue for the government must be made up by individuals; hence, the rise of individual tax contributions to the Treasury to over 48 percent of total receipts. When we read stories of the multinationals exporting jobs to low-wage societies, therefore, we should keep in mind that workers at home and owners of small businesses are in effect subsidizing their operations with their taxes, as well as losing work opportunities.

Higher prices and resource scarcities are occurring in part because the U.S. economy has, since World War II, relied for growth on military production, food exports, and multinational investments and financial services. The rising cost of housing and personal credit, for instance, stems partly from the increased interest rates multinational banks are charging on home loans and credit cards to make up for the bad loans they made to underdeveloped countries. Diminished domestic production of energy, manufactured goods, and even certain farm products (such as tomatoes, strawberries, and pineapples) means these must be imported, adding to inflation and intensifying dependence on overseas sources of raw materials.

The resort to violence as an accepted norm of international conduct eventually finds its way home. The Vietnam War led directly to the National Guard attacks on students at Kent State and Jackson State. The overthrow of Salvador Allende led to the murders in Washington, D.C., of Chilean opposition leader Orlando Letelier and his research assistant. Ex-CIA agents, who may have retained their contacts with the Agency, have worked in the United States and abroad as assassins and saboteurs for Libyan dictator Moammar Kadafi. Numerous U.S.-trained soldiers have turned up as mercenaries in the pay of the South African, Zairian, and other repressive regimes. Private armies today train in Florida and California in hopes of restoring anticommunist regimes in Cuba and Nicaragua.

Military interventions and deployments abroad have *physically and psychologically maimed* many thousands of soldiers. Exposed to toxic chemicals such as Agent Orange or addicted to drugs, they return home to lead twisted lives. Among Vietnam veterans, for instance, there is an extraordinary incidence of suicides, criminal arrests, alcoholism, and drug overdoses.

The *civil liberties* of U.S. citizens and visitors are constantly threatened by intelligence activities directed at "enemy agents." Privacy and freedom of movement and association have long been compromised by U.S. government surveillance and cooperation with agents of allied governments who operate here. The phenomenon of McCarthyism—the witch hunts for communists, the purges of officials, and the loyalty oaths—is synonymous with the cold war. Since then, the CIA and the FBI have engaged in numerous instances of spying, infiltrating, and "black bag" operations against citizens and groups suspected of being subversive. These have been well documented since the Watergate "affair" came to light; they are likely to increase in the 1980s as restrictions on CIA domestic spying are removed. Somewhat less well known are the activities of foreign intelligence agents who spy on their own nationals residing in the United States—activities clearly known to and permitted by U.S. agencies. This is not surprising when we realize that the American CIA set up and trained several of these foreign spy outfits, including the Chilean DINA, the South Korean KCIA, and SAVAK, the secret police of the Shah of Iran. In short, as James Madison said, the greater are perceived or manufactured threats from abroad, the closer does the nation approach a garrison state.

Bribery to obtain military or other contracts from foreign governments is commonly practiced by multinational corporations. Not only do Americans pay for bribery through taxes foregone, the bribery itself often comes home (as the "Koreagate" and "Abscam" scandals showed) in payoffs to U.S. public officials.

Contaminated food and other dangerous products are imported from the Third World after having been treated with U.S.-manufactured pesticides or chemicals banned for sale at home. The multinationals dump these lethal items abroad on unsuspecting, often illiterate workers; but the goods make their way back home in contaminated coffee and tomatoes, fish products that were exposed to irradiated or polluted water (from U.S. nuclear reactors or vessels), and chemically treated clothing.

Refugees from war-torn countries in which the United States intervened (for example, from Indochina, Cuba, and El Salvador), or from authoritarian states long supported by the United States (such as Haiti and Guatemala), put additional pressure on a society already wracked by unemployment and housing shortages. The treatment many refugees and undocumented workers (some tellingly labeled "aliens") receive from public agencies such as the U.S. Immigration and Naturalization Service is shockingly racist and contrary to law.

Secrecy, as we have discussed, is an essential tool of the national security state. Reducing media access to officials and the flow of information to the public actually has little to do with national security. But such restrictions do enhance the security of *the state*: They prevent embarrassing leaks, preserve hostile stereotypes, keep out uncomfortable questions, and promote a benign image of authoritarian allies. Supplementing them is the classification system itself. In light of the Pentagon Papers and other secret documents that have come into the public domain, we are led to conclude that classified information hides the truth from the American public far more than it keeps vital secrets from the Russians.

The impact of a militarized foreign policy on all levels of American *education*, finally, is especially profound. Some of that impact is readily identifiable, such as the coopting of teachers to do "defense-related" research or consulting; the endowments and grants of multinational firms to higher education; and the orientation of curricula to conflict, power, and war rather than to conflict resolution and alternatives to war. The subtler impact is also the more far reaching: The inculcation of militarist and nationalist values, of negative assumptions about human nature and conflict potential, and of distorted, patronizing, and often racist images of Third World societies.

In short, Americans pay dearly for the overseas adventures and global reach of government and big business. The bill would seem to cover the basics of ordinary life: Diet, health, education, jobs, energy, justice. These activities abroad reflect and are reflected in declines in the quality of life at home: The subversion of the Constitution, the celebration of martial virtues, the increasing gap between rich and poor, the ever-tightening relationship between big business and big government ("friendly fascism" as Bertram Gross has called it in a book of the same title), the increasing powerlessness of minorities, the elderly, and numerous other groups, and the mad search to create new "needs" and wants that will perpetuate American globalism.[56]

One might conclude that U.S. behavior in the Third World brings out the worst features of our system and its predominant values. But that suggests that if we can recover the best of America—its traditions of community, self-reliance, creativity, responsibility, appreciation of nature and of diversity—foreign policy can be transformed to serve humane ends. With a different interpretation of what it takes to make America secure, restoring the integrity and quality of life at home, the nation might again become the shining example Americans since Thomas Jefferson have regarded as their best contribution to the world.

NOTES

1. Speech by Richard L. McCall, Assistant Secretary of State for International Organization Affairs, October 14, 1980; U.S. Department of State transcript.

2. According to U.S. government statistics, between 1973 and 1980 the United States and its allies (mostly NATO) have on average accounted for 58 percent of all government arms deliveries to the Third World. (Warsaw Pact countries account for the other 42 percent.) The

U.S. share (an average of 33 percent) would be even higher if U.S. commercial arms sales and military grants were included. (In 1976, for instance, U.S. companies sold $1.56 billion in arms to Third World governments.) These figures do not include arms backlogs—arms sales concluded but not yet carried out. One informed estimate is that the United States in 1982 had a backlog of $50 billion in arms sales.

3. Willy Brandt et al., *North-South: A Program for Survival* (Cambridge, Mass.: MIT Press, 1980).

4. Gerald O. Barney, ed., *The Global 2000 Report to the President: Entering the Twenty-first Century*, vol. 1 (Harmondsworth, England: Penguin, 1982).

5. David Rockefeller, cited in Thomas Ferguson and Joel Rogers, "Another Trilateral Election?" *The Nation*, June 28, 1980, p. 784.

6. Andrew Young, quoted in Holly Sklar, ed., *Trilateralism: The Trilateral Commission and Elite Planning for World Management* (Boston: South End, 1980), p. 564.

7. Speech by Cyrus Vance, secretary of state, March 27, 1980; State Department transcript. See also Secretary of State George Schultz's foreign aid report for fiscal 1984 in a presentation to Congress on February 16, 1983.

8. Richard Allen, quoted in *The Nation*, December 13, 1980, p. 636.

9. Reagan quotes the letter in a speech before the National Press Club in Washington, D.C., November 18, 1981; State Department transcript.

10. Jeane Kirkpatrick, "Dictatorships and Double Standards," *Commentary*, November 1979, pp. 34–45.

11. *Los Angeles Times*, March 12, 1981, p.15.

12. Shortly after these words were written, a *Los Angeles Times* report from El Salvador cited these words of a Catholic church official there: "Why does Reagan light candles for Poland's nine dead and complain about Poland's living two months under martial law? In El Salvador 30,000 have been killed and we have been under martial law for two years. Why does he light the candles for Poland and not for us?"

13. Lyndon Johnson, quoted in Richard Barnet, *Intervention and Revolution: The United States in the Third World* (Cleveland: World, 1968), p. 25.

14. The $2 trillion figure does not include the cost of interest on the national debt when the government borrowed to finance its aid programs. Senator Jesse Helms, in a report of May 1982, insisted that any true accounting of the foreign-aid program should take account of the fact that it almost always has been funded in years of government

budgeting deficits. Helms estimated that U.S. aid from 1946 to 1980 was $2.3 trillion, with interest comprising nearly 88 percent of the total.

15. Henry Kissinger, *Nuclear Weapons and Foreign Policy* (Garden City, N.Y.: Doubleday Anchor, 1958), p. 244, emphasis supplied.

16. Albert Einstein, cited in *New York Times Magazine*, August 2, 1964.

17. In Melvin Gurtov, *The United States against the Third World: Antinationalism and Intervention* (New York: Praeger, 1974), ch. 1.

18. Harry S. Truman, quoted in Noam Chomsky, *American Power and the New Mandarins* (New York: Pantheon, 1967), p. 268.

19. *Los Angeles Times*, March 19, 1981, p.10.

20. Walt W. Rostow, *The View from the Seventh Floor* (New York: Harper & Row, 1964), p. 53.

21. Speech by Henry Kissinger to the American Society of Newspaper Editors, April 17, 1975; State Department transcript.

22. Richard Nixon, "Asia after Viet Nam," *Foreign Affairs*, 46, no. 1 (October 1967), p. 123.

23. Henry Kissinger, quoted in James Petras and Morris Morley, *The United States and Chile: Imperialism and the Overthrow of the Allende Government* (New York: Monthly Review, 1975), p. vii.

24. Brzezinski said much the same thing in an interview with *Time* (May 29, 1978, p. 18): "A big country like the U.S. is not like a speedboat on a lake. It can't veer suddenly to the right or left. It's like a large ship. There's continuity to its course . . . . However, each Administration imposes its own stamp on foreign policy, by turning a little bit from one side to the other."

25. Some of these "shared images" are drawn from Morton Halperin et al., *Bureaucratic Politics and Foreign Policy* (Washington, D.C.: Brookings Institution, 1974), pp. 11–12. Halperin, in turn, relied heavily for these images on Graham Allison's "Cool It: The Foreign Policy of Young America," *Foreign Policy*, no. 1 (Winter 1970–1971), pp. 144–160.

26. Dean Acheson, quoted in Gilbert G. Gutierrez, "Dean Rusk and Southeast Asia: An Operational Code Analysis" (University of California, Riverside, doctoral dissertation, April 1974), pp. 136–137.

27. *San Francisco Chronicle*, May 10, 1980.

28. Henry Kissinger, *American Foreign Policy* (New York: Norton, 1974), p. 30.

29. Dean Rusk, cited in Roger Hilsman, *To Move A Nation:The Politics of Foreign Policy in the Administration of John F. Kennedy* (New York: Doubleday Publishing Co., Inc., 1967), p. 219.

30. *San Francisco Chronicle*, May 27, 1980, p. 8.

31. See, for example, testimony by Marshall D. Shulman, special

adviser to the secretary of state on Soviet affairs, before a House of Representatives subcommittee, in Department of State, *Current Policy*, no. 33 (September 1978), p. 2.

32. Amory B. Lovins, L. Hunter Lovins, and Leonard Ross, "Nuclear Power and Nuclear Bombs," *Foreign Affairs*, vol. 53, no. 5 (Summer 1980), p. 1175.

33. The full text of Eisenhower's memorandum may be found in Seymour Melman, *Pentagon Capitalism: The Political Economy of War* (New York: McGraw-Hill, 1970), pp. 231–239.

34. Although the focus here is on the Pentagon, the reader should keep in mind that other U.S. government agencies, especially the Department of Energy (which spends nearly half its budget on nuclear weapons and energy), are equally critical parts of the national-security establishment.

35. For example, Gordon Adams's study, *The Iron Triangle* (New York: Council on Economic Priorities, 1981), shows that between 1970 and 1979, 1,942 persons transferred between the eight top military contractors and the Department of Defense or the National Aeronautics and Space Administration.

36. Clark Clifford, quoted in Richard J. Barnet, *Roots of War* (New York: Atheneum, 1972), p. 100.

37. Ibid.

38. Zbigniew Brzezinski, "How the Cold War Was Played," *Foreign Affairs*, vol. 51, no. 1 (October 1972), p. 204.

39. Wayne Biddle, "The Silo Busters," *Harper's*, December 1979, pp. 43–58.

40. Secretary of State Haig in fact said during 1981 that one way the United States could respond to the threat of a Soviet invasion of Western Europe would be to explode a "demonstration" nuclear weapon in Europe in hopes of making the Russians desist.

41. On the nuclear industry's early history, and the critical role of government in it, two studies that are readily available can be recommended: John J. Berger, *Nuclear Power: The Unviable Option*, rev. ed. (New York: Dell, 1977), and Barry Commoner, *The Poverty of Power* (New York: Knopf, 1975).

42. Berger, *Nuclear Power*, p. 159.

43. Sources for this section on nuclear proliferation are: Lovins, Lovins, and Ross, "Nuclear Power and Nuclear Bombs," pp. 1137–1177; a speech by Victor Gilinsky, NRC commissioner since 1975, reprinted in *Not Man Apart* (San Francisco), May 1981, pp. 16–17; U.S. Arms Control and Disarmament Agency, *Arms Control 1979* (Washington, D.C.: U.S. Government Printing Office, 1980); Joseph R. Egan, "The Mask Is Off the 'Peaceful Atom,' " *In These Times*, November 18–24,

1981, pp. 6–22; "500-Mile Island—The Philippine Nuclear Reactor Deal," *Pacific Research*, vol. 10, no. 1 (1979), pp. 1–45.

44. Lovins, Lovins, and Ross, "Nuclear Power and Nuclear Bombs," p. 1139.

45. Speech by James L. Malone, assistant secretary of state for oceans and international environmental and scientific affairs, December 1, 1981; U.S. Department of State, *Current Policy*, no. 354, (same date).

46. *Ibid.*

47. Cited in William A. Williams, "Is the Idea and Reality of America Possible without Empire?" *The Nation*, August 2–9, 1980, p. 114.

48. Speech by Cyrus Vance, July 23, 1979; State Department transcript.

49. Arthur M. Schlesinger, Jr., *A Thousand Days: John F. Kennedy in the White House* (Boston: Houghton Mifflin, 1965), p. 769.

50. U.S. Congress, House of Representatives, Committee on Foreign Affairs, Subcommittee on International Security and Scientific Affairs, *Changing Perspectives on U.S. Arms Transfer Policy: Report by the Congressional Research Service, Library of Congress*, 97th Cong., 1st Sess. (Washington, D.C.: U.S. Government Printing Office, 1981), p. 32.

51. Jeane Kirkpatrick, statement at confirmation hearing, January 15, 1981.

52. Quoted in House, *Changing Perspectives on U.S. Arms Transfer Policy*, p. 36.

53. Cited in *These Times*, March 1982.

54. Hence, the United States played major roles not only in putting in office South Vietnam's Ngo Dinh Diem, Nguyen Cao Ky, and Nguyen Van Thieu; the Shah of Iran; Anastasio Somoza in Nicaragua; Cuba's Fulgencio Batista; and South Korea's Park Chung Hui, but also in bringing about their removal. In most of these cases the United States compensated its friends by allowing them to live a comfortable retirement here; but in a few cases—Diem for certain, as the Pentagon Papers document; and possibly Park as well—the United States acquiesced in their assassination. Both their successors, Ky and Chun Doo Hwan, were military officers trained in the United States.

55. Franklin Roosevelt, quoted by Marcus Raskin, "Progressive Liberalism for the '80s," *The Nation*, May 17, 1980, p. 591.

56. Bertram Gross, *Friendly Fascism*, rev. ed. (Boston: South End Press, 1984).

BIBLIOGRAPHY

Since the major textbooks on U.S. foreign policy contain extensive bibliographies, we can concentrate here on books of particular value for the critical perspective they offer on ideas, institutions, and policy instruments.

For thoughtful critiques of U.S. foreign-policy priorities and the concepts that underlie them, we recommend: Richard J. Barnet, *Roots of War* (New York: Atheneum, 1972) and *Real Security: Restoring American Power in a Dangerous Decade* (New York: Simon and Schuster, 1981); George Kennan, *The Cloud of Danger* (Boston: Little, Brown, 1977); Robert W. Tucker, *The Purposes of American Power: An Essay on National Security* (New York: Praeger, 1981); Robert C. Johansen, *The National Interest and the Human Interest: An Analysis of U.S. Foreign Policy* (Princeton, N.J.: Princeton University Press, 1980); William Appleman Williams, *Empire as a Way of Life* (New York: Oxford University Press, 1980); Gabriel Kolko, *The Roots of American Foreign Policy* (Boston: Beacon, 1969); and Arthur Macy Cox, *The Myths of National Security: The Peril of Secret Government* (Boston: Beacon, 1975). Each of these works represents a different school of foreign-policy analysis, but each is well informed and clearly written.

The origins of the cold war are quite germane to an understanding of U.S. policy toward the Third World, as the next chapter suggests. Among the many such histories, we recommend Daniel Yergin's *Shattered Peace: The Origins of the Cold War and the National Security State* (Boston: Houghton Mifflin, 1977) for its definitions of "Yalta" and "Riga" thinking in the evolution of U.S. policy toward the Soviet Union; Fred Block's *The Origins of International Economic Disorder: A Study of United States International Monetary Policy from World War II to the Present* (Berkeley and Los Angeles: University of California Press, 1977), for its trenchant portrayal of the interplay of economic and political post–World War II planning to ensure American predominance; Walter LaFeber's comprehensive *America, Russia, and the Cold War 1945–1980*, 4th ed. (New York: Wiley, 1980); John G. Stoessinger's *Nations in Darkness: China, Russia, and America* (New York: Random House, 1971), for the light it sheds on misperceptions between major-power leaders; and Gregg Herken's *The Winning Weapon: The Atomic Bomb in the Cold War, 1945–1950* (New York: Random House, 1981), on atomic diplomacy.

Particular features of the foreign-policy process also have a distinguished critical literature. Irving L. Janis, in *Victims of Groupthink: A Psychological Study of Foreign Policy Decisions and Fiascoes*, 2d ed. (Boston: Houghton Mifflin, 1982), applies social psychology to understanding the group dynamics behind several major cold war decisions. *"Lessons" of the Past: The Use and Misuse of History in American Foreign Policy* (London: Oxford University Press, 1973), by Ernest R. May, examines the mistaken application of history's "lessons" to those decisions. Morton H. Halperin, Priscilla Clapp, and Arnold Kanter, in *Bureaucratic Politics and Foreign Policy* (Washington, D.C.: Brookings Institution, 1974), stress the salience of bureaucratic roles and missions, as well as shared images, in policymaking. G. William Domhoff's long-standing interest has been in the question, who rules America? Of his several works on that subject, see in particular *The Powers That Be: Processes of Ruling-Class Domination in America* (New York: Random House, 1978) for excellent essays on the theory and practice of elites that influence decision making. (Laurence Shoup's *The Carter Presidency* [Palo Alto, Calif.: Ramparts, 1980] is a useful application of Domhoff's work to understanding the significance of the Trilateral Commission.)

The literature on American institutions is enormous, but very little of it critically evaluates their specific role in the foreign-policy process. On the press, see Ben H. Bagdikian's *The Media Monopoly* (Boston: Beacon, 1983) on corporate control of the news along with James Aronson's *The Press and the Cold War* (Boston: Beacon, 1970). Their analyses should be supplemented by other works that document the control of news and information generally by Western, and especially American, news services and technology. Two of these works are *The Geopolitics of Information: How Western Culture Dominates the World* (London: Faber and Faber, 1980), by Anthony Smith, and *Who Knows: Information in the Age of the Fortune 500* (Norwood, N.J.: Ablex, 1982), by Herbert I. Schiller. On other institutions, see Thomas M. Franck and Edward Weisband, *Foreign Policy by Congress* (New York: Oxford University Press, 1979), and John Spanier and Joseph Nogee, eds., *Congress, the Presidency and American Foreign Policy* (New York: Pergamon, 1981), on executive-congressional relations; John E. Mueller, *War, Presidents and Public Opinion* (New York: Wiley, 1973); Seymour Melman, *The Permanent War Economy: American Capitalism in Decline* (New York: Simon and Schuster, 1974), and Gordon Adams, *The Iron Triangle: The Politics of Defense Contracts* (New York: Council on Economic Priorities, 1981), on the military-industrial complex; and, on the CIA, Victor Marchetti and John D. Marks, *The C.I.A. and the Cult of Intelligence* (New York: Knopf, 1974), Philip Agee, *Inside the Company: CIA Diary* (Baltimore: Penguin, 1975), and Thomas Powers, *The Man Who Kept the Secrets: Richard Helms and the CIA* (New York: Pocket Books, 1979).

The literature on the U.S. economic and military role in Third World politics and economies is really central to our analysis. On the economic side, there are important writings on multinational corporations and international political economy such as Harry Magdoff's *The Age of Imperialism: The Economics of U.S. Foreign Policy* (New York: Modern Reader, 1969), which is dated but still conceptually valuable; Richard J. Barnet and Ronald E. Muller, *Global Reach: The Power of the Multinationals Corporations* (New York: Simon and Schuster, 1974); Robert J. Gilpin, *U.S. Power and the Multinational Corporations* (New York: Basic Books, 1975); and C. Fred Bergsten, Thomas Horst, and Theodore Moran, *American Multinationals and American Interests* (Washington, D.C.: Brookings Institution, 1978). Several monographs clarify the interplay of private and international capital in the Third World, including Cheryl Payer's *The Debt Trap: The International Monetary Fund and the Third World* (New York: Monthly Review, 1974); Teresa Hayter, *Aid as Imperialism* (Harmondsworth, England: Penguin, 1971), which focuses on Latin America; Penny Lernoux's study of the politics of the big banks, *In Banks We Trust* (New York: Doubleday, Anchor, 1984); and Robert J. Engler, *The Politics of Oil* (New York: Macmillan, 1976).

On the military side, there are several valuable studies of U.S. interventions in and arms sales to the Third World. Besides Melvin Gurtov's study, *The United States Against the Third World* (New York: Praeger, 1974) already cited, see Richard J. Barnet, *Intervention and Revolution: The United States in the Third World* (Cleveland: World, 1968), and J.L.S. Girling, *America and the Third World* (London: Routledge and Kegan, 1980), on interventions. Concerning U.S. arms and economic aid to repressive governments, see Noam Chomsky and Edward S. Herman, *The Washington Connection and Third World Fascism* (Boston: South End, 1979), and Michael T. Klare and Cynthia Arnson, *Supplying Repression: U.S. Support for Authoritarian Regimes Abroad* (Washington, D.C.: Institute for Policy Studies, 1981). Andrew J. Pierre's *The Global Politics of Arms Sales* (Princeton, N.J.: Princeton University Press, 1982) puts the matter in international political perspective and provides useful figures. Those wishing to see comparative figures on military and economic spending and on the arms traffic should consult any of three annual publications: Ruth Leger Sivard, *World Military and Social Expenditures* (published by World Priorities, Box 1003, Leesburg, Va. 22075); *World Military Expenditures and Arms Transfers*, published by the U.S. Arms Control and Disarmament Agency; and the *SIPRI Yearbook* of the Stockholm International Peace Research Institute. The Center for Defense Information (600 Maryland Avenue, S.W., Washington, D.C. 20024) and the Congressional Research Service of the Library of Congress also publish periodic analyses of U.S. conventional arms transfers.

2

The United States in Iran

> On your first question, Mr. Chairman, the issue of whether our intelligence was adequate, let me say this: I don't believe it is accurate or indeed fair to the intelligence community to attribute the problem of American perceptions of events in Iran to a failure of intelligence. I think the problem is a much broader one than that.
>
> —Harold H. Saunders,
> Assistant Secretary of State for Near Eastern,
> African, and South Asian Affairs,
> *Hearings before Subcommittee on Europe and the Middle East, House of Representatives*, January 1979

In January 1979, a popular revolution, within a year from its inception, overthrew the regime of Mohammad Reza Pahlavi, the "King of Kings" and the "Light of the Aryans." Shortly after, Ayatolla Rouhollah Khomeini, a prominent religious leader, who had been sent to exile in 1964 by the Shah, returned to Tehran and created the Islamic Republic of Iran. These events are probably one of the most dramatic episodes of the late twentieth century: They affected not only the lives of 36 million Iranians, but they also influenced regional and international politics.

The United States was affected more than any other country by the Iranian revolution. On the political level, a very reliable and strong ally was overthrown. Less than a year after the ouster of the Shah, Iranian-American relations were severed, the

American Embassy in Tehran was taken over by a group of Iranian students, and over fifty Americans were taken hostage.

The demise of the Shah also had significant economic consequences for the United States. For almost twenty-five years, Iran was one of the major importers of American goods and services. From 1955 to 1978, $21 billion in military sales were negotiated between Tehran and Washington (see Table 2). This included the purchase of some very sophisticated military equipment by the Shah's government (see Table 3).

The United States also exported substantial amounts of consumer and industrial goods to Iran, including wheat, rice, pharmaceuticals, automobiles, and other items. In late 1977 the U.S. Department of Commerce described business opportunities in Iran in these terms: "Iran's rapid economic growth has established a business climate characterized by expansion and keen competition, which should continue for several years to come. United States suppliers hold a leading position in the Iranian market . . . [and] excellent opportunities continue for sales of U.S. capital goods and services to Iran" (see Tables 4, 5, and 6).

Iran under the Shah was a major exporter of oil to the Western world. Although the United States received only 5.5 percent of its oil consumption from Iran, Washington's allies did receive a more substantial portion of their oil needs from Iran. Japan and West Germany, for example, each imported 17.2 percent and 13 percent of their oil consumption from Iran, respectively (see Table 7).

While the Western world's dependence on Iranian oil was substantial and significant in itself, there was still another dimension to the Iranian-American relations: Over the years, the Shah had become a strong leader in the development of the Organization of Petroleum Exporting Countries (OPEC). He was a moderating force that Washington could count on to stabilize the price of OPEC oil. Given that in 1978, the United States alone imported an average of 5.6 million barrels of oil from OPEC countries per day, the Shah was a valuable friend to Washington; he could help American trade and foreign exchange.

Despite the extensiveness of political and economic relations between Tehran and Washington under the Shah, the United

Table 2

United States and Iran, Military Sales and Services (in Thousands of Dollars; fiscal years)

	Foreign military sales agreements	Foreign military sales deliveries	Military assistance program deliveries expenditures including military assistance service funded and excluding training	International military education and training program deliveries including military assistance service funded	Summary of students trained under international military education and training program, including military assistance service funded.
1969.......	235,821	94,881	45,343	3,247	765
1970.......	134,929	127,717	12,791	2,447	504
1971.......	363,884	78,566	4,290	2,230	354
1972.......	472,611	214,807	6,277	885	186
1973.......	2,171,355	248,391	2,621	.....	.....
1974.......	4,325,357	648,461	191	.....	.....
1975.......	2,447,140	1,006,131	2	.....	.....
1976[1]......	1,794,487	1,927,860	.....	.....	.....
1977.......	5,713,769	2,433,050	.....	.....	.....
1978.......	2,586,890	1,792,892	.....	.....	.....
1955-78....	20,751,656	8,715,810	766,733	67,445	11,025

[1]Includes transitional quarter.

Source: U.S., Congress, Joint Economic Committee, Economic Consequences of Revolution in Iran, Joint Committee Print (Washington, D.C.: Government Printing Office, 1980), p. 8.

Table 3

Major Items of Military Equipment Delivered to the Government of Iran

	Quantity
Aircraft:	
C-130	13
KC-707	13
F-4	209
F-5	217
F-14A	80
P-3	6
RF-4	12
AH-1 helicopter	202
UH-1 helicopter	56
Naval craft:	
Destroyers	5
Patrol craft	20
Submarine	1
Ground forces:	
Armored cargo carriers	435
Armored personnel carriers	878
Tanks	461
155-mm howitzers (self-propelled)	440
175-mm guns (self-propelled)	37
8-in howitzers (self-propelled)	51
Munitions (missiles):	
TOW	([1])
Dragon	([1])
Harpoon	([1])
Hawk	([1])
Maverick	([1])
Phoenix	([1])
Sidewinder	([1])
Sparrow	([1])
Standard (surface-to-air)	([1])

[1]Quantities classified

Note: The above list includes only major items sold and delivered to the Government of Iran under foreign military sales procedures. Additional quantities of some aircraft, in particular, were sold directly by private companies and are not included. Since delivery, attrition and usage have reduced the quantities available to Iran.

Source: House of Representatives, Committee on Foreign Affairs, Subcommittee on Europe and the Middle East, Hearings. U.S. Policy Toward Iran, January 1979, pp. 67-68.

Table 4
Iran Trade Patterns, 1971–1977 (in Millions of U.S. Dollars)

	1971	1972	1973	1974	1975	1976	1977
Iran - Exports:							
United States	136	199	344	2,133	1,398	1,483	2,756
Federal Republic of Germany	300	340	582	1,126	1,334	1,807	1,696
Japan	1,241	1,376	1,754	4,331	4,526	4,049	3,881
United Kingdom	242	282	532	1,093	1,412	1,709	1,245
France	136	174	284	651	1,150	1,309	998
European Economic Community	1,243	1,587	2,582	7,286	7,139	8,256	7,751
U.S.S.R.							
Iran's Total Exports	3,298	3,958	6,078	16,620	16,959	18,613	18,327
Iran - Imports:							
United States	530	614	474	974	2,051	2,133	3,004
Federal Republic of Germany	403	459	655	991	1,824	2,304	3,014
Japan	262	360	484	847	1,662	2,098	2,136
United Kingdom	209	318	338	450	877	992	1,256
France	101	135	163	217	415	630	751
European Economic Community	942	1,225	1,488	2,137	4,022	5,505	6,753
U.S.S.R.	67	74	180	212	231	126	22
Totals	2,514	3,185	3,782	5,828	11,082	13,788	16,936

Source: U.S., Congress, Joint Economic Committee, _Economic Consequences of Revolution in Iran_, Joint Committee Print (Washington, D.C.: Government Printing Office, 1980), p. 11.

Table 5

Iran Trade Patterns, 1971–1977 (Percentage share of the Iranian market by major trading partners)

	United States	Federal Republic of Germany	Japan	United Kingdom	France	EEC	U.S.S.R.
1971:							
Exports	3.9	8.5	35.3	6.9	3.9	35.4	...
Imports	24.0	18.3	11.9	9.5	4.6	42.7	3.0
1972:							
Exports	4.8	8.1	33.0	6.8	4.2	38.9	...
Imports	22.2	16.6	13.0	11.5	4.9	44.2	2.7
1973:							
Exports	5.4	9.2	27.7	8.4	4.5	40.8	...
Imports	14.0	19.4	14.3	10.0	4.8	44.0	5.3
1974:							
Exports	11.3	6.0	22.9	5.8	3.4	38.6	...
Imports	18.0	18.2	15.6	8.3	4.0	39.4	3.9
1975:							
Exports	7.7	7.3	24.8	7.7	6.3	39.1	...
Imports	19.8	17.6	16.1	8.5	4.0	38.9	2.2
1976:							
Exports	7.2	8.8	19.7	8.3	6.4	40.2	...
Imports	16.6	17.9	16.3	7.7	4.9	42.7	1.0
1977:							
Exports	12.8	7.9	18.0	5.8	4.6	36.0	...
Imports	19.1	19.1	13.6	8.0	4.8	42.9	1.1

[1]Estimate.

Source: U.S., Congress, Joint Economic Committee, Economic Consequences of Revolution in Iran, Joint Committee Print (Washington, D.C.: Government Printing Office, 1980). p. 11.

Table 6
United States Share of Selected Commodities Imports to Iran, 1975–1976 (in Thousands of U.S. Dollars)

	Total	U.S. share	Percentage
Wheat	22,681	15,631	69.0
Rice	10,519	10,334	98.0
Pharmaceuticals	14,064	2,054	15.0
Tools	2,630	507	19.0
Mining and construction equipment	25,906	12,289	47.0
Tractors	7,955	3,408	43.0
Autos	9,895	945	9.5
Agricultural equipment	2,571	261	10.0

Source: U.S., Congress, Joint Economic Committee, *Economic Consequences of Revolution in Iran*, Joint Committee Print (Washington, D.C.: Government Printing Office, 1980), p. 12.

Table 7
Users of Iranian Oil

Importer	1978 percent of-- Users' Oil Supplies	Iran's Output
Japan	17.2	16.0
United States	5.6	15.9
West Germany	13.0	6.2
Italy	16.0	5.0
Netherlands	62.4	4.7
United Kingdom	13.5	4.2
France	9.0	3.6
Belgium	32.7	2.7
Canada	7.6	2.3

Source: Petroleum Intelligence Weekly, Jan. 22, 1979, p. 8.

States was not prepared for the Iranian Revolution that toppled the Shah's regime. According to all available data, the overthrow of Shah Mohammed Reza Pahlavi in Iran in early 1979 caught the Carter administration completely by surprise. Just a year before the Shah's departure, Carter referred to Iran as "an island of stability in one of the more troubled areas of the world."[1] Even after the trouble had started, and just a few months before the Shah's demise, a Central Intelligence Agency study concluded that Iran was not "in a revolutionary or even pre-revolutionary situation." This top secret report (completed in August 1978) advised the White House that: "Those who are in opposition in Iran, both violent and nonviolent, do not have the capability to be more than troublesome . . . there is dissatisfaction with the Shah's tight control of the political process, but this does not threaten the government."[2] What the Americans had not predicted, said CIA Director Admiral Stansfield Turner in February 1979, was that "a single man, a 78-year-old cleric who had been in exile for 15 years, would be a catalyst that would bring all these forces together, and we had a huge volcano, a truly national revolution."[3]

A review of various news analyses reveals a very interesting phenomenon: The failure to predict the Iranian situation went beyond the Carter administration. Not only were the CIA and the State Department caught by surprise, but so too were the U.S. Congress, academicians, journalists, and businessmen. For over a decade, Iran had been considered one of the most stable governments in the Middle East.[4] This was reflected in the American sale of billions of dollars worth of sophisticated military hardware to Iran and the movement of numerous financial institutions from Beirut to Tehran after the eruption of the Lebanese Civil War in 1975.

How does one explain the official U.S. attitudes toward Iranian politics and America's surprise over the depth and breadth of the anti-Shah feelings in Iran? The fact that many people in the United States, including the CIA and the State Department, overestimated the Shah's ability to meet the challenge of the opposition was no accident. It certainly was not due to the lack of potentially relevant intelligence data. The American Embassy in Tehran during the 1970s was staffed by a highly experienced group of foreign-service personnel, including the ex-chief of the CIA, Richard Helms, who served as the American ambassador to Iran for several years. In addition, for over a decade Iranian students in Europe and the United States used various means to sensitize the outside world to the Iranian political situation. Thus, the existence of a pervasive opposition to the Shah's regime should not have been so entirely unexpected.

We reject the simplistic explanation of U.S. policy in terms of an "intelligence failure."[5] Such charges, as a congressional report pointed out, "blind us to the importance of user attitudes in any warning process. In the case of Iran, long-standing U.S. attitudes towards the Shah inhibited intelligence collection, dampened policymakers' appetite for analysis of the Shah's position, and deafened policymakers to the warning implicit in available current intelligence."[6]

It is our thesis that the failure of U.S. policy in Iran can be traced to American ideas regarding the Third World countries generally and to instruments and institutions of the American foreign-policy system. In short, the failure was no accident: It was inevitable, and its roots lay in the foundation of U.S. foreign policy. In order to demonstrate this point, a review of American Third World policy is in order.

U.S. POLICY IN THE THIRD WORLD: THE ROLE OF IDEAS, INSTRUMENTS, AND INSTITUTIONS

American foreign policy in the Third World over the past three decades has had a slow and uneven development. With the exception of Latin America, where the United States has been involved in extensive political, economic, and military activities since the early 1800s, American involvement with the underdeveloped world was relatively limited until the early 1950s. To the extent that trade and other interaction did occur with the Third World, it occurred in the context of U.S. support for the colonial system. Nevertheless, there are identifiable patterns and continuities in the overall U.S. policy toward the Third World during the past thirty years which, we will argue, contribute to an understanding of the failure of American relations with Iran, Nicaragua, and Vietnam. Specifically, it would appear that the cold war origin of U.S. Third World policies, the security and economic dimensions of American interests in the Third World, and the underlying assumptions of U.S. policymakers about the requirements of political stability in developing nations all help to explain Washington's inclination to support authoritarian regimes abroad. We will develop each of these points separately.

The Origins of U.S. Third World Policy

American concern for Africa, the Middle East, and Asia grew directly out of the early years of the cold war and has been strongly influenced by the thinking behind the Truman Doctrine, the Marshall Plan, and the containment policy as it evolved under Secretary of State John Foster Dulles. Even with the loosening of bipolarity and the strengthening of the nonaligned movement among developing countries by the 1960s, American foreign policies in the developing world continued to incorporate attitudes and assumptions which had taken shape during the late forties and early fifties.

The Truman Doctrine articulated in 1947 in response to civil war in Greece and the perception of a Soviet threat to Turkey signaled the first comprehensive American commitment to assist in the defense of countries outside the Western hemisphere. The doctrine stressed the importance of American economic and financial aid to countries threatened by internal disorder, which, according to the conventional wisdom of the time, was the work of international communist subversion. It also led to an emphasis on building up the military forces of developing countries to promote internal and external security. In the following years, the Truman Doctrine provided the rationale for the formation of several regional security pacts in the developing world directly or indirectly supported by American economic and military foreign assistance. Between 1965 and 1974 alone, the United States transferred over $27.5 billion in military supplies to its allies in the Third World—a figure that represented about 54 percent of all military supplies received by the Third World during this period.[7] Washington's willingness to supply military aid to countries with virtually no consideration for their domestic political systems encouraged many U.S. Third World allies to rely disproportionately on forces to maintain internal order rather than on political institutionalization. The process became circular as U.S. officials began to perceive that countries with strong military organizations tended to be the most "stable" and developed closer relations with these countries. Thus, President Johnson stated in 1965 that "Our past investment in the defense of the Free World through the Military Assistance and Supporting Assistance Program has paid great dividends. Not only has it foiled aggression, but it has brought stability to a number of countries."[8]

Military aid was, as Walter LaFeber has put it, only "half of the walnut."[9] The United States also became convinced of the necessity of economic development in the Third World as a requirement for the stability of U.S. allies. This policy was first developed in relation to the reconstruction of Europe after the war. The Marshall Plan was predicated on the notion that "It is logical that the United States should do whatever it is able to do to assist in the return of normal economic health in the world, without which there can be no political stability, and no assured peace."[10] Its objective was to rehabilitate European capitalism to reduce the influence of domestic communist parties within the Western alliance. The spectacular success of economic aid for Europe in reestablishing political stability without communist takeovers encouraged U.S. policymakers later to apply the same solution to the Third World, beginning in 1949–1950 with the modest $27 million Point Four program. By the mid–1950s, U.S. foreign aid to Third World countries began to increase so that between 1953 and 1977 total U.S. foreign economic aid amounted to over $89.7 billion.[11] Most of this assistance was directed to U.S. Third World allies to promote domestic stability through economic development along capitalist ("free market") lines. But as Maghroori and Gorman have argued,

> Somewhere along the way, the critical distinction between rebuilding collapsed economies and reinforcing existing democratic tradition (as occurred in Western Europe) was confused with building economies from the ground up and creating liberal political attitudes where none had existed before (as was the objective in the underdeveloped world).[12]

The ability of U.S. economic aid to foster the type of political stability that Washington desired in the Third World was further complicated by a reliance on "trickle down" development theory. That is, U.S. aid went mainly to large businesses, property holders, and activities on the assumption that benefits from expanding national and international markets, production, and investments would inevitably reach the lower classes through higher wages and more consumer goods. The belief that economic growth of that kind would produce stability, while at the same time neglecting who within a country actually benefited from such "growth," caused U.S. officials to place far too much faith in aggregate economic statistics (such as GNP and per capita income) as indicators of a developing country's progress and stability.

By the mid–1950s there existed a shared image of the Third World within the U.S. foreign-policymaking establishment. As Morton Halperin has explained, U.S. officials came to believe that:

> The Third World really matters, because (a) it is the battleground between Communism and the Free World; (b) Western capital will generate economic development and political stability with a minimum of

violence; and (c) instability is the greatest threat to progress in the Third World.[13]

By far, the strongest proponent of this outlook during the fifties was Secretary of State Dulles, who, according to LaFeber, was intent on applying the solutions contained in the Truman Doctrine and Marshall Plan to trouble spots in the Third World.

He hoped to build into those areas many of the same military and political institutions which had established the *status quo* in Europe. This policy moved from *the assumption that disturbances anywhere outside the Iron Curtain usually worked against American interests sooner or later*.[14]

This outlook led quite naturally to an attitude in the Eisenhower administration toward the Third World, which "saw communism as the ultimate winner in any revolution . . . ."[15] The legacy for American foreign policy has been Washington's disposition to assist antirevolutionary forces throughout the Third World, regardless of the political attributes of the regimes that may receive aid under such a policy. The challenge this poses for American Third World policy is that, as Robert Heilbroner suggested some time ago, it invariably places the United States in opposition to the inherent forces of political change in the developing world.[16]

U.S. Security and Economic Interests in the Third World

Without attempting to be comprehensive, we can identify at least three primary U.S. interests in the developing world: Access to strategic materials for ourselves and our important allies (for example, Japan), protection of American foreign investments, and access for American products to Third World markets. These interests were subsumed under the objectives of free trade and capitalist development in the developing world. Admittedly, the United States also has a military interest in certain strategically located countries, but geopolitical considerations will be left for later since they normally cloud (but do not negate) the issues we wish to address here.

One of the most basic American interests is access to strategic materials in the Third World that are absolutely essential to the U.S. military establishment. As the secretary of defense reported in 1977, "The United States is not an economic island. We depend for our standard of living and economic security increasingly on raw materials imported from abroad, *and some of these imports have strategic value as well*."[17] He went on to identify twelve strategic materials for which the U.S. is 70 to 100 percent dependent on imports.[18] American access to some of these materials (which are essential for the production of many advanced weapons systems) is becoming increasingly difficult because of developments in the Third World. In 1979, *Business Week* noted that "Most ominous is the growing U.S. dependence on foreign supplies. Such vital metals as cobalt, chromium, and platinum are almost entirely imported from unstable or potentially hostile nations in southern Africa or from the Soviet Union."[19] As research by Stephen Gorman suggests, there exists a strong correlation between the amount of strategic materials a Third World country produces and exports to the United States and the distribution of American military and economic aid among Third World countries.[20] Hence, there is sufficient evidence to accept the importance of Third World strategic resources to the United States without even raising the question of oil, whose importance is readily apparent.

On the question of American investment abroad, there is considerable disagreement concerning the relative importance of underdeveloped and developed countries to the American economy. S. M. Miller, Roy Bennett, and Cyril Alpatt have correctly argued that U.S. business invests more heavily in other developed countries and earns higher profits there than in the underdeveloped world, while Paul Sweezy, Harry Magdoff, and others have developed different data showing the economic importance of the Third World to specific sectors of the U.S. economy.[21] Whatever the case may be, the United States had a total of over $100 billion in direct foreign investments by the late 1970s. And according to the State Department, "The 'book value' (original value) of American private direct investment *in the Third World* is over $30 billion, and market value is perhaps double that. Earnings from these investments amount to about

5% of total U.S. corporate profits."[22] This does not take into consideration the hidden profits that are repatriated through pricing transfer arrangements between parent companies in the United States and their subsidiaries in developing host countries. The reader may draw his or her own conclusions about the significance of this amount. But more important for our immediate purpose is the fact that U.S. policymakers are determined to promote and protect American direct investment in the Third World, which reinforces Washington's support for regimes like those that existed in Iran and Nicaragua and which welcomed American capital.

In a recent publication, the Department of State explained that "It is the U.S. Government's policy to encourage private investment in the developing countries . . . ."[23] As a justification for this policy, it was asserted that:

> There are many who consider the multi-national [corporations] to be a uniquely powerful engine of development: " . . . only the international companies have the capital, trained personnel, and entrepreneurial capacity to develop other countries and integrate them into the world economic structure." There is no substitute.[24]

This is a relatively accurate summation of U.S. policymakers' attitudes over the past three decades, whose more ominous side was revealed in a statement by Secretary of State Dean Rusk in 1962: "The United States Government is prepared to intercede on behalf of American firms and make strong representations to host governments in cases of economically unjustified expropriation or harrassment" of American firms.[25] Without delving into the variety of available U.S. actions when such "strong representations" fail, it is enough to say that Washington has consistently viewed governments that protect and encourage American investment as, for all purposes, automatically acceptable. By the same token, U.S. officials have neglected or overlooked the unsavory side of governments that cooperate with American capital—their authoritarianism and anticonstitutionalism, for instance, and even their willingness to subordinate "free market" mechanisms to those typical of a command economy when it has suited the political needs of ruling elites.

Aside from strategic materials and direct investment, the Third World has been an important market for American products. As the State Department has noted, "About one-third of American exports already go to the less developed countries. With further development, these same countries could provide a considerably larger market."[26] To argue that the United States has a policy interest in maintaining and expanding trade with the developing countries need not lead to an endless debate over whether the United States is an "imperialist" country or whether American capitalism can function without access to foreign markets where it can unload its "surplus production."[27] All that is necessary to support the present argument (that U.S. officials view free trade in the Third World as an important goal) is to show that, rightly or wrongly, U.S. policymakers have perceived a necessity for American access to foreign markets.

The liberal belief in the benefits of free trade has a long tradition and has been especially strong in the United States since the Second World War. As Joan Edelman Spero writes:

> The most extreme expression of belief in free trade was to be found in the United States in the person of Secretary of State Cordell Hull . . . . His argument for a more open system was transplanted into U.S. State Department policy and thereby into American foreign policy.[28]

Spero goes on to quote the secretary as stating in a memo that:

> A great expansion in the volume of international trade after the war will be *essential* to the attainment of full and effective employment in the United States . . . , to the preservation of private enterprise, and to the success of an international security system to prevent future wars.[29]

This perceived necessity for the American economy to enjoy free trade continued under Secretary of State Acheson, who held that "we cannot expect domestic prosperity under our system without a constantly expanding trade with other nations."[30] For that reason, Lawrence Shoup's study of the Council on Foreign Relations in the 1940s has shown that the Council worked with the State Department to sketch out a "Grand Area" for the postwar era that, it was safely assumed, would be dominated by U.S. capital, scientific know-how, and productivity.[31] It was to be Luce's "American Century."

This perspective in government has been reinforced by opinions in the U.S. business community. For example, W. Gifford, from the Detroit Board of Commerce, testified before the Senate Banking and Currency Committee that "The Detroit area . . . is the major producer in the world of industrial goods destined for foreign markets. The well-being of the city and the state of Michigan depends on a high level of international commerce and a relative freedom and possibility of competing in world markets."[32] Such testimony reinforces existing images. Hence, whether U.S. trade with the Third World is or is not essential to the survival of American capitalism, there is a strong inclination in government to assume that it is. Therefore, there is a nearly automatic support for foreign governments that protect and promote American trade, regardless of their internal politics.

The U.S. Preoccupation with Third World Stability

From the foregoing, it should not be difficult to appreciate the American concern for stability in the Third World or the limits to which the United States has been prepared to go to preserve order in the developing countries. As Gabriel Kolko observed:

> It is the American view of the need for relative stability within the poorer nations that has resulted in a long list of United States interventions since 1946 into the affairs of numerous nations, from Greece to Guatemala, of which Vietnam is only the consummate example—but in principle no different than numerous others.[33]

One rationalization that has been offered by U.S. officials for such interventionism is that a peaceful international order cannot evolve without domestic stability in Third World nations. This attitude gains expression in the notion that "the first fundamental rule of American foreign policy thinking relates the security of American institutions to the prevention of 'disturbances' overseas."[34] The United States is concerned that Third World government maintain domestic order not only because this increases "national security" and facilitates American investment and trade in their economies, but also because Washington officials are convinced that only under stable political conditions can the poorer countries achieve "development." Here, we come to the most important element of our thesis. The American preoccupation with domestic order in developing countries has resulted from a one-sided view of what development involves and has caused U.S. officials either to excuse authoritatively imposed order as a necessary expedient for development and/or to mistake it for political stability.

The readiness of leading American foreign policy experts to excuse the authoritarianism of certain Third World allies is exemplified in a comment by Henry Kissinger:

> In recent decades, no totalitarian regime has ever evolved into a democracy. Several authoritarian regimes—such as Spain, Greece, and Portugal—have done so. We must therefore maintain the moral distinction between aggressive totalitarianism and other governments which, with all their imperfections, are trying to resist foreign pressures and subversion and thereby help preserve the balance of power in behalf of all free people.[35]

In short, Kissinger views communist-backed dictatorships as "totalitarian," while U.S.-backed dictatorships are merely "authoritarian." The dominant assumption in Washington has been that authoritarian regimes are sometimes a necessary evil in order to impose the level of domestic order required to develop backward economies. Once economic development gains momentum, so the argument goes, the government will acquire increasing legitimacy in the eyes of the populace and will be able to reduce its reliance on coercion to maintain domestic tranquility.

U.S. RELATIONS WITH IRAN

A review of U.S. relations with Iran under the Shah illustrates the existence of the attitudes we have attributed to the American foreign-policymaking establishment and demonstrates how such perceptions contribute to inflexibility in the conduct of U.S. foreign policy. In this section we will review the background of American involvement with the government of Shahanshah Mohammad Reza Pahlavi, examine why American officials viewed his government as stronger than its opposition even in the face of mounting evidence to the contrary, and, finally, assess the adequacy of the explanations that have been advanced for the failure of U.S. policy in Iran.

The United States moved quickly after the Second World War to displace British influence in Iran in order to promote the twin objectives of containing Soviet influence in the region and gaining participation for American firms in Iranian oil production. In 1947 an agreement was signed for American military aid to Iran, and in 1950 a modest amount of economic aid was begun.[36]

In 1953, the United States participated in a military coup on behalf of the Shah and against Prime Minister Mohammed Mossadeqh, a popular nationalist leader. This coup, planned by Allen Dulles, the director of the CIA, and John Foster Dulles, the secretary of state, and executed by Kermit Roosevelt at a cost of $1 million, resulted in the overthrow of Mossadeqh's government. Many Americans have forgotten the extent of American involvement in Iran in the early 1950s and its consequences for Iranian politics. But to most Iranians, this interference resulted in destruction of the Iranian nationalist movement, in the centralization of power in the royal court, and in the increase of American influence in Iranian society. Indeed, as some have argued, U.S. involvement in the 1953 coup in Tehran was the backdrop of the Iranian revolution in 1978 and the main rationale used to justify the seizure of the American Embassy in November 1979.[37] In this context, a closer look at American involvement in Iranian politics in the early 1950s is crucial.

Early in 1951, the Iranian Parliament passed a bill that nationalized the Iranian oil industry. The bill was signed by the Shah, who did not have the right of veto. Soon after, the architect of the nationalization bill, Dr. Mohammad Mossadeqh, became the prime minister and thus responsible for implementing the nationalization policy.

The main target of the nationalization bill was the Anglo-

Iranian Oil Company, which operated the Iranian oil industry in the southern part of the country. The major stockholder in this company was the British government, which controlled 52 percent of its stocks. The remaining 48 percent was owned by private British companies.[38] According to some analysts, ". . . the Anglo-Iranian Oil Company invited its own nationalization by refusing to consider Iranian requests for a rate of royalty payment commensurate with that received by other oil-producing states in the Middle East at the time."[39]

Initially, the British did not take the nationalization seriously: They believed that Iran was dependent on Anglo-Iranian Oil Company. Many felt that the operation of the Iranian oil industry was beyond the comprehension of a primitive country such as Iran; that the Iranians would "come crying back to the company for help in a very short time."[40]

Although Iranians did have difficulty operating their oil industry without the British, they did not go crying back to them. They did suffer economic problems; but the nationalization was only partially motivated by economic considerations: To many Iranians, the nationalization implied the beginning of their political independence. As the Shah was reported to have said in an interview some twenty-five years later: "We were hearing that the oil company was creating puppets—people just clicking their heels to the order of the oil company—so it was becoming in our eyes a kind of monster—almost a kind of government within the Iranian government."[41]

After several months of unsuccessful negotiation between the British government and Mossadeqh, the Anglo-Iranian Oil Company closed down its operation in Iran. The Iranian oil production came to a near halt. Iran did attempt to export oil, but few foreign buyers were willing to face British threats "to sue any purchases of oil that [they] considered to be 'hot.' "[42] In the following months, the oil production fell sharply from 660,000 barrels a day in 1950 to less than 30,000 in 1952. This reduction in the oil production had severe consequences for the Iranian economy. The national income fell by 30 percent, and the government lost 60 percent of its foreign exchange revenues.

Mossadeqh turned to the United States, hoping that it would

purchase Iranian oil or might give Iran economic assistance that would help the government to cope with its loss of oil revenues. In a letter to President Eisenhower in May 1953, Mossadeqh wrote:

> The Iranian nation hopes that with the help and assistance of the American Government the obstacles in the way of sale of Iranian oil can be removed, and that if the American Government is not able to effect a removal of such obstacles, it can render effective economic assistance to enable Iran to utilize her other resources. This country has natural resources other than oil. The exploitation of these resources would solve the present difficulties of the country. This, however, is impossible without economic aid.[43]

It took a month before the United States informed Iran that it would not assist her: It would neither purchase Iranian oil nor would it give economic aid. The reason, President Eisenhower wrote Mossadeqh on June 29, 1953, was that:

> There is strong feeling in the United States, even among American citizens most sympathetic to Iran and friendly to the Iranian people, that it would not be fair to the American taxpayers for the United States Government to extend any considerable amount of economic aid to Iran so long as Iran could have access to funds derived from the sale of its oil and oil products if a reasonable agreement were reached with regard to compensation whereby the large-scale marketing of Iranian oil would be resumed. Similarly, many American citizens would be deeply opposed to the purchase by the United States Government of Iranian oil in the absence of an oil settlement.[44]

While Eisenhower's response did outline some of the reasons behind his decision, there were other considerations that were not mentioned.

American perception of Iranian government at this time reflected Washington's growing fear of Soviet expansionism. It was agreed in the United States that Mossadeqh was not a communist; but many top officials in the Eisenhower administration felt that Mossadeqh's dependence for support on the Iranian communist party (Tudeh) would eventually make him dependent on the Soviet Union. Some even believed that the Soviets were planning to take over the Iranian political scene through the deployment of the same tactics that were used in Czechoslovakia.[45] This belief was reinforced when early in 1953, the Soviets appointed Anatol Laurentieve—the man who had masterminded the communist takeover of Czechoslovakia in 1948—as the new Soviet Ambassador in Tehran. As far as Americans were concerned, Iran was slipping: Mossadeqh was viewed "as the stalking horse of a Communist takeover."[46]

American refusal to aid Iran accentuated Mossadeqh's economic difficulties; he began to lose support among some of this domestic coalition (the National Front). As a result he became increasingly dependent on the Tudeh party. On July 21, the party staged a demonstration in support of Mossadeqh; some 100,000 people attended the rally. According to Eisenhower, "reports were coming in that Mossadeqh was moving closer and closer to the Communists. . . ." One report said "he was looking forward to receiving $20 million from the Soviet Union, which would keep his treasury afloat for the next two or three months."[47]

It was decided in Washington that Mossadeqh had to go. The go-ahead was given at a meeting in Secretary of State Dulles's office late in June. Those participating in this meeting, in addition to the secretary, were Allen Dulles (director of the CIA), Kermit Roosevelt (a CIA official), Charles Wilson (secretary of defense), Loy Henderson (American ambassador to Iran), and several other State Department officials. It was decided that Roosevelt would be dispatched to Iran to organize an anti-Mossadeqh coup. The CIA provided $1 million in Iranian currency.[48]

Kermit Roosevelt arrived in Iran in July. He visited the Shah clandestinely on August 1. Roosevelt informed the king of the American plan to topple Mossadeqh's government. The Shah was delighted: In the last two years, the Shah had come under pressure to relinquish most of his power. Early in 1953, for example, Mossadeqh had tried to get the parliament to pass legislation making him commander in chief of the Iranian Army, replacing the Shah (the parliament refused). Further, there were rumors in Tehran that Mossadeqh was planning to abolish the institution of monarchy in Iran and replace it by a republican form of government. Thus, the Shah saw the American plan as an excellent opportunity to dispose of a very strong enemy. He promised Roosevelt his full cooperation: He signed a decree dismissing Mossadeqh and replacing him by General Fazlollah Zahedi. Meanwhile, Roosevelt made contacts with several Iranian agents; he dispersed some $100,000 among an assortment of weight lifters, musclemen, and athletic thugs.

On August 19, several hundred men, organized with the CIA funds, marched toward Mossadeqh's residence. Along the way, they were joined by hundreds of recruits. They crashed through the gate of the prime minister's house. Mossadeqh escaped. By late afternoon, General Zahedi, who had been in hiding since his appointment as the prime minister, surfaced and assumed control of the government. The Shah, who had left the country a few days earlier, returned to Iran. Mossadeqh was arrested, tried, and convicted of rebelling against the Shah and several other constitutional violations. He was sentenced to three years' imprisonment. The Mossadeqh era was ended.

It is difficult to assess the role of the CIA in the overthrow of Mossadeqh's government. John Foster Dulles's sympathetic biographer, John Robinson Beal, attributed the overthrow of the Iranian prime minister to "an act of God."[49] But many Iranian nationalists disagreed. They believed that without the American intervention Iran's history would have been different.[50] Even if Mossadeqh's government had fallen, he might have been replaced by another member of the National Front; the Shah might have abdicated, never returning to Iran.

Instead, after the coup, the Shah began to centralize power in his court, eliminating his domestic opponents; the Shah increasingly became the sole ruler. According to Barry Rubin:

> Without the restraining hands of the parliament and of a strong prime ministership, Iran now moved toward a one-man dictatorship in which the Shah relied for his political survival on the passivity of the peasantry and on the energy of the armed forces and of SAVAK (the State Organization for Intelligence and Security), the secret police organization.[51]

SAVAK was organized in 1957 by the CIA at the behest of the Shah.[52] It was set up as a security organization responsible for domestic and foreign intelligence collection. But over the years, SAVAK evolved into an organization whose primary function was to identify and eliminate the Shah's opponents. SAVAK officers received their advanced training in Washington, D.C., at the International Police Academy (IPA) and the International Services School. The number of SAVAK officers receiving training in the United States is subject to controversy. But according to one State Department document, between 1963 and 1973, some 1,979 Iranians were trained in the United States.

In fulfilling its objectives, SAVAK did not hesitate to use illegal means, including intimidation, bribery, torture, and murder. Again, there are conflicting figures, but informed sources have estimated that between 10,000 and 15,000 people lost their lives at the hands of the Shah's police between the 1953 coup and the Shah's ouster in 1979. It is difficult to establish the number of those who were tortured. According to one estimate, at least half a million people were beaten, whipped, or tortured by SAVAK. A gruesome exposé of the torture under the Shah was depicted by Reza Baraheni, an Iranian poet and novelist, in *The Nation*, March 1, 1980. Baraheni, who himself was imprisoned and tortured by SAVAK, wrote:

> Six-year-old children were tortured to betray the identity of their parents' guests. I speak of horrors I saw with my own eyes or was told about. Women were given electric shocks with prods placed in their private parts. A woman screamed in cell 22 of the first ward of the Komite prison for more than ten hours, crying, "The electric prods have dried my breasts, give me a glass of milk to feed my baby!" . . . A guard in the Komite prison told me that the body of a young man who weighed no more than 60 pounds lay in the torture chamber of the second floor of the Komite. Earlier he had been in my cell for a few brief moments. In one instance I carried to the men's room the half-scorched body of a prisoner who had undergone what might be called "purification by fire." Afterward he hated the smell and sight of food with meat in it. It reminded him of the smell of his own flesh. I also met a worker who had been raped by a torturer . . . . [53]

The extent of the CIA involvement with SAVAK and its knowledge of torture and other human-rights violations in Iran has been debated widely in the United States in recent years. As late as 1976, Alfred Atherton, then assistant secretary of state, told a congressional committee that he did not believe there was torture in Iran, although he admitted there was "harsh treatment." But others disagree. Jesse Leaf, a former CIA political analyst with extensive involvement in Iranian matters told *The Nation* in early 1980: "The Atherton '76 statement was bullshit. Of course we were aware of [SAVAK torture.] It was common knowledge. Being based in Washington, I constantly heard 'war stories' from returning agents about SAVAK torture . . . . In 1972 when a lot of stuff came out from Amnesty International and other sources about SAVAK torture, I wanted to pull the information together for a CIA memo on the subject. I was told not to prepare the report."[54] Leaf further maintained that the CIA set up seminars in Tehran in extensive interrogation techniques.

Iran under the Shah maintained friendly relations with the United States. Tehran joined the U.S.-sponsored Baghdad Pact in 1955, it extended economic and political ties to Israel, and in 1959 an executive agreement between the Shah and President Eisenhower gave Washington the right to intervene militarily in Iran in the case of outside aggression against the country.[55]

Although U.S. economic aid and military grants to Iran were suspended in 1967 because of the country's increasing oil prosperity, the United States continued to provide technical assistance and sell military equipment to the Shah's government after that date. The United States and its developed allies also began to play an important role in the nonoil sectors of the Iranian economy. The so-called White Revolution initiated by the Shah in the early 1960s eradicated the feudal structure of agriculture in the country and contributed to the expansion of the urban-industrial sectors of the economy in which multinational firms became actively involved.[56] Between 1966 and 1975, for example, the developed Western countries invested nearly $300 million in the nonoil sector of the Iranian economy, and by 1977 there were over 31,000 Americans working in Iranian industry and commerce.[57] Iran also became an important market for Western exports, with approximately 55 percent of the country's nonmilitary imports coming from only three developed countries: West Germany, Japan, and the United States.[58] With the deterioration in the American balance of trade in the late seventies, the Iranian market became increasingly important to the United States. As a State Department official noted, "The Iranian market became critical as Iran used its new oil revenue from Europe and Japan to buy from the U.S. Iran spent nearly $2 on U.S. goods for every $1 the U.S. spent on Iranian oil."[59]

In the area of military sales by the United States to Iran, the real watershed was the Nixon Doctrine, which relied on the forces of American allies around the world to contain communist expansion. The Nixon administration singled out Iran as the most important American military ally in the Persian Gulf and adopted a policy permitting the sale of sophisticated weapons to the Shah's government after 1970. When Iran's oil revenue increased dramatically after the 1973 oil embargo, the volume of Iranian military purchases rose precipitously. Between 1971 and 1977, Iran placed orders for military hardware from the United States totaling more than $11.8 billion.[60] The Shah's commitment to maintaining a strong military was reflected in the fact that defense accounted for 30 percent of central government expenditures or 17 percent of the gross domestic product.[61] The apparent utility to the United States of a strong Iranian army was demonstrated in the early 1970s when Iranian forces intervened in neighboring Oman to prop up the U.S.-backed monarchy in that country in the face of domestic disorder.[62] Indeed, the Shah's military forces were viewed by the U.S. government as surrogates for American forces in the protection of the West's vital oil supply route.

The obvious advantages for the United States in maintaining a close working relationship with the Shah's government led inevitably to a systematic effort to downplay negative reporting on Iran within the foreign-policy establishment. As one State Department official wrote after the revolution, "The Embassy, State Department, U.S. military team in Iran, and intelligence community quickly learned that no one in the White House really wanted any negative information about Iran's Shah, its stability, or the military buildup."[63] On the contrary, official reports throughout the sixties and seventies repeatedly stressed Iran's apparent stability and economic prosperity.

The Shah's program of economic development seemed, in terms of Washington's standards, to be achieving significant results. As the U.S. government's area handbook on Iran reported in 1978, the country had a 1976 GNP of $57.5 billion (fifteenth largest in the noncommunist world), a 1977 per capita income of $2,200, and an annual growth rate of 29 percent in constant prices between 1971 and 1974.[64] Although it was admitted in the area handbook that "not all groups or regions have shared equally from economic growth," it was stressed that "the aim of the Pahlavi dynasty had been to achieve equality in the benefits of development."[65] The direction of government programs were viewed as working toward spreading the benefits of development. Recent studies, however, indicate that income gaps widened in Iran during the 1960s and 1970s. According to Nikki R. Keddie, " . . . income inequalities in Iran which were already great on a world scale, increased, and this increase was particularly dramatic after 1974, when oil income shot up after the great price rise."[66] The widening of income inequality was accompanied by high inflation, housing shortages, and an increase in repression and centralization of authority.[67] In March 1975, the Iranian political parties were dissolved; a new party was formed (Rastakhiz). It was headed by Prime Minister Amir Abbas Hoveyda. By 1977, poor economic planning and a reduction in oil revenues created an economic recession in Iran. Unemployment rose, particularly among unskilled workers. And as the economic conditions worsened, the opposition to the Shah grew, initially among the lower classes and eventually spreading to all segments of the Iranian population.[68]

Some have attributed the timing of the Iranian Revolution to the impact of President Carter's human-rights policy. According to this view, Carter's human-rights campaign, enunciated in January 1977, (which implied that countries guilty of human-rights violations might be deprived of American arms and aid), gave courage to Iranian dissidents to express their opposition to government openly.[69] While this argument may be in part correct, there is no doubt that opposition to the Shah would have occurred soon, since the Shah's government lacked the most fundamental ingredient of stability: Legitimacy.

Early in 1978, there were major riots in Iran, including one in Qom in January and one in Tabriz a few weeks later. Some of these riots included clashes between military forces and the demonstrators. Despite these indications, however, as late as summer 1978, Americans did not believe that the Shah's government was in any danger. Remember the CIA report completed in August concluding that Iran "is not in a revolutionary or even a pre-revolutionary situation."[70] Thus, until early fall, the Carter administration supported the Shah's government and refused to open up lines of communication with opposition groups, which by this time had rallied around Ayatollah Khomeini.[71] According to President Carter, " . . . there was no question in my mind that [the Shah] deserved our unequivocal support. Not only had the Shah been a staunch and dependable ally of the United States for many years, but he remained the leader around whom we hoped to see a stable and reformed government organized and maintained in Iran."[72] Further, many Americans, including Carter's National Security Adviser Zbigniew Brzezinski, believed that the Shah should use his military to suppress the revolution.[73] There also is some evidence to suggest that the Carter administration even considered arranging a military coup against the revolution.[74]

By late fall, it had become clear to the Shah that his regime was in serious danger. Hoping to save his throne and not recognizing the extent of opposition to his government, he appointed a new prime minister—Shahpour Bakhtiar, a moderate member of National Front. On January 16, the Shah left Iran for Egypt. With his departure, the Pahlavi era ended in Iran.

Khomeini, who under the Shah had spent several years in exile, returned to Iran on February 1, 1979. A few days later, he appointed Mehdi Bazargan as the "real" prime minister. After a major clash between Khomeini's supporters and Bakhtiar's forces on February 10 and 11, the power was effectively transferred to Khomeini and Bazargan. Bakhtiar and the members of Majlis (Iranian Parliament) resigned. The Khomeini era had begun.[75]

Despite the American Embassy's recommendation against inviting the Shah to the United States, the Carter administration allowed him an entry in October 1979. The justification was that the Shah was seriously ill and that he needed medical treatment, although this justification may have been a pretext. According to President Carter, the Shah "wanted to come to the United States, where he had some enthusiastic advocates."[76]

These included Henry Kissinger, David Rockefeller, and Zbigniew Brzezinski.

The Shah's trip to the United States resulted in several major anti-American demonstrations throughout Iran. On November 4, 1979, the American Embassy in Tehran was overrun by about 3,000 militant students; over fifty Embassy staff members were taken hostage. Although the hostages were released early in 1981, the event marked the downfall of the American era in Iran: Diplomatic relations were broken, all Americans were expelled from Iran, and trade and economic relations came to a halt.[77] Iran, once one of the most reliable allies, became the center of anti-Americanism in the region.

CONCLUSION

What explains this turnabout in American position in Iran? What explains the failure of American decision makers to foresee correctly the direction of Iranian politics and the inevitability of the Iranian Revolution? According to the available data, the inability to foresee the potential for revolution in Iran spread to all areas of American government during the 1970s. As the report of the Permanent Select Committee on Intelligence concluded in early 1979:

> As U.S. policy in the Persian Gulf became more dependent on the Shah, risk of offending the Shah by speaking with the opposition became less acceptable. No CIA intelligence reporting based on sources within the religious opposition occurred during the two-year period ending in November 1977, and Embassy political reporting based on contacts with the opposition was rare and sometimes contemptuous.[78]

According to this explanation of the failure of U.S. policy in Iran, Washington's "close identification with the Shah limited the opportunities for U.S. officials to hear from Iranians who opposed him, thereby causing Iran to resemble a closed society from the U.S. perspective, with even clandestine collection on Iranian politics discouraged."[79] The result was a succession of positive evaluations of Iranian stability during the 1970s carried out by different branches of the foreign policy and intelligence communities.

For example, a 1970 congressional report on Iran stressed the success of economic development programs and concluded that "The study mission believes Iran has done an excellent job in developing a sound economy and *viable social order*."[80] This view persisted right up to the eve of the revolution, with Carter describing Iran just a year before the Shah's overthrow as "an island of stability in one of the more troubled areas of the world."[81]

The fall of the Shah in January 1979 led to a review of American foreign policy to identify the reasons why U.S. perceptions of Iranian political conditions had been so at variance with actual conditions within the country. At first, the failure of U.S. policy in Iran was attributed to an intelligence breakdown that prevented Washington-based policymakers from appreciating the true situation in Iran in the period leading up to the revolution. But the focus gradually shifted to the presumed "special importance" of Iran that had caused Washington officials to strengthen relations with the country regardless of its government's domestic policies. It is our position, however, that neither of these explanations goes far enough in identifying the root causes of American policy toward Iran.

The origins of American failure in Iran can be traced to a number of faulty assumptions regarding the relationship between economic and political variables. More specifically, American policymakers have tended to define the problems of political stability in terms of insufficient economic development. This has led to either the subordination or total neglect of political considerations within Third World countries in preference to a concentration on economic modernization as the crucial determinant of stability. And to the extent that there has been interest in purely political development, it has been misconceived: Societal order has been equated with political development. Thus, the Shah's government was considered stable—even after several months of serious challenge—because by American economic standards, Iranian aggregate economic conditions had indeed improved under the Shah's regime. Therefore, many Americans believed that Iran was also developed politically. They tended to equate societal order—imposed by an effective secret police force—with acquisition of legitimacy by the Shah's regime. Such views were clearly reflected in the report to the House of Representatives presented by a group of Congressmen who visited Iran in 1970. After reporting on the success of Iranian economic projects, the document concluded that "the Shah has the structure for a more democratic system of government and the ultimate institution of more democratic procedures will complete Iran's impressive success story."[82]

There is no indication anywhere in the report that "political requirements" were taken into account in arriving at this optimistic conclusion.[83] Yet even a cursory examination of Iranian political institutions would have revealed that the country did not possess even the most elementary structures normally associated with stable political democracy: Power was centralized and hierarchical, political parties were restricted and purely formalistic, and structures for interest aggregation and articulation were nonexistent. The only "political" factor that the report referred to was order.[84] Hence, the Shah's ability to maintain absolute order in Iran through the use of an extensive secret police and a modern military apparatus was accepted by the American government as a demonstration of the political stability of his regime. The Shah prepared his country for democracy by systematically repressing even the most rudimentary expressions of popular political organization. The eventual overthrow of the Shah illustrated that his regime was not stable, and it could not have been stable because, in spite of thirty-seven years in power, he was not able to legitimize his rule. Without legitimacy, even the "impressive economic gains" of Iran under the Shah could not invest his regime with stability (not to mention the fact that those economic gains were enjoyed by only a select minority).

There is actually little theoretical basis in the literature on political development to support either the American assumption of the primacy of economic development or the equation of "order" with "political stability." On the contrary, a review of the major works in comparative politics leads to quite different conclusions.

We may begin to clear up the issue by recognizing, as Seymour Martin Lipset has argued, that:

> The stability of any given democracy depends not only on economic development but also upon the effectiveness and the *legitimacy of its*

> *political system.* Effectiveness means actual performance, the extent to which the system satisfies the basic functions of government *as most of the population . . . see them.* Legitimacy involves the capacity of the system to engender and *maintain the belief that the existing political institutions are the most appropriate ones for the society.*[85]

Lipset goes on to note that emerging nations often times experience crises in legitimacy as they pass from traditionalism to modernity. Without getting too deeply into the issue of exactly what constitutes traditionalism or modernity, we can nevertheless agree with Lipset that legitimacy crises occur most often from an insufficient institutionalization of new political relationships. This leads him to the conclusion that " . . . one main source of legitimacy lies in the continuity of important traditional integrative institutions during a transitional period in which new institutions are emerging."[86] Thus, legitimacy is not an automatic attribute of regimes that impose order and economic growth. American concentration on order and economic development as determinants of political stability therefore misses the consentual and affective nature of real political stability. It also ignores the reality that authoritarian regimes that undermine "important traditional integrative institutions" in their exercise of power and/or pursuit of economic development promote the very conditions that favor political instability.

Authoritarian regimes are not automatically unacceptable simply because they employ coercion, since nearly all political regimes depend to some extent on at least implied threats of coercion to perpetuate themselves. But what makes authoritarian regimes like those that existed in Vietnam, Iran, and Nicaragua suspect is the degree to which they rely exclusively on coercion to the exclusion of the institutional requirements for lasting political stability. As David Apter has noted, regime types differ, *inter alia,* in terms of their relative dependence on either coercion or information as the basis of their control: " . . . Different politics employ different mixtures of coercion and information in trying to maintain authority, achieve stability, and increase efficiency."[87] He goes on to argue that developing political systems require an equilibrium between coercion and information but with a steady decrease in coercion and increase in information as the regime's capacity to act effectively on information increases. The mounting evidence that the Shah was becoming increasingly dependent on coercion to retain authority after years in power should have indicated that he was not promoting effective political development.

A regime can only increase its ability to collect and to act on information effectively through political institutionalization. There is nearly unanimous agreement in the literature that, aside from the legitimacy of a government, the most important determinant of its viability is its level of political institutionalization. As Samuel Huntington has stated succinctly, "Complexity produces stability."[88] Authoritarian regimes are in reality usually autocracies and as such are actually quite simple, rigid, and therefore inherently unstable. In seeking to assist authoritarian regimes to develop their economies as a basis for stability, the United States has actually helped promote political instability. Economic development mobilizes formerly marginalized, traditional sectors of society who must then be integrated into the existing political system. As Huntington has explained, modernization (understood as social mobilization) can, in the absence of political institutionalization to accommodate increasing popular interest in government, lead to political decay.[89] But the problem for a self-styled modernizing leader who attempts to develop his economy authoritatively is that to achieve political stability he must create parallel political institutions that diminish his own personal power. "The would-be institution-builder needs personal power to create institutions but he cannot create institutions without relinquishing personal power."[90]

From what has been presented to this point, we may conclude that legitimacy and institutionalization are the primary ingredients of political stability. Legitimacy derives from the compatibility of the regime's societal goals (and means of achieving those goals) with the cultural values of the wider society. Only in a society whose single overriding value is rapid economic development can a regime obtain legitimacy solely on the basis of its developmental achievements. But development for its own sake tends to be a specifically Western, middleclass ethic and therefore may have a less universalistic appeal than Washington has assumed. Institutionalization, in turn, means the creation of formal and informal organizations, channels, and procedures that integrate individuals into an increasingly complex social reality. Only in a society whose entire spectrum of social interactions take place within a strictly economic setting can economic development in itself produce the institutionalization necessary for political stability. The ideological and religious forces that have toppled U.S.-supported authoritarian regimes, however, reveal that other values besides economic development exist in the Third World. Thus, "modernizing oligarchies," which have been looked upon so approvingly from abroad, are not always appreciated by those who are subjected to their policies.

This brings us to a consideration of the "congruence" between governmental values and authority patterns on one side, and the values and authority patterns of the broader society on the other side. Harry Eckstein has suggested that "a government will tend to be stable if its authority pattern is congruent with the other authority patterns of the society of which it is a part." Conversely, "governments will be unstable . . . if the government authority pattern is isolated."[91] Put another way, "Incongruity between the authority patterns of a society, *like any other incongruity among social patterns,* is an obvious source of strain, and through strain of anomie, and through anomie of behavior potentially destructive to the stability of any pattern of government."[92] For our present purposes, we may interpret this to mean that no amount of economic development or enforced order can engender political stability when the government's values and authority patterns are at variance with those of society at hand. Therefore, the greatest consideration in evaluating the viability of a regime should be how well it promotes the aspirations of its underlying culture or at least the dominant forces of that culture. Yet a review of American relations with any number of U.S.-backed authoritarian regimes ranging from South Korea to the Philippines, and from Nicaragua to Iran, easily illustrates that policymakers have overlooked this complex requirement in preference for the more immediately manageable concepts of order and economic development.

We may summarize our critique of American foreign policy

toward Iran by agreeing with Robert Morrison MacIver, who observed more than forty years ago that:

> Dictatorship solves the problem of government by cutting out one half of it. The permanent problem of government is to reconcile fundamental liberties with a fundamental order. Liberties cannot be assured without order, but order can be assured, and often is immediately assured, by the sacrifice of liberties. Democracy is the only principle that really seeks to solve the total problem.[93]

The American preoccupation with order has missed the deeper complexities of civil society and the requirements of political stability. The problem may be reducible to the observation that foreign-policy officials and foreign-service officers are principally concerned with protecting and advancing American interests abroad and not with the issue of political development as a separate and distinct issue. It may in fact be easier to deal with strong leaders in foreign countries over the short run, rather than face the difficult task of adjusting American interests with governments involved in a sometimes confusing (to Americans) political transition. But over the long run it may become imperative that U.S. foreign policymakers acquire a more sophisticated understanding of the dynamics of development in the Third World, especially in the face of rising nationalism abroad.

American policy toward Iran is merely a single example of a larger pattern of U.S. support for authoritarianism throughout the Third World. Such support is offered by deliberate choice because Americans have traditionally paid more attention to economic factors than political variables in their assessment of Third World development—as long as the regime has been anticommunist. Authoritarianism has been accepted because, in American thinking, it can facilitate economic modernization and it can evolve into democracy. Thus, American policy toward Iran is not an isolated case. As the next two chapters will show, support for authoritarian governments is an integral part of U.S. foreign policy. We can best support this thesis by turning to the Nicaraguan revolution, which toppled another U.S.-backed dictatorship only six months after the Shah's overthrow.

NOTES

1. See "Toast of the President and the Shah at a State Dinner, December 31, 1979," *Presidential Documents*, vol. 13 (January 2, 1977), p. 1975; Jimmy Carter, *Keeping Faith: Memoirs of a President* (New York: Bantam Books, 1982), p. 437.

2. "The Failure of America's Iranian Intelligence Is Nothing New," *Los Angeles Times*, January 14, 1979, Part 1, p. 6; Carter, *Keeping Faith*, p. 438.

3. "CIA Inaccurate on Iran, Director Concedes," *Los Angeles Times*, February 5, 1979, Part 1, p. 4.

4. In 1973, for example, Joseph Sisco, then the assistant secretary of state, told a congressional hearing that Iran was one of the two major stable governments in the Middle East. See Frances Fitzgerald, "Giving the Shah Everything He Wants," *Harper Magazine*, November 1974, p. 78.

5. Such a view was reflected in various news coverages of the Iranian Revolution. It was also reflected in various testimonies before congressional committees. See, for example, House Committee on Foreign Affairs, Subcommittee on Europe and the Middle East, *U.S. Policy toward Iran, January 1979*, 96th Cong., 1st sess., January 17, 1979. Also see Bernard Gwertzman, "House Panel Blames Intelligence Agencies and Policy Makers over Iran," *New York Times*, January 25, 1979, Part 1, p. 8.

6. U.S., Congress, House, Permanent Select Committee on Intelligence, *Iran: Evaluation of U.S. Intelligence Performance prior to November 1978*, January 1979, p. 7.

7. United States Arms Control and Disarmament Agency, *World Military Expenditures and Arms Transfers, 1966–1975* (Washington, D.C.: U.S. Government Printing Office, 1975), pp. 77–80.

8. *Public Papers of the President of the United States: Lyndon Johnson, 1965* (Washington, D.C.: U.S. Government Printing Office, 1966), p. 674.

9. See Walter LaFeber, *America, Russia, and the Cold War: 1945–1975* (New York: John Wiley, 1976), ch. 3.

10. "European Initiative Essential to Economic Recovery," *Department of State Bulletin*, 26 (June 15, 1947), p. 1160.

11. U.S. Bureau of the Census, *Statistical Abstract of the United States* (Washington, D.C.: U.S. Government Printing Office, 1978), p. 871.

12. Ray Maghroori and Stephen Gorman, "The Conceptual Weakness of American Foreign Policies toward Authoritarian Third World Allies," *Towson Journal of International Affairs*, 14 (Spring 1980), p. 63.

13. Morton H. Halperin, *Bureaucratic Politics and Foreign Policy* (Washington, D.C.: Brookings Institution, 1974), p. 12.

14. LaFeber, *America, Russia, and the Cold War*, p. 156, emphasis added.

15. Melvin Gurtov, *The United States against the Third World* (New York: Praeger, 1974), p. 49.

16. Robert L. Heilbroner, *The Great Ascent: The Struggle for Economic Development in Our Time* (New York: Harper, 1963), ch. 8.

17. *Annual Defense Department Report, FY 1978* (Washington, D.C.: U.S. Government Printing Office, 1977), p. 16.

18. *Ibid.*, p. 17.

19. "Now the Squeeze on Metals," *Business Week*, July 12, 1979, p. 46.

20. Stephen M. Gorman, "Strategic Materials and U.S. Relations with the Third World," unpublished paper.

21. See S. M. Miller, Roy Bennett, and Cyril Alpatt, "Does the U.S. Economy Require Imperialism," in Robert J. Art and Robert Jervis, eds., *International Politics: Anarchy Force, Imperialism* (Boston: Little, Brown, 1973); Paul Sweezy and Paul Baran, *Monopoly Capital* (New York: Monthly Review Press, 1968); and Harry Magdoff, *The Age of Imperialism* (New York: Monthly Review Press, 1969).

22. Ralph Stuart Smith, *The United States and the Third World: A Discussion Paper* (Washington, D.C.: State Department, 1976), p. 3.

23. *Ibid.*, p. 55.

24. *Ibid.*

25. Dean Rusk, "Trade, Investment and United States Foreign Policy," in Marvin D. Bernstein, ed., *Foreign Investment in Latin America* (New York: Knopf, 1966), p. 183.

26. Smith, *United States and the Third World*, p. 3.

27. For arguments on this point, see V. I. Lenin, "Imperialism, the Highest Stage of Capitalism," in James E. Connor, ed., *Lenin on Politics and Revolution* (New York: Pegasus, 1968); or J. A. Hobson, "The Economic Taproot of Imperialism," in Art and Jervis, *International Politics*.

28. Joan Edelman Spero, *The Politics of International Economic Relations* (New York: St. Martin's Press, 1977), pp. 65–66.

29. *Ibid.*, p. 66, emphasis added.

30. LaFeber, *America, Russia and the Cold War*, p. 10.

31. Lawrence Shoup, *Imperial Brain Trust: The Council on Foreign Relations and United States Foreign Policy* (New York: Monthly Review Press, 1977).

32. W. Gifford, quoted in Pablo Gonzalez Casanova, "The Ideology

of the United States concerning Foreign Investment," in Bernstein, *Foreign Investment in Latin America*, p. 236.

33. Gabriel Kolko, *The Roots of American Foreign Policy* (Boston: Beacon Press, 1969), p. 89.

34. Gurtov, *United States against the Third World*, p. 4.

35. Henry Kissinger, "Morality and Power: The Role of Human Rights in Foreign Policy," *Washington Post*, September 25, 1977.

36. Richard F. Nyrop, ed., *Iran: A Country Study* (Washington, D.C.: American University, 1978), pp. 58–59.

37. Barry Rubin, *Paved with Good Intentions: The American Experience in Iran* (New York: Penguin Books, 1980), p. 55. Also see Sepehr Zabih, *The Mossadeqh Era: Roots of the Iranian Revolution* (New York: Lakeview Press, 1982).

38. For a review of the agreement between Iran and the Anglo-Iranian Oil Company, see Robert B. Stobaugh, "The Evolution of Iranian Oil Policy, 1925–1975," in George Lenczowski, ed., *Iran under the Pahlavis* (Stanford: Hoover Institution Press, 1978), pp. 201–252.

39. Robert L. Paarlberg, "The Advantageous Alliance: U.S. Relations with Iran 1920–1975," in Paarlberg, Eul Y. Park, and Donald L. Wyman, eds., *Diplomatic Dispute: U.S. Conflict with Iran, Japan, and Mexico* (Cambridge: Center for International Affairs, Harvard University, 1978), p. 35.

40. Stobaugh, "The Evolution of Iranian Oil Policy," p. 208.

41. Cited in *ibid.*, p. 206.

42. *Ibid.*, p. 210.

43. Yonah Alexander and Allan Nanes, eds. *The United States and Iran: A Documentary History* (Frederick, Md.: Aletheia Books, 1980), p. 233.

44. Dwight D. Eisenhower, *Mandate for Change: 1953–1956* (Garden City, N.Y.: Doubleday, 1963), p. 162.

45. *Ibid.*, p. 163.

46. Rubin, *Paved with Good Intentions*, p. 62.

47. Eisenhower, *Mandate for Change*, p. 163.

48. For a review of the American decision and subsequent events see Kermit Roosevelt, "How the CIA Brought the Shah to Power," *Washington Post*, May 6, 1979; Rubin, *Paved with Good Intentions*, pp. 54–90; David Wise and Thomas B. Ross, *The Invisible Government* (New York: Bantam Books, 1964), pp. 116–121.

49. John Robinson Beal, *John Foster Dulles: A Biography* (New York: Harper and Brothers, 1957), p. 251.

50. See, for example, Bahman Nirumand, *Iran: The New Imperialism in Action* (New York: Monthly Review Press, 1969).

51. Rubin, *Paved with Good Intentions*, pp. 93–94.

52. Carl Kaplan and Fred Halliday, "The SAVAK-CIA Connection," *The Nation*, March 1, 1980, p. 229.

53. Reza Baraheni, "The SAVAK Documents," *The Nation*, February 23, 1980, p. 198.

54. Kaplan and Halliday, "SAVAK-CIA Connection," p. 229.

55. For details, see R. K. Ramazani, *The United States and Iran: The Pattern of Influence* (New York: Praeger, 1982).

56. For details, see Ervand Abrahamian, *Iran between Two Revolutions* (Princeton, N.J.: Princeton University Press, 1982); Amin Saikal, *The Rise and Fall of the Shah* (Princeton, N.J.: Princeton University Press, 1980); James A. Bill, "Modernization and Reform from Above: The Case of Iran," *Journal of Politics*, 32 (February 1970), pp. 19–40; Eric Hooglund, *Land and Revolution in Iran, 1960–1980* (Austin: University of Texas Press, 1982).

57. Nyrop, *Iran*, p. 231.

58. *Ibid.*, p. 259.

59. Abul Kasim Mansur, "The Crisis in Iran: Why the U.S. Ignored a Quarter Century of Warning," reprinted in Chau T. Phan, ed., *World Politics, 80/81* (Guilford, Conn.: Duskin Publishing Group, 1980), p. 205.

60. Nyrop, *Iran*, p. vii.

61. *Ibid.*, p. xix.

62. Robert Graham, *Iran: The Illusion of Power* (London: Croom Helm, 1978), pp. 178–179; Ramazani, *United States and Iran*.

63. Mansur, "Crisis in Iran," p. 205.

64. Nyrop, *Iran*, p. xvii.

65. *Ibid.*

66. Nikki R. Keddie, *Roots of Revolution: An Interpretive History of Modern Iran* (New Haven, Conn.: Yale University Press, 1981), p. 174. Also see Ervand Abrahamian, "Structural Causes of the Iranian Revolution," *MERIP Reports*, no. 87 (May 1980), pp. 21–26; Robert E. Looney, *Economic Origins of the Iranian Revolution* (New York: Pergamon Press, 1982).

67. Graham, *The Illusion of Power*, ch. 8–10; Fred Halliday, *Iran: Dictatorship and Development* (New York: Penguin Books, 1979).

68. For a review of various perspectives on the causes of the Iranian Revolution see Keddie, *Roots of Revolution*, ch. 9; Abrahamian, *Iran between Two Revolutions*; Looney, *Economic Origins of Iranian Revolution*; Hooglund, *Land and Revolution in Iran*; David H. Albert, ed., *Tell the American People: Perspectives on the Iranian Revolution* (Philadelphia: Movement for a New Society, 1980).

69. Keddie, *Roots of Revolution*, p. 231.

70. Carter, *Keeping Faith*, p. 438.

71. According to some reports, by early fall, some members of the Carter administration had become convinced that the Shah would fall and therefore began opening lines of communication with the opposition groups. William H. Sullivan, American ambassador to Tehran, was among those who believed the Shah's government would collapse. But he states that "when the State Department advanced the view that the Shah's regime would not survive, there were many others in the Washington bureaucracy, particularly on the National Security Council (where the revolt was simplistically believed to be an Islamic revolution), who attributed State's perception, and by indirection that of the embassy, to an expression of wishful thinking on the part of those whose vision was blurred by their zeal for human rights." William H. Sullivan, "Dateline Iran: The Road Not Taken," *Foreign Policy*, no. 40 (1980), p. 177. Also see Sullivan's book, *Mission to Iran* (New York: Norton, 1981) and Carter, *Keeping Faith*, pp. 443–447. About Sullivan's earlier position see *Keeping Faith*, p. 439.

72. Carter, *Keeping Faith*, p. 440.

73. Sullivan, "Dateline Iran," p. 179.

74. *Ibid.*, pp. 183–185.

75. For details, see Keddie, *Roots of Revolution*, p. 257.

76. Carter, *Keeping Faith*, p. 452.

77. For details of the hostage crisis, see *ibid.*, pp. 452–596; Sullivan, *Mission to Iran*; Rocky Sickman, *Iranian Hostage: A Personal Diary of 444 Days of Captivity* (New York: Crawford Press, 1982).

78. House Permanent Select Committee on Intelligence, *Iran: Evaluation of U.S. Intelligence Performance prior to November 1978*, p. 2.

79. *Ibid.*, p. 3.

80. House Committee on Foreign Relations, *Report of Special Study Mission to Asia*, 91st Cong., 1st sess., April 1970, p. 29, emphasis added.

81. See "Toast of the President and the Shah at a State Dinner, December 31, 1977," in *Presidential Documents*, p. 1975.

82. U.S. Congress, House Committee on Foreign Relations, *Report of Special Study Mission to Asia*, 91st Cong., 2d sess., April 1970, p. 9.

83. The next several paragraphs are based on Maghroori and Gorman, "Conceptual Weakness of American Foreign Policies," pp. 68–72.

84. *Ibid.*

85. Seymour Martin Lipset, *Political Man: The Social Basis of Politics* (New York: Doubleday, 1963), p. 64. Emphasis added.

86. *Ibid.*, p. 66.

87. David Apter, *The Politics of Modernization* (Chicago: University of Chicago Press, 1965), p. 40.

88. Samuel P. Huntington, "Political Development and Political Decay," *World Politics,* 17 (April 1965), p. 401.

89. See Samuel P. Huntington, *Political Order in a Changing Society* (New Haven, Conn.: Yale University Press, 1968.

90. Huntington, "Political Development and Political Decay," p. 423.

91. Harry Eckstein, "A Theory of Stable Democracy," in Eckstein, ed., *Division and Cohesion in Democracy: A Study of Norway* (Princeton, N.J.: Princeton University Press, 1966), p. 204.

92. *Ibid.*, pp. 255–256, emphasis added.

93. Robert Morrison MacIver, *Leviathan and the People* (Baton Rouge: Louisiana State University Press, 1939), p. 19.

BIBLIOGRAPHY

The causes of the Iranian Revolution are too complex. But Nikki R. Keddie's *Roots of Revolution: An Interpretive History of Iranian Revolution* (New Haven, Conn.: Yale University Press, 1981) provides a balanced analysis. Keddie puts into perspective the cultural, socio-economic, and religious factors needed to understand the Iranian Revolution of 1978–1979. Also, Amin Saikal's *The Rise and Fall of the Shah* (Princeton, N.J.: Princeton University Press, 1980) is a useful source. Saikal argues that despite the Shah's achievements, his goals and policies were full of inherent contradictions and weaknesses, were unresponsive to the needs of Iran, and failed to achieve their own objectives. These problems, coupled with the traditional nature of his throne and the repressive behavior of his regime, ultimately led to the Iranian Revolution. Ervand Abrahamian, *Iran between the Two Revolutions* (Princeton, N.J.: Princeton University Press, 1982) is also quite useful. In *Iran since the Revolution* (Baltimore: Johns Hopkins University Press, 1982), Sepehr Zabih reviews some of the factors leading to the Iranian Revolution, as well as some of its consequences. He places the overthrow of the Shah in the context of a protracted struggle for democracy dating back to the early twentieth century. Robert E. Looney's *Economic Origins of the Iranian Revolution* (New York: Pergamon Press, 1982) is devoted to an analysis of Iran's economic strategy before the fall of the Shah, including a detailed discussion of the problems caused by the post–1973 oil boom. Eric J. Hooglund, *Land and Revolution in Iran, 1960–1980* (Austin: University of Texas Press, 1982), looks at the Iranian land reform program. He argues that the Iranian land reform between 1962 and 1971 was one of the most ambitious undertakings in the Middle East. But, he points out, beneath apparent statistical success, the actual accomplishments of the program were negligible. Later, the resulting widespread discontent of thousands of Iranian villagers would contribute to the Shah's downfall. Also, Homa Katouzian's *The Political Economy of Modern Iran: Despotism and Pseudo-Modernism, 1926–1979* (New York: New York University Press, 1981) is a useful source and should be consulted.

For a general review of Iranian politics under the Shah, consult Ervand Abrahamian, *Iran between the Two Revolutions* (cited above); James A. Bill, *The Politics of Iran: Groups, Classes and Modernization* (Columbus, Ohio: Charles E. Merrill, 1972); and Robert Graham, *Iran: The Illusion of Power* (London: Croom Helm, 1978). For a Marxist interpretation, see Fred Halliday, *Iran: Dictatorship and Development* (New York: Penguin Books, 1979), and Marvin Zonis, *The Political Elite of Iran* (Princeton, N.J.: Princeton University Press, 1971).

In recent years, *MERIP Reports* has devoted several issues to a critical review of the Iranian political system under the Shah. In particular, issues number 69, 71, 75/6, 86, 87, 88, 98, and 104 are quite helpful and should be consulted. Contributors to these issues include Eric Rouleau, Patrick Clawson, Fred Halliday, and Ervand Abrahamian. In addition, these issues contain revealing interviews with Iranian officials.

For a review of the Iranian-American relations, see R. K. Ramazani, *The United States and Iran: The Pattern of Influence* (New York: Praeger, 1982). Ramazani examines the U.S.-Iran influence relationship during the Shah's regime, emphasizing the intimate linkage between Iran's domestic politics and its foreign policy toward the United States and revealing the contribution of that relationship to the Iranian Revolution. For a personal account of American-Iranian relations, see Jimmy Carter, *Keeping Faith: Memoirs of a President* (New York: Bantam Books, 1982). William H. Sullivan, the American ambassador to Iran, in his memoirs, *Mission to Iran* (New York: Norton, 1981), provides a revealing account of American foreign policy during the Shah's last days in power.

In addition to the above sources, students of Iranian-American relations should also consult government documents and publications. If read with care, government publications are usually insightful. The following is a list of relevant and helpful government publications: House, Permanent Select Committee on Intelligence, *Iran: Evaluation of U.S. Intelligence Performance Prior to November 1978*, 96th Cong., 1st sess.,

1979; Senate, Hearing before the Committee on Foreign Relations, *The Situation in Iran*, 96th Cong., 2d sess., 1980; House, Hearing before the Subcommittee on Europe and the Middle East, *U.S. Policy toward Iran, January 1979*, 96th Cong., 1st sess., 1979; Joint Economic Committee, *Economic Consequences of the Revolution in Iran*, 96th Cong., 1st sess., 1979; House, Committee on Foreign Relations, *Report of Special Study Mission to Asia*, 91st Cong., 2d sess., 1970.

3 *Stephen M. Gorman*

Nicaragua

> The aberration of the North American government is what perpetuates traitors and mercenaries in power in my country by fire and blood . . . .
>
> —Augusto Cesar Sandino, leader of the 1927–1933 rebellion against U.S. military occupation of Nicaragua

> Ahead Compañeros! . . . we fight against the Yankees, the enemies of humanity.
>
> —From Nicaragua's new national anthem

In July 1979, the government of Anastasio Somoza, a close American ally, was overthrown in Nicaragua and a revolutionary junta with suspected Marxist tendencies was established. The event was not only politically embarrassing to the Carter administration, whose somewhat confused human-rights policy was credited with helping to destabilize the Somoza regime, but it also suggested an inability on the part of the U.S. foreign-policymaking establishment to deal effectively with developments even in an area long recognized as an American sphere of influence. In many respects, the Nicaraguan Revolution was an even greater embarrassment than the fall of the Ira-

---

Stephen Gorman died unexpectedly in July 1983 after having completed a first version of this chapter. It was updated through February 1984 by Ward Schinke, a doctorate candidate in political science at the University of California, Riverside. Mr. Schinke is completing his dissertation on Nicaragua.

nian Shah, occurring as it did in a region where the United States has a long history of successful interventionism and, presumably, a greater understanding of political dynamics. Unlike the Iranian Revolution, the overthrow of the pro-American government in Nicaragua was a protracted process that seemed to offer numerous opportunities for U.S. involvement to head off the formation of a hostile regime. Yet, at every critical juncture, Washington's response to the deepening crisis in Nicaragua strengthened the momentum toward radical change in the country.

In the aftermath of the Nicaraguan Revolution, U.S. policy toward the new Sandinista government followed a tortuous path. From early attempts to force the Sandinista government to moderate its policies through the application of traditional instruments of control in the region (manipulation of trade relations and development credits), U.S. policy drifted inexorably toward an open intention to destabilize the postrevolutionary regime by a variety of means, including the use and threatened use of military force. Throughout this process, the entire question of U.S.-Nicaraguan relations was progressively subsumed under the new Reagan administration's broader concern with Soviet expansionism. As a consequence, Washington's ability to understand the true nature of the Nicaraguan Revolution and devise sound and reasonable policies toward it all but disappeared. This, in turn, reduced the ability of the American policymaking establishment to comprehend and to respond to developments in the region as a whole.

A meaningful analysis of U.S.-Nicaraguan relations is almost impossible outside the context of American foreign policies toward the Caribbean and Central America in general. This region, which is increasingly referred to now as the "Caribbean Basin," was one of the first extracontinental areas in which the United States successfully asserted political, military, and financial influence during its rise to great power status.[1] Not long after the Spanish-American War, U.S. policymakers had come to view the Caribbean Basin as a secure sphere of interest within which a pax Americana was to be enforced by whatever expedients required. This led, naturally enough, to a high level of direct interventionism during the first three decades of this century and sporadic direct and indirect interventionism thereafter. In many respects, Nicaragua presents a microcosm of U.S. relations with the area as a whole, both in terms of the nature of U.S. interests there and the various means adopted for furthering those interests. In the same vein, the more recent difficulties that Washington has experienced in controlling or responding to developments in Nicaragua may presage a broader deterioration in Washington's regional relations. An understanding of the precise reasons for what must be considered the American foreign-policy debacle in failing to prevent the Nicaraguan revolution, or influencing the direction of the postrevolutionary regime, requires at least a modicum of historical perspective.

AN OVERVIEW OF U.S.-NICARAGUAN AND CARIBBEAN BASIN RELATIONS

As is true for the region as a whole, U.S. relations with Nicaragua have passed through at least four distinct periods since the turn of the century. Each period has been characterized by a slightly different set of interests, changing assumptions about the internal and external political dynamics of the country, and the application of alternative instruments of control and influence.

Direct Interventionism

The first period, lasting from 1912 to 1933, was one of direct military interventionism intended to halt the violent political turmoil between the liberal and conservative factions of the Nicaraguan creole elite and impose a stable political order within which U.S. interests could be secured.[2] Those interests were of two basic types: Economic and geopolitical. During the early years of direct U.S. military occupation of Nicaragua, one of the important objectives of American policy was to ensure the repayment of loans obtained by Nicaragua from private New York banks. Far more important, however, was Washington's strategic interest in the country, both as a potential site for a second transisthmian canal and as a base for protecting the approaches to the Panama Canal itself. The U.S. objectives were achieved through an alliance with the conservative faction of the Nicaraguan elite, whose governments were preserved in office through overt American endorsements and the protection of a small contingent of U.S. Marines.

The assumptions that guided U.S. policy in Nicaragua throughout this period were relatively simplistic and straightforward. First, it was presumed that the endemic political chaos of the country was culturally inherent in the creole society and resulted more from petty factionalism and personal rivalries than substantive ideological schisms. Second, it was taken for granted that no government could realistically hope to survive in the face of open diplomatic hostility from Washington, just as those governments that were supported by Washington were expected to be more or less immune from serious armed challenges. The presence of U.S. Marines was intended more as a trip wire than an actual military deterrent against armed attacks on American-backed regimes: They symbolized Washington's will and determination to defend the status quo. Finally, the U.S. government considered political calm to be a good in itself and, therefore, a goal that justified the means of direct interventionism. Political calm, if not actually mistaken for democracy, was certainly considered the next best thing. And, at any rate, there was a "sincere, if naive, belief in some circles that U.S. involvement could somehow help bring democracy to the country."[3] While a preoccupation with political calm (or stability) has remained a constant in American foreign policy throughout this century, during this period it was less sophisticated. While it was implied that domestic tranquility would lead generally to the improvement of Nicaraguan society, the connection was left ambiguous. In later years, political stability would be advanced in more complex arguments as a necessary prerequisite to political and economic development, regardless of how that stability was achieved (or, more accurately, imposed).

The "Good" Neighbor

The second period in U.S.-Nicaraguan relations developed during the early 1930s and lasted through the immediate post-World War II years. U.S. actions during this phase were oriented by President Franklin Roosevelt's "Good Neighbor Policy," which aimed at relieving America of its more direct and embarrassing involvement in the internal affairs of Caribbean Basin countries, and institutionalizing new arrangements for protecting American interests throughout the region.[4] The earlier direct interventionism of the United States had carried certain costs, both politically and financially, and posed the danger of inciting nationalist opposition to American interests and influence (as, indeed, occurred in Nicaragua with the Sandino Rebellion between 1927–1933). Under the Good Neighbor Policy, Washington sought to invest pro-American regimes with the political, financial, and military resources necessary to sustain themselves, which in Nicaragua led to the consolidation of a pseudo-democracy under the domination of an American protégé, Anastasio Somoza Garcia. After training and equipping a National Guard (intended to perform as an apolitical constabulatory), U.S. Marines withdrew from Nicaragua in 1933. By 1936, Somoza had utilized his command of the National Guard to seize control of the presidency without the slightest dissent from Washington.

Somoza's pro-American regime differed significantly from earlier governments of the same political ilk in that he skillfully constructed an autonomous power base. Somoza's authority was rooted in an expanded state apparatus, a politically corrupted military, and a wholly acquiescent national congress dominated by a political party entirely subservient to the dictator. Washington, while not totally insensitive to political appearances, was pragmatically inclined to embrace and support the Somoza regime. As Eduardo Crawley writes:

> It is said that when Secretary of State Cordell Hull showed Roosevelt the list of Heads of State to be invited to Washington, the President picked out Somoza's name and asked, "Isn't that man supposed to be a son of a bitch?" "He sure is," replied Cordell Hull, "but he is *our* son of a bitch."[5]

The United States was motivated to accept, even encourage, such political arrangements in Caribbean Basin countries out of two basic considerations. First, they were thought to be the lesser of two evils; the alternative being intra-elite conflict of the variety that had destabilized the region during the early decades of the century. Second, such regimes, given their thin veneer of legitimacy and popularity, were especially sensitive to the new instruments of American influence in the region: Preferential trade relations, diplomatic recognition, and private foreign investments and loans. Hence, they were amenable to manipulation.

The expansion of American interests in the region added weight to both of these considerations. In addition to continued strategic concerns, expanding trade and business relations with the Caribbean Basin placed a premium on cooperative governments. The approach, nevertheless, was not entirely cynical: Washington officials perceived Nicaragua and neighboring countries as extremely backward societies still incapable of governance under more liberal political structures. Just when they might be ready for more open political systems, however, or how the transition from authoritarianism to democracy was to be achieved, were not salient issues in the American foreign policy of the day.

The Institutionalization of the Cold War

The third identifiable phase in U.S.-Nicaraguan relations coincides with the early cold war period of the 1950s. As Soviet-American rivalry escalated, Washington's concern with protecting its nearly exclusive influence in the Caribbean Basin intensified, and new policies were adopted to that end. But while Washington employed a mixture of economic and military assistance to contain the spread of communism in Western Europe, Latin America was given, as Walter LaFeber puts it, "only one-half of the walnut." When the Latin American states met in 1947 to discuss U.S. proposals for hemispheric defense, Washington made it clear that they would receive only military aid and not economic aid.[6]

Washington's military relations with Latin America were formalized in the 1947 Inter-American Treaty of Reciprocal Assistance (Rio Pact), principally designed to defend the hemisphere from internal and external communist threats. Political relations were formalized in the following year with the creation of the Organization of American States (erected on the foundations of the older Pan-American Union). Washington's success in institutionalizing its political-military relations with Latin America tended to obscure the very real antagonisms that were coming into existence. The postwar era was one of deepening socio-political problems for the region.

> As a consequence, most governments in Latin America tended to look to the United States less and less for leadership in the international fight against Communism, and more and more for help, chiefly in the form of economic assistance, with their domestic socio-political problems. This fundamental difference over priorities was to plague Washington policymakers in dealing with Latin America throughout the entire Truman (1945–53) and Eisenhower (1953–61) administrations.[7]

For a variety of reasons, however, Washington's policy remained one of guns, not butter, for Latin America.

Midway through this period, however, the political imperatives of responding to Latin America's needs for development assistance gained more attention. Under Eisenhower, a debate emerged between Secretary of Treasury Humphrey and Secretary of State Dulles over how to respond to the Soviet economic offensive in developing countries. Humphrey wanted to rely primarily on private capital for investment, the World Bank for long-term capital investment loans, and the Export-Import Bank for regional import needs. "Dulles attempted to show Humphrey that this approach would be insufficient, arguing that, because of the growing importance of the newly emerging nations, an agency must be formed 'to make political loans and 'soft' loans on a long-term basis.' "[8] The primary emphasis on military assistance, nevertheless, remained unchanged until Humphrey's departure from the cabinet in 1957.

Interestingly enough, Washington's relations with the Somoza regime reached a low at the beginning of this era. In the early postwar period, the Truman administration strongly objected to Anastasio Somoza Garcia's open intentions of seeking a third presidential term in direct violation of the Nicaraguan constitution, a somewhat embarrassing prospect in the immediate aftermath of a war fought in defense of "democracy." Yet after Somoza's political coup was an accomplished fact, U.S. opposition faded quickly, and diplomatic relations were normalized by 1948.[9] With the onset of the cold war, Somoza's calculated anticommunism reestablished strong American support for his regime. In 1956, Nicaragua entered a formal military assistance program with the United States and subsequently received both training and material for the National Guard. As was true for all other Latin American nations, the U.S. military assistance received by Nicaragua was more suited to internal control than effective defense against external aggressions (even though the justification for the entire program was to strengthen hemispheric collective security). The elder Somoza's assassination in 1956, and his replacement by his son Luis Somoza as president (revealing the dynastic nature of the political regime), did not alter the close relations that had developed between Nicaragua and the United States.

The Cuban Spectre

The fourth major period in U.S.-Nicaraguan relations extended through the second half of the cold war and into the early 1970s, and was shaped by American responses to the perceived threat of communist subversion throughout the region. The Cuban Revolution, and Fidel Castro's turn toward Marxism-Leninism, convinced the Kennedy administration of the need to mount a massive development assistance program for Latin America to eradicate the socio-economic conditions that were perceived to breed Cuban-style revolutions.

> On March 13, 1961, less than two months after assuming office, President Kennedy called upon the people of the Western Hemisphere to join in a new "Alliance for Progress." He proposed "a vast cooperative effort, unparalleled in magnitude and nobility of purpose, to satisfy the basic needs of the American people."[10]

This was to be accomplished by a combination of bilateral and multilateral loans and the stimulation of increased foreign and domestic investment in Latin American economies. The program, although it fell far short of being a Marshall Plan for the

Western Hemisphere, went a long way toward improving U.S.-Latin American relations. It also signaled a willingness in Washington to support loans for social investments in such areas as education, health, and sanitation.

But the Alliance for Progress was seriously flawed in a number of areas. Its reliance on private foreign and domestic investments was unrealistic for many countries, including Nicaragua, and served in many cases to strengthen dependent ties between the United States and Latin American economies. And the reliance on trickle-down benefits meant that the bulk of the population in countries like Nicaragua would have to wait a considerable time for only marginal improvements in employment and income. More significantly, as Edwin Lieuwen observed, because of Washington's "apparent failure to make any distinctions between high-handed military dictatorships and struggling civilian democracy in granting aid, the United States was criticized in Latin America for holding up the normal political evolution of the area."[11]

In practice, the Alliance for Progress received increasingly less attention under President Johnson as more and more resources were channeled to the escalating war in Indochina. Also, the administration looked to expanding Latin American imports of U.S. products to help offset growing American trade deficits with Japan and Western Europe. Accordingly, attention began to shift during the mid–1960s toward once again maximizing U.S. economic advantages in the region. This coincided with a growing acceptance in Washington of military regimes in Latin America as effective instruments for promoting economic development and creating the preconditions for eventual political democracy.

Relations between the United States and Nicaragua were especially good during this entire period. Luis Somoza was an enthusiastic participant in the Alliance for Progress, and his technocratically inclined regime was considered a model for the region as a whole. Under his leadership, Nicaragua achieved impressive rates of growth and American investments in the country increased considerably. Luis Somoza also instituted a variety of cosmetic reforms designed to enhance the "democratic" image of the country: Actions which seemingly vindicated supporters in Washington who had argued that the authoritarianism of the Somocista system was paving the way to greater political liberties in the future. Power and wealth, however, remained highly concentrated while the masses began to experience a revolution of rising expectations.

Aside from a new willingness to support the developmental efforts of Latin America, this period was also distinguished by Washington's new concern with counterinsurgency measures to prevent any future Cubas. The military assistance programs of the earlier period remained in force, but a new emphasis was placed on training and equipment suited for internal security actions. As a direct consequence of the new American resolve to stem the tide of radical political change in Latin America (most clearly articulated in the militant anticommunism of the 1965 Johnson Doctrine), Washington also became more willing to openly intervene in the internal affairs of regional nations. The U.S. military intervention in the Dominican Republic and the covert operations to topple the Salvador Allende government in Chile illustrate the extremes to which Washington was prepared to go to prevent the spread of "communism" in the hemisphere. For the most part, though, control of development credits, trade, and military assistance proved sufficient levels of influence in U.S. dealings with Caribbean Basin nations.

The international political, economic, and military environments within which U.S.–Latin American relations unfolded began to change by the opening of the seventies, however. The approaching U.S. political-military defeat in Indochina, the emergence of detente in Soviet-American relations, and the expanding political, commercial, and even military relations of Latin American nations outside the hemisphere all lessened American influence in the region. Also, as the political shock wave of the Cuban Revolution receded into history, Washington's concern with Latin American developments dissipated. Thus, programs like military assistance (which had been largely concessionary since the mid–1950s) were placed increasingly on a payment basis, and the overall number of U.S. military advisers throughout the region began to decline. And in the area of development assistance, private banks and multilateral agencies gradually assumed an expanding share of the burden, although U.S. policymakers still retained the ability to influence the availability of resources to Latin American countries from these two sources.

While the international context of U.S.–Latin American relations began to undergo change, socio-political developments within the region were also taking place. In particular, social mobilization in nations like Nicaragua was imposing new standards of accountability on governments and making clientelistic relations with Washington a political liability where once they were an asset. Equally important, the incorporation of formally marginalized social groups into the mainstream of political-economic life increased pressures on regional governments to respond more directly and effectively to the material needs of the majority. This meant that the U.S.-sponsored model of development based on "open" economies and capitalist accumulation (with anticipated "trickle down" benefits for the masses) came under increasing criticism from opposition politicians. In Nicaragua, the Somoza dictatorship, with its close association with the United States and reliance on a supposedly "free market" to meet the needs of its population, began to suffer a steady decline in legitimacy. But the United States refused to view Somoza-style dictatorships as anachronisms. Rather, in a period of political uncertainty in the region, U.S. policymakers derived a certain sense of security from the continued friendly ties between Washington and such "strong" and "dependable" allies.

As the following section will demonstrate, the inability of American officials to understand internal developments within Nicaraguan society, together with their unwillingness to disassociate the United States from the Somoza regime, produced a counterproductive policy orientation toward the evolving revolution in that country. In the end, U.S. actions were material in bringing about precisely those conditions in Nicaragua that were most feared.

THE DECLINE OF SOMOZA AND THE U.S. RESPONSE

By the time Richard Nixon assumed the presidency in 1969, the Alliance for Progress had become a dead letter and Washington's concern with Latin America had slackened considerably. As Paul E. Sigmund observes, U.S. foreign policy during the first half of the seventies was characterized by "a 'low profile' in Latin America, and (with the exception of the Chilean covert interventions of 1970–73 and a half-hearted attempt to develop a 'New Dialogue' with Latin America in the mid–1970s) an almost total disregard for the area by Henry Kissinger during his tenure as Secretary of State . . . . "[12] Within this context, U.S. relations with Nicaragua were such that the internal policies of the Somoza dictatorship were conveniently ignored and the advisability of overtly close and cordial U.S. ties with such a repressive regime went entirely unquestioned. Nicaragua settled into a comfortable pattern of commercial and military relations with the United States that, from a pragmatic standpoint, seemed to provide tangible benefits to both sides at relatively low costs. The United States served simultaneously during this period as Nicaragua's largest single trading partner (purchasing over one-third of all Nicaraguan exports and supplying almost half of all imports), and its primary arms supplier (providing over 70 percent of its military imports, or about $11 million between 1967 and 1976).[13] These figures were substantially above the regional average. Overall, Nicaragua under the Somozas appeared to be a reliable and, equally important, stable American ally in the region.

The Last Somoza

Anastasio Somoza Debayle, second eldest son of the founder of the Somoza dynasty and third member of that family to rule the country, became president of Nicaragua in 1967. Relying on his command of the National Guard, Anastasio Somoza engineered his own "election" over the objections of his elder brother, Luis (who, as it turned out, died the same year), and proceeded to return the nation to the more heavy-handed political practices that had characterized his father's extended rule. While many of the trappings of formal liberal democracy were retained, Anastasio Somoza systematically undermined even the limited reforms that had been achieved under his brother, and resorted to an intensification of corruption and coercion to consolidate power and silence critics of his administration. Nevertheless, U.S.-Nicaraguan relations became even closer than before, and U.S. Ambassador Turner Shelton assumed the role of one of Somoza's staunchest defenders within both Nicaragua and Washington policymaking circles. He also became one of Somoza's closest political advisers.[14]

Ambassador Shelton's enthusiasm for Anastasio Somoza's openly authoritarian regime derived largely from the widely held belief that economic development directed from the top down would have to precede the institution of effective democracy in nations like Nicaragua. In the meantime, it was in America's best interest to work closely with governments that, at a minimum, promoted "open economies" and contributed to the security of the region. The pragmatic acceptance of authoritarian governments implicit in this perspective was clearly enunciated in a remarkable document submitted by President Richard Nixon to the U.S. Congress in 1973. In this report, *U.S. Foreign Policy for the 1970s: Shaping a Durable Peace*, Nixon acknowledged his administration's decision to "deliberately reduce our visibility on the hemispheric stage," and argued that a greater willingness on the part of the United States to allow Latin American governments to respond to their pressing socio-economic problems with indigenous solutions would, in the long run, produce greater results than in the past.[15] He went on to state that:

> Accomodation to the diversity of the world community is the keystone of our current policy. That does not diminish our clearly stated preference for free and democratic process and for governments based thereon. Nor does it weaken our firmly held conviction that an open economic system and the operation of the market economy are the engines that best generate economic advance. But it does mean that we must be prepared to deal realistically with governments *as they are*, providing, of course, that they do not endanger security or the general peace of the area.[16]

As Richard Millett has written, the U.S. State Department was under no illusions about the true character of the Somoza regime.[17] But any concerns with the corruption and repression of the Nicaraguan political system were far outweighed by worries over which direction political change might take if the strong hand of Somoza were removed.

Under the Somozas, Nicaragua had been an obedient ally, participating in the preparation and execution of the 1961 Bay of Pigs invasion and contributing forces to the U.S. intervention in the Dominican Republic in 1965. Indeed, Anastasio Somoza Debayle even offered in 1967 to "send a contingent to Vietnam in support of United States efforts there."[18] Such close relations with Washington was one of the ways in which the Somozas maintained their firm grip on the National Guard and cowed political opponents. But dictatorships are seldom simplistic autocracies. On the contrary, they frequently demand considerable political skill on the part of the ruler, who must engage in constant political maneuvers to head off rivals and maximize authority. More importantly, dictatorships, like other political systems, are not static: The political fortunes of autocrats rise and fall, and recurrent crises are not uncommon. During the first presidential term of Anastasio Somoza Debayle, the dictatorship came close to collapse.

The deterioration of the Somoza dictatorship in the early 1970s is significant for a number of reasons, but most importantly because it illustrates a curious point of confusion in American foreign policy toward authoritarian Third World allies. A common rationale (apologia) offered in defense of U.S. ties with dictatorships in developing nations is that strong leaders are needed to guide such societies through difficult periods of political and economic transition. Yet as in the case of Nicaragua, it must be questioned just how strong some of these leaders are when in practice they must fall back on various forms of U.S. assistance to retain power when serious challenges to their rule materialize. At the very least, U.S. policymakers were guilty of not recognizing the political crisis that confronted Anastasio Somoza in the early 1970s as an early indication of the inherent fragility and instability of the entire Somocista system. U.S. actions at this point, then, constituted the first critical error in its policy toward Nicaragua that would help precipitate the Sandinista revolution of 1979.

The crisis that confronted Somoza, and the U.S. response, was symptomatic of broader problems in American foreign policy toward Latin America. Anastasio's brother, Luis, had presided over a period of economic expansion, political reform, and modernization of the state apparatus. Traditionally, the three pillars of Somocista power had been command of the National Guard, control of the National Liberal party and occupation of the executive. Luis Somoza, responding to the changing sociopolitical realities of Nicaragua, had attempted to remove the family from direct control of the state by gradually surrendering formal powers and ruling through political allies. Thus, after serving one term as president, he placed a family business associate, Rene Shick, in the presidency. He also attempted to pressure Anastasio Somoza to relinquish his command of the National Guard. His approach was to depend on the military to protect the prevailing political and economic order within which the Somoza family enjoyed entrenched privileges but to make the family's power and influence less obvious and, therefore, ultimately more secure. Such policies, had they been pursued past the death of Luis Somoza, might have been a superficial vindication of U.S. policies inasmuch as authoritarianism would have yielded gradually to political liberalization. After Luis Somoza's death, however, U.S. policy did nothing to further these trends.

Anastasio Somoza Debayle's political approach was atavistic.[19] His determination to "run the nation like an extension of the Guardia," as Richard Millett notes, produced disaffection not only among the traditional opponents of the regime, but likewise among many of its supporters.[20] In the first instance, Anastasio Somoza returned to the earlier practice of his father of guaranteeing the officers of the National Guard virtual immunity for any crime committed against opponents of the regime. Additionally, systematic corruption was not only permitted but encouraged as a means of tying the military more closely to the dictatorship.[21] In the second instance, Somoza lacked the political instincts of either his father or elder brother. His treatment of critics was too direct and brutal for the new political realities of the country, and his abuse of the state administrative apparatus was too clumsy and obvious after a period of bureaucratic professionalization. Finally, his open intentions of circumventing the constitutional proscription against successive terms to gain a second presidential term in the approaching 1971 elections helped unify his opponents. Accordingly, Somoza's political capital within Nicaragua was at its nadir in 1970 when U.S. actions staved off what might have been an internal decomposition of the dictatorship.

> As had happened in the past, the Somoza dynasty was again saved, at least in part, through the intervention of the United States, this time operating through the new Ambassador, Turner Shelton. A trip to the United States, including a private dinner with President Richard Nixon and a public meeting with United Nations General Secretary U Thant was arranged. Nixon . . . considered Somoza a firm American ally, deserving of all possible support.[22]

Somoza utilized this warm embrace by Washington to consolidate his control within the National Guard and convince members of the entrepreneurial class that he was still America's preferred representative in Nicaragua. Following up on this political reprieve, Somoza initiated a plan to write a new constitution that would enable him to serve another term as president. While the document was being drafted, Somoza turned over executive authority to a triumvirate (containing two of his own personal appointees) but retained his direct command of the National Guard.

Increasing Corruption

The second critical turning point in U.S.-Nicaraguan relations came in the aftermath of the December 23, 1972, earthquake that leveled downtown Managua and inflicted massive casualties. Acting on the direct advice of the U.S. ambassador, Somoza seized on the event to reassume absolute powers to direct "reconstruction." Ruling by decree, Somoza placed all international relief under the administration of the National Guard.[23] This was a significant move. "The widespread destruction removed some traditional areas of graft for the Guardia, but the massive amounts of foreign aid, from both government and private sources, which flowed into Nicaragua during 1973 more than made up for this."[24] These new opportunities for corruption came at just the right moment for Somoza. In spite of the Somoza family's patronistic administration of the Guardia, a certain degree of professionalization had begun to take place which fostered resentments against politically motivated promotions. The newly expanded opportunities for graft following the 1972 earthquake allowed Somoza to accommodate the interests of a larger number of officers. He also decreed pay raises for enlisted personnel and gave them priority in receiving earthquake relief.

The U.S. government chose to ignore the use to which Somoza put international relief. This was not a dangerous error simply because it neglected the human suffering that Somoza's policies permitted to continue. Rather, it was a disastrous error because it overlooked the fact that Somoza was beginning to change the very rules of economic activity in Nicaragua that had traditionally led the middle and upper classes to acquiesce in the continuation of the dictatorship. As Millett reports, "As the work of reconstruction progressed, the Somozas and high-ranking officers increasingly found ways to use the disaster as a means of increasing their own wealth."[25] In itself, this was certainly not out of the ordinary for Nicaragua (or other Latin American countries, for that matter). But Somoza's greed led him virtually to monopolize business opportunities following the earthquake, thereby excluding important support groups from their normal participation in economic activities. In some areas, Somoza even took over economic activities from elites who were not permitted to recover from the natural disaster.[26] In effect, Somoza isolated himself from key support groups, and relied increasingly on the National Guard to preserve his position.

It would not be completely accurate to suggest that the United States accepted this increasing authoritarianism with absolute equanimity. But the nature of the U.S. response illustrates the indecisiveness of American foreign policy in its approach to friendly dictatorships. This indecisiveness would later prove fatal to American interests in Nicaragua during the crucial stages leading up to the 1979 revolution.

In 1974, Somoza arranged his election to a second presidential term under the provisions of a new constitution. Oddly, the United States—which had not objected to Somoza's diversion of earthquake relief to himself and the Guardia—found something amiss with this heavy-handed political ploy. The response, however, was low keyed: Ambassador Shelton, over the strong objections of Somoza, was replaced in early 1975. Precisely what this gesture was intended to accomplish is unclear, since in all other respects U.S.-Nicaraguan relations (including military assistance, trade relations, and foreign aid) remained normal. Practically speaking, all that was accomplished was to deprive Somoza of one of his innermost political advisers who had helped him through several political crises. Aside from this mild political reproach, Washington's political support for the dictatorship continued as before, but only under increasing criticism within the United States.

America's Grooved Thinking

By 1975 a series of columns by Jack Anderson concerning the brutality and corruption of the Somoza regime had made U.S.-Nicaraguan relations a point of embarrassment for the State Department. But strong backing from conservative supporters in the U.S. Congress kept U.S. policy toward the dictatorship on its traditional course. One such supporter, Representative John Murphy (D-N.Y.) issued a defense of Somoza on the floor of the House of Representatives that described the dictator as one of the few true American allies in the hemisphere. Murphy explained that:

> As international relationships have shifted with the winds of detente it has become difficult to distinguish steadfast allies from those opportunistic nations seeking special economic advantage while barely hiding their contempt for the United States. So it troubles me when a longtime friend is pointlessly vilified . . . . [27]

The U.S. State Department, for its part, responded to the allegations of corruption involving U.S. assistance by sending an open letter to the Nicaraguan ambassador in Washington, assuring him that the U.S. government did not have any basis for investigating such accusations.[28] Both the address in Congress and the State Department letter received prominent coverage in the Somoza-controlled press agencies in Nicaragua.

The political situation in Nicaragua by this time, however, demanded a careful reevaluation of American public identification with the Somoza regime. Already by 1974 the Catholic church in Nicaragua, under the leadership of the new Archbishop Miguel Obando y Bravo, had publicly disavowed the Somoza government and had boycotted Somoza's inauguration to a second presidential term. The defection of this pivotal institution in a predominantly Catholic country should have tipped off the U.S. foreign-policymaking establishment that Somoza was alienating even those groups whose acceptance of the existing order would normally be taken for granted. On top of this, the dictatorship, while keeping the situation militarily under control, had proven incapable of destroying an embryonic revolutionary group (the Sandinista Front of National Liberation) that continued to harass and embarrass the government. Finally, as criticism of his government mounted, "the dictator's responses became increasingly erratic."[29] From an objective standpoint, Somoza's presidency did not appear to be the best vehicle for furthering U.S. interests in the country. But Washington's backing continued.

By the mid–1970s, the very legitimacy of the Somocista political system was in serious doubt, and this should have been evident to U.S. observers. Within the Nicaraguan church, a so-called Theology of Liberation had firmly taken hold that led a significant number of the clergy to identify with the impoverished masses and to criticize the government openly for its neglect of basic needs.[30] Within the middle classes, intellectuals became more active in their opposition to the dictatorship at the same time that entrepreneurs began reacting to Somoza's monopolization of new and existing economic activities. Most significant, however, was the increasing receptivity of a broad cross sector of Nicaraguan society to the ideology of the Sandinista Front of National Liberation.[31]

The ideological platform of the dictatorship and its supporting political infrastructure was simple and, increasingly, unappealing to the bulk of the population. Somocismo stood for close political-economic relations with the United States, a "free market" approach to capitalist development in which benefits for the majority were expected to trickle down from the activities of leading entrepreneurs, and strong centralized authority dedicated to ensuring the level of internal order deemed indispensable for development. Noticeably lacking was any effective appeal to national sentiments, nor were there any perceptible populist undercurrents in the political platform of the Somoza dictatorship. As such, it was especially vulnerable to any political movement that could successfully develop these dual themes. Nationalism and populism had been on the rise throughout the Third World for some time, and American foreign policymakers should have been more sensitive to their potential significance in Nicaragua given recent developments elsewhere in the Third World. The Sandinista Front began to attract considerable attention and popularity at this stage of U.S.-Nicaraguan relations as a direct consequence of its nationalistic and highly populistic political program.[32] Washington, nevertheless, remained closely tied to what could only be described as a politically uninspiring tyranny.

INSURRECTION AND U.S. POLICY: 1977–1979

The Sandinista Front of National Liberation (FSLN) that would eventually overthrow the Somoza regime was founded in 1961. One of the original organizers, Carlos Fonesca Amador, attempted to combine the lessons of the recent Cuban Revolution with the nationalism and populism of an indigenous political folk hero, Augusto Cesar Sandino. Sandino had fought a protracted guerrilla campaign against the North American military presence in Nicaragua between 1927 and 1933. After the withdrawal of American Marines in 1933, Sandino ended hostilities against the government, but was assassinated on the orders of Anastasio Somoza Garcia (commander of the new U.S.-trained and equipped National Guard) in 1934. While Augusto Cesar Sandino's political ideology was, in truth, little more than a militant populism with strong religious overtones, Carlos Fonesca Amador selected him as the symbol under which to launch a Marxist guerrilla campaign against the Somoza dictatorship.[33]

The Sandinista Front was dominated by young Marxists during its formative period and received direct assistance from the Cuban government in the form of training and logistical support. Throughout the sixties, however, the FSLN suffered repeated military setbacks within Nicaragua and failed to establish a political following among the rural population where it concentrated its activities. Progressively after 1967, the strategy and even the ideology of the Sandinista Front underwent a gradual reorientation that brought about increased organizational activities in urban centers and political associations with non-Marxist progressive groups, including the reform wing of the Catholic church in Nicaragua. The Sandinista Front finally acquired national recognition in the politically charged atmosphere of the postearthquake period. In December, 1974, the FSLN carried out a commando action that captured a number of key figures in the Somoza regime, who were then exchanged for the freeing of political prisoners, the broadcast of political communiqués, and a $1 million ransom. This action brought the FSLN to the attention of American foreign policymakers, and sparked a major counteroffensive by the National Guard that lasted until mid–1977.[34]

The Escalation of Internal War

In the period between December 1974 and October 1977, the Somoza dictatorship came under mounting foreign criticism not only for its open corruption, which has already been discussed, but also for its increasingly arbitrary repression. In its efforts to eradicate the FSLN, the National Guard was allowed to turn entire areas of the countryside into free-fire zones. Political liberties and human rights in the urban centers were also severely and systematically repressed. These actions on the part of the Somoza dictatorship, which were aided and supported by U.S. policy toward Nicaragua, had three important consequences. First, the extreme dislocation and brutality inflicted on the rural population increased recruits for the FSLN. Second, the middle class experienced a growing political alienation and many key intellectuals moved closer to the political position of the Sandinista Front. Finally, the FSLN underwent further tactical and ideological change under the intense pressure of the National Guard offensive that made future alliances with the progressive middle class possible. In particular, a new majority faction emerged within the FSLN known as the Insurrectionists, who called for a political alliance with all anti-Somoza groups and the creation of a new political system based on pluralism and a mixed economy. Thus, while the Somoza regime was undermining many of its traditional bases of support, the Sandinista Front was broadening its own.[35]

While the FSLN had come close to extinction during the period of intense repression between December 1974 and mid–1977, in the end it not only survived but grew in strength. With the election of Jimmy Carter to the American presidency, and the new U.S. emphasis on human rights that followed, the Somoza government finally yielded to pressure to end its nearly three-year-old state of siege in October 1977. In the following month, the FSLN launched a major nationwide insurrection against the government, which escalated even beyond the expectations of many Sandinistas as unorganized sectors of the population joined spontaneously in the revolt. While the National Guard ultimately succeeded in putting down the insurrection after several weeks and thousands of lives, the severity of the political crisis in Nicaragua had been made obvious to officials in Washington. But after extensive debate in the U.S. Congress, military aid to Nicaragua was continued, and the White House publicly affirmed that progress was being made toward improving human rights in Nicaragua.[36]

In January 1978, the political crisis in Nicaragua deepened still further when the dictatorship's leading private-sector critic, Pedro Joaquin Chamorro, was assassinated. Chamorro had been instrumental in providing damaging information to Somoza's detractors in the United States, and it was generally assumed in Nicaragua that his death had been ordered by the dictator. Immediately, the leading representatives of the middle and upper classes organized the Broad Opposition Front (FAO) to force the dictator to resign. The FAO (consisting of many of the leading centrist political parties, labor unions, opposition political personalities, and economic elites) initiated a general strike and looked to the United States to provide the decisive push to remove Somoza from the presidency. The U.S. response was ambivalent. As one observer would later comment: "Without knowing which direction events would take, the Carter government adopted the most opportunistic of policies: it maintained ties with both the FAO and the Somocista regime, without understanding the actual divisions that existed between them."[37] The formation of the FAO meant that Somoza now had two major centers of opposition. The Sandinista Front (with its primary base among peasants, rural proletarians, and urban workers) pursued a strategy of armed opposition intended to bring about a highly nationalistic and somewhat socialistic system in Nicaragua. The FAO represented a centrist coalition committed to nonviolent protests to force Somoza out of office. But aside from promises to strengthen democratic practices, the FAO did not advocate sweeping economic or social reforms nor was it the least bit hostile to the United States.

The FAO represented both an opportunity to the United States and a potent political threat to the FSLN. By the middle of 1978, Somoza, along with his closest associates and the National Guard, was all but isolated from the nation as a whole. Decisive action by the United States at this moment to withdraw any and all forms of visible U.S. support for the dictator might have enhanced the prospects for a peaceful transition of power to the FAO. Such a change in government would clearly have been in America's interest. Indeed, the leader of the FAO, millionaire industrialist Alfonso Robelo, was recognized in Washington as an able and attractive replacement for Somoza. U.S. actions, nevertheless, made it impossible for the FAO to compete with the FSLN for the political allegiances of the population as a whole.

The Failure of Reformism

The Sandinista Front's assertion that only armed action could bring down the dictatorship gained wider acceptance as the FAO proved unable to enlist effective U.S. support in forcing Somoza to relinquish power peacefully. The first half of 1978, then, constituted another opportunity missed by American policymakers to stem the accelerating political deterioration in Nicaragua. Three possible explanations for Washington's indecisiveness at this critical juncture can be offered.

First, and perhaps most decisively, the Somoza family had

long maintained an extensive network of lobbyists and political consultants in the United States to guarantee support for the dictatorship.

> Among their North American friends were senators, congressmen, top administrators, and influential entrepreneurs. Two of the most loyal supporters that Somoza had were Representatives John Murphy (D-NY) and Charles Wilson (D-TX). The former had been a friend of Tacho's (Somoza Garcia) at West Point.[38]

The Somozas also retained the services of leading public relations firms, such as Norman, Laurence, Patterson, and Farrell of New York, with extensive influence in Washington policy circles.[39] This network of personal friends and hired supporters repeatedly helped counteract efforts in Congress or the bureaucracy to reduce aid to the Somoza regime or withhold political backing.

A second explanation for Washington's lethargy in responding to developments in Nicaragua concerns the mounting influence of a new conservative intellectual establishment during this period (which would later come to full fruition with the election of Ronald Reagan in 1980). Included in this conservative establishment were such institutions as the Heritage Foundation, the Hudson Institute, and the Council on American Affairs; and such individuals as future U.S. Ambassador Jeane Kirkpatrick, political commentator Jeffrey St. John, and Senator Carl T. Curtis (R-Neb.). Already, by 1978, the new conservative establishment was reacting against the Carter administration's limited attention to human rights and arguing in favor of unwavering support for proven U.S. allies regardless of the internal characteristics of their regimes. In 1978, for example, Jeffrey St. John wrote that the real issue in the debate over U.S. aid to Nicaragua was "the use of the Human Rights issue as an 'ideological sledgehammer' to destroy long-term allies and friends of the United States."[40] In the process of downplaying the salience of human rights as an issue in U.S. relations with Nicaragua, the new conservatives alternately either denied the authoritarian nature of the Somoza regime, or defended it as necessary and within acceptable limits. For example, Senator

Curtis (echoing the views expressed by Kissinger and Kirkpatrick) argued that there was a significant difference between dictatorships that "seek to control every aspect of citizens' lives, and authoritarian governments which, while strong, nevertheless allow individuals to exercise freedom of choice with regard to most aspects of everyday life. Nicaraguan citizens exercise complete freedom . . . ."[41]

The third explanation for the reluctance of the United States to act decisively to head off the collapse of the prevailing political system and the rise of radical forces in Nicaragua concerns an inherent characteristic of the American foreign-policymaking establishment: Grooved thinking. Since at least 1936, American influence and interests in Nicaragua had been secured by one after another of the Somozas. Hence, it was only natural for policy experts to accept intuitively the outlook of Jeffrey B. Gayner that:

> Nicaragua has had the most stable and durable government in the region. Those who desire to change the nature of this government undoubtedly believe that if they are successful in this particular case, other governments in the area will eventually succumb to similar pressures in the years ahead. Thus, Nicaragua becomes both the substance and the symbol of a general effort to transform the nature of a nation and a region. Consequently, the role of the United States in either influencing or acceding to the direction that Nicaragua takes may constitute a major battle in the ideological struggle in the hemisphere.[42]

Ignoring for the moment the incoherence of the statement as a whole, what it illustrates is the policy analysts' almost instinctive preference for existing relations and ingrained fear that change, of almost any nature, may become uncontrollable. What this perspective ignored was the relative need for, or likelihood of, change within Nicaragua and whether, or to what extent, the United States might be able to influence the direction of that change (as opposed to resisting change altogether). In other words, the natural reflex of American foreign policymakers and policy analysts when confronted with evidence that the Somoza regime was in serious trouble was to concentrate on all the reasons why change should not, or could not, be tolerated.

Thus, preference for a continuation of the status quo influenced evaluations of the durability of the Somoza regime.

The political crisis in Nicaragua took still another turn toward revolution in August and September 1978 that finally forced U.S. political intervention in an effort to mediate Somoza's surrender of power to the FAO. In August, the Sandinista Front captured the National Palace and held about 1,500 Somocista politicians and administrators captive. The hostages were eventually released in return for the freeing of political prisoners, the broadcast of political communiqués, and payment of a ransom.[43] The Sandinista commandos were granted safe passage out of Nicaragua and were cheered by thousands of Nicaraguans as they were driven to the airport to depart the country. In the next months, coordinated FSLN military actions sparked a massive nationwide popular insurrection that threw the Sandinistas into pitched battles with the National Guard to defend the population from arbitrary reprisals by the government. Several major towns fell under Sandinista control, and the guerrillas were joined in combat spontaneously by people from all social strata. Although Somoza's National Guard had quelled the revolt by month's end, the political position of the dictatorship remained tenuous. The atrocities committed by the National Guard during the insurrection, moreover, led the Carter administration to suspend military aid. (Israel, however, was permitted to meet most of Nicaragua's military needs thereafter.) Under these conditions, the FAO renewed its efforts to enlist the support of the United States in forcing Somoza out of office before the expiration of his term in 1981. What followed in the next five months between October 1978 and February 1979, however, constituted the United States' most costly mistake in Nicaragua.

The American "Peace" Initiative

In October 1978, Somoza responded to the mounting indications that the United States might demand his replacement by the FAO by offering to hold a plebiscite to determine whether he should serve the remainder of his presidential term. Protracted negotiations between the United States, the FAO, and the Somoza government over the conditions and the timing of the plebiscite ensued. During the same period, however, Somoza's National Guard continued to prosecute its counterinsurgency campaign against the FSLN throughout the country. The first obstacle to the plebiscite was the U.S. demand that it be supervised by an international agency, such as the Organization of American States, to guarantee the validity of the vote. This was eventually rejected definitively by Somoza. Next, the United States attempted to force Somoza to accept an impartial body within Nicaragua to supervise the electoral process. This proposition was also rejected by Somoza after extended conversations. Finally, after the National Guard appeared to have restored nearly complete military control, Somoza withdrew his offer of a plebiscite altogether. The United States responded by formally cancelling economic and military aid to Nicaragua (actions that were considered a mere slap on the wrist for Somoza) but failed to recall the American ambassador. The continuing presence of the U.S. ambassador indicated to most observers a willingness on the part of the Carter administration to work with Somoza. This had the effect of discrediting the FAO as a viable political force and a realistic alternative to Somoza.

The inability or unwillingness of the United States to force Somoza to follow through with a plebiscite destroyed whatever prestige and appeal the FAO had enjoyed and brought about a wholesale defection of centrist groups to the FSLN. The Sandinista thesis that only armed action could bring down the dictatorship had been convincingly demonstrated by Washington's continuing inability to renounce Somoza fully in favor of the FAO, and the progressive middle class reluctantly threw its support behind the Sandinista Front after February 1979. From this point forward, the situation in Nicaragua was well beyond the control of the United States, which had completely lost its sense of political realities in the country.[44]

In April 1979, the Sandinista Front again took the military offensive, this time with broad-based political backing from virtually every major social sector of the country, including the Catholic church, businessmen, centrist political groups, and, of course, the lower classes. The American response can only be described as a desperate attempt at "damage control." That is, it was belatedly accepted that Anastasio Somoza could not retain power, and U.S. policy now sought to achieve the alternative of a broadly based middle-class government of "national reconciliation," which was actually no longer an obtainable option. The Sandinistas viewed the U.S. efforts as a thinly veiled plan to bring about the "Somoza system without Somoza," and therefore rejected out of hand any form of mediated political settlement.[45] The U.S. betrayal of the FAO during the critical period between October 1978 and February 1979 had brought about the disintegration of the only moderate political force in the country with which the United States might have been able to cooperate in replacing Somoza. Thus, Washington's search for an alternative to Somoza turned to the National Guard.

Throughout the month of April, the United States endeavored to promote an "inside coup" that would depose Somoza but leave the Somocista political apparatus intact. While there were some dissident officers within the Guardia who, together with many of the political and economic interests associated with the dictatorship, favored this course of action, the coup never materialized. Had it taken place, the palace coup would likely not have ended the Sandinista offensive. The FSLN had long since rejected anything short of the destruction of the Somocista system as a whole. Thus, Washington's policy in Nicaragua at this moment was wholly unrealistic. American foreign policymakers had delayed acting until events passed beyond the point that a simple change in personnel could save the U.S.-backed political system in the country. Washington's actions showed that American policymakers still did not fully grasp the depth of the social upheaval in the country, the new political alliances that were taking shape, or the growing appeal of the Sandinista platform. The intended coup was a stopgap measure that was pursued in the absence of an intelligent long-term policy toward Nicaragua.

In May 1979, the Sandinistas launched their "final offensive" against the dictatorship, which was supported politically by the majority of the middle and upper classes and militarily by the lower classes. In response, Somoza ordered indiscriminate bombings of major cities and called upon the United States for direct military assistance. The deteriorating situation in Nicaragua sparked an intense debate within the Carter administration. On one side, National Security Adviser Zbigniew Brzezinski advocated immediate U.S. military intervention; on the other side, Secretary of State Cyrus Vance argued for a less unilateral response to the crisis.[46] By June 1979, the Carter administration had decided in favor of military intervention but sought to gain approval and cooperation for such a move from the Organization of American States. The expectation that the OAS would legitimize direct U.S. military intervention in Nicaragua was yet another example of how confused Washington's understanding of the situation had become. By this point in the Nicaraguan insurrection, several Latin American states, including the Andean Pact nations, had recognized the FSLN as a legitimate belligerent force in Nicaragua. Other nations, like Mexico and Costa Rica, actively defended the right of the Nicaraguan people to determine their own political destiny even if this meant revolution. Thus, the United States met steep opposition when it brought its proposal before the OAS in June.

Secretary of State Cyrus Vance presented a six-point proposal to the OAS. First, the United States called for the formation of a Government of National Reconciliation acceptable to all "relevant" social groups. This point was both unrealistic and unnecessary in the view of many since it (1) clearly intended to exclude the Sandinistas from any new government and (2) ignored the fact that the FSLN had just named such a broadly based provisional government. Second, the United States called for the sending of an OAS delegation to Nicaragua to mediate a peaceful resolution of the conflict acceptable to all "important" groups. In this regard, the United States sought to ensure that the interests of the National Guard as an institution would be included in any eventual settlement. Third, the United States called for an immediate cease-fire in place; a proposal clearly intended to prevent the complete military liquidation of the National Guard at the hands of the insurgents. Fourth, there should be a total arms embargo to all parties—a move that the United States anticipated would harm the Sandinistas more than the well-provisioned National Guard. Fifth, Washington called for coordinated international assistance to aid in the reconstruction of the war-torn nation. Finally, and most crucially from the American standpoint, Secretary Vance called for the dispatch of an "Inter-American Peace-Keeping Force," which, it was made clear, would consist of a large contingent of U.S. Marines.[47]

With Mexican leadership, the U.S. proposals were narrowly defeated. The Mexican representative's position was straightforward. "No organization or country has the right to intervene in the internal affairs of another. He said also that the government of Somoza had 'violated in a massive, flagrant, persistent, and systematic manner the human rights of that unfortunate country.' "[48] The American diplomatic defeat in the OAS forced Washington to abandon the idea of direct military intervention. Had the United States made the same proposals at an earlier point in the Nicaraguan crisis—during the September 1978 Insurrection, for example—when the political-military outcome was less certain, the plan would likely have been approved. In fact, Venezuela had actually sought U.S. backing for such an Inter-American Peace-Keeping Force in September 1978, but at that time the Carter administration was still committed to mediating some transfer of power from Somoza to others who might perpetuate the Somocista system under a new guise.[49] The U.S. proposals brought before the OAS, then, represented another critical error in timing of U.S. initiatives in Nicaragua.

As we have observed up to this point, the United States had sought to preserve a pro-American government in Nicaragua by three different means. In late 1978, Washington half-heartedly sought to pressure Somoza into a plebiscite from which the centrist FAO might have emerged victorious. The fact that in the end Somoza stymied this approach and did not bring about any serious rupture in U.S. relations with his government, demonstrates a recurrent tendency of American foreign policymakers to allow weaker allies to dictate policy in areas of critical interest to the United States. Then, in April 1979, the United States attempted to engineer an internal coup that would have replaced Somoza with the National Guard; a policy completely oblivious to the fact that by this time the bulk of the Nicaraguan population was equally opposed to Somoza and the National Guard. Finally, when the prospect of a Sandinista military victory became evident to Washington officials, the United States belatedly proposed direct military intervention, thinly disguised as a humanitarian action intended to end the bloodshed and bring about a "just" political settlement. When Somoza appeared to hold the upper hand militarily only six months before, the United States had been unconcerned with the intensity of fighting or the level of civilian casualties. Hence, the cynicism of the June proposals was clearly evident to all parties concerned, and the United States found itself constrained from acting in the only remaining way it knew how to save the Somocista system in Nicaragua.

With the option of U.S. military intervention temporarily removed, the Sandinista Front pressed its assault on the dictatorship. By early July, a Sandinista victory appeared all but certain. Within this context, the United States attempted one last time to exert leverage in a situation entirely out of control. Washington worked out a plan under which Anastasio Somoza Debayle resigned the presidency on July 17 and went into exile in the United States. Somoza's deputy, Francisco Urcuyo Malianos, was left in charge of a caretaker government with instructions to (1) negotiate an immediate cease-fire in place, (2) arrange for high-level meetings between the military leaders of the National Guard and the FSLN to work out an integration of forces, and (3) surrender power to the Sandinista-appointed provisional government within seventy-two hours.[50] The provisional five-member junta that had been named by the FSLN in June was reluctantly accepted by the United States since two of its members represented the private sector and another was considered centrist. But precisely how Urcuyo Malianos was supposed to induce the FSLN to accept a cease-fire in place and agree to integrate its forces with the Guardia was not thought out. Again, the U.S. objective was to prevent a complete Sandinista victory on the battlefield and preserve the existence of the National Guard as a "stabilizing" influence in the postinsurrectionary political system. Yet, with the option of a military intervention becoming increasingly remote, why the Sandinistas should agree to these terms remained a complete mystery. The United States had been reduced to wishful thinking.

In any event, this final U.S. plan to salvage the situation in

Nicaragua fell through immediately. While Somoza resigned and left the country per Washington's instructions, he had left orders with his loyal replacement to attempt to salvage the situation militarily (assuming that the United States would be forced into defending this "new" regime and leaving the door open to an eventual return to power by Somoza himself). Thus, no cease-fire was called, and no negotiated surrender of power took place. Instead, fighting intensified and within thirty-six hours the Sandinistas captured the capital after the total collapse of the Guardia and state apparatus.

In the final analysis, American hesitation and lack of understanding in its response to the Nicaragua revolution contributed to a complete and unconditional Sandinista victory. Washington's tardy "damage control" policies in the final stages of the insurrection had failed to preserve even a shadow of the institutions through which American influence had previously operated.

AMERICAN RELATIONS WITH THE SANDINISTA REGIME: 1979–1983

The Sandinista Front of National Liberation took power on July 19, 1979, after an insurrection that cost over 40,000 lives and an estimated $3 billion in damage. The fighting left the nation's export industries in serious disorder, large segments of the population unemployed, and the government virtually bankrupt. An urgent need for foreign assistance confronted the new regime, which had also inherited a massive foreign debt (much of which was related to borrowing by Somoza to support his war effort). Within this context, a normalization of Nicaragua's foreign relations was one of the first orders of business taken up by the new rulers.

The United States recognized the new government of Nicaragua on July 24, 1979, and shortly thereafter the Carter administration proposed $75 million in aid to help rebuild the economy. The primary objective of the United States in offering assistance was to strengthen the private sector and provide an inducement to the new government to remain within a moderate course of action. The immediate postinsurrectionary political situation within the country was viewed as extremely fluid by the United States. Accordingly, Washington endeavored to strengthen the position of bourgeois moderates within the new governmental apparatus. The actual political relationships within Nicaragua following the fall of Somoza, however, were not nearly as susceptible to outside manipulation as Washington assumed.

Before the fall of Somoza, the National Directorate of the FSLN had named a five-member Government of National Reconstruction (JGRN) composed of one known Sandinista, two middle-class intellectuals who were assumed by Washington to be more liberal than radical, and two members of the private sector (including Alfonso Robelo), who were expected to project a generally conservative influence. Upon the Sandinista victory, the JGRN assumed formal executive powers, and it was with this political entity that the United States expected to deal. Real political power, however, was vested in a nine-member Sandinista National Directorate (DNC), which made all key appointments and approved all legislation (or decrees). Of particular importance, the DNC retained exclusive control over the new Sandinista Popular Army that replaced the National Guard, and made all foreign policy decisions. The JGRN—whose role and influence within the new political system the United States hoped to expand—remained entirely subservient to the DNC and essentially performed a ceremonial and consultative function. As the reality of absolute Sandinista authority in the post-insurrectionary government became clear to Washington, U.S.-Nicaraguan relations became more problematic.

Early Tensions

During the first year and a half, the main issues that arose in U.S.-Nicaraguan relations were: (1) what conditions would be attached to economic assistance, (2) Washington's concern with the presence of Cuban social and military advisers, (3) the preservation of a "pluralistic" political system and a "mixed" economy, and (4) the alleged militarism of the Sandinistas and their involvement in the mounting civil strife of neighboring El Salvador. From one angle, the general policy of the Carter administration toward the new Nicaraguan regime appeared to emphasize conditional cooperation based on a pragmatic acceptance of a fait accompli. Attitudes within the foreign-policymaking establishment itself as well as the Congress—coupled with a continuing misunderstanding about the true revolutionary nature of the change that had transpired within Nicaragua—served to frustrate the entire process of rebuilding mutually beneficial relations. An alternative way of looking at the Carter administration's response to the Sandinista victory, according to Susanne Jonas, is that it opened the door to so-called soft-line interventionists who hoped to use conditional aid for damage control in Nicaragua. From this perspective, the U.S. offer of aid was intended to keep Nicaragua out of the Soviet orbit and guarantee American investment capital access to the country.[51] Whatever the true motives for the Carter administration's policies toward Nicaragua, however, relations became progressively strained beginning with the issue of economic assistance.

The congressional debate over the Nicaraguan aid package was intense. Conservative forces in both the House and Senate succeeded in attaching a number of conditions to the bill which were designed to make the assistance unacceptable to Nicaragua. In the first version of the bill passed in February 1980, four key conservative provisions were inserted: (1) That 60 percent of the aid go to the private sector (to strengthen the entrepreneurial class); (2) that distribution of the assistance be conditional on an overall observance of human rights; (3) that no money be used to support programs or facilities employing Cuban advisers; and (4) that Nicaragua abstain from terrorist or subversive activities aimed at other nations. These general provisions, along with others designed to be offensive to the Sandinista government, were retained in the final bill passed in June 1980. The very delay in passage of the aid package itself was a major point of irritation given the immediacy of the socioeconomic problems confronting Nicaragua. The delay was also counterproductive from the standpoint of the Carter administration's objectives since by mid–1980 Nicaragua had secured enough assistance from other nations to reduce significantly any political leverage Washington might hope to derive from its own offer of assistance. Mexico, Venezuela, and West Germany, in particular, provided the bulk of Nicaraguan foreign aid through late 1980.[52]

The second issue we have noted that interfered with American relations with the postinsurrectionary government in Nicaragua was the question of the role of Cuban advisers in the country. In January 1980, U.S. intelligence operatives in Nicaragua had reported that although the Sandinistas were constructing a "socialist" system modeled after Cuba, it did not have the same type of penetrative security apparatus nor dependency on the Soviet Union.[53] The precise role of Cuban advisers within the country, it was also reported, remained uncertain. The Sandinistas openly acknowledged the presence of Cuban doctors, teachers, and health experts, but the American concern centered on the 200 to 300 military advisers that were training, and in some cases reportedly commanding, units of the new Sandinista Popular Army. By December 1980, U.S. intelligence reported that there were between 3,600 and 4,200 civilian-military Cuban advisers in Nicaragua, information that tended to indicate to Washington the existence of a Soviet-Cuban-Nicaraguan connection.[54] American suspicions were also raised by a number of high-level Nicaraguan visits to Cuba, and the participation by Fidel Castro in Nicaragua's celebration of the first anniversary of the revolution in July 1980. Underlying Washington's general agitation on this subject was a growing U.S. annoyance with the strong nationalistic, anti-imperialistic "rhetoric" espoused by the ranking members of the Sandinista government. The American response, nevertheless, remained within the realm of official protests and, increasingly, private threats.

The third area of stress in U.S.-Nicaraguan relations in the year and a half following the revolution involved doubts about the Sandinistas' commitment to "pluralism" and a "mixed" economy. While the Sandinistas had expropriated the property of Somoza and his closest supporters upon taking power (giving the state control of up to one third of the economy), they also pledged to respect private enterprise. Likewise, the Sandinista National Directorate promised that the revolution would be "generous" with its opponents and respect the rights of free political organization, balanced representation, and public discussion of government policies. To that end, it had been announced that a Council of State consisting of thirty members from more than twenty different political groups would be convened as soon as possible to serve in a quasi-legislative capacity. In a somewhat hypocritical stance (given Washington's prior disinterest in the relative political openness of the Somocista regime), U.S. officials concentrated critical attention on the representation of private sector interests in the new political institutions, particularly the Government of National Reconstruction and Council of State. And, from the American perspective, problems of representation emerged relatively quickly.

The first serious political crisis to strike the postinsurrectionary government was the resignation in April 1980 of the two private-sector representatives on the JGRN: Industrialist Alfonso Robelo (former leader of the FAO and current leader of the Nicaraguan Democratic Movement, MDN) and Violeta Barrios de Chamorro (widow of Pedro Joaquin Chamorro). While the latter resigned ostensibly for reasons of health, Robelo's departure was openly political. Aside from disagreement with various Sandinista policies, Robelo objected to the expansion in membership of the Council of State from thirty members to forty-seven and the allocation of the vast majority of the new seats to pro-Sandinista organizations (which, in reality, represented the overwhelming majority of the population). Robelo's MDN, together with virtually all of the other private-sector groups allocated seats in the new Council of State, boycotted the body in spite of expanded powers of legislation and review of government policies granted to the Council by the DNC. The United States responded swiftly to these political developments, accusing the DNC of authoritarianism and disregard for political pluralism. Under intense U.S. pressure, the Sandinista National Directorate quickly appointed two new private-sector representatives to the JGRN, but the self-imposed boycott of the Council of State by conservatives and leading business organizations continued.

The last issue that complicated U.S. relations with the Sandinistas was the purported militarization of the country and suspected Sandinista involvement in the Salvadoran civil war.

The fact that Somoza's Nicaragua had spent more than any other country in the region on its military did not deter the United States from objecting to the military buildup under the Sandinistas (which in terms of forces in uniform did not appreciably surpass that of the National Guard under Somoza even after the first year and a half). And the reality that the social upheaval in El Salvador predated the Sandinista victory did not prevent Washington from assessing blame on Nicaragua for the political breakdown in that country.

With respect to the question of Nicaraguan militarization, Washington's primary concerns were with (1) the Sandinistas' stated intention of training a 200,000 man reserve (known as Sandinista Popular Militias) and (2) reports that sophisticated weapons were to be transferred from Cuba to Nicaragua. On the first point, Washington conveniently overlooked the new regime's legitimate security needs. After the fall of Somoza, somewhere between 2,000 and 5,000 members of the National Guard escaped into Honduras where they continued to pose a military threat along the entire northern frontier (limited military incursions and assassinations remained routine throughout this period, presumably with the acquiescence of the Honduran military).[55] Washington's preoccupations also ignored the use to which Sandinista Popular Militias were put: Sanitation work, health services, and emergency labor in reconstruction and harvesting. The effort to institutionalize the widest possible mass participation in the new order which the militias, *inter alia*, represented should have been recognized by Washington as an essential dimension of the revolutionary process through which the country was passing, and not as an indication of militarism or expansionist tendencies.

On the matter of anticipated Cuban transfers of sophisticated weapons, the U.S. drew conclusions from inadequate intelligence and faulty analysis. When construction to expand the Bluefields Airport (on the Atlantic coast) was discovered by CIA operatives in Nicaragua in April 1981, the report that followed stated definitively that the enlargement of the runway was to accommodate Mig–23s. Similar reports had been dispatched to Washington since at least mid–1980, but as of mid–1982, no such aircraft had been transferred to Nicaragua by Cuba. Subsequently, it would be theorized by U.S. intelligence experts that the enlargement of the airstrip in Bluefields was to accommodate cargo planes bringing in weapons for clandestine shipment to insurgents in El Salvador. This latter determination, of course, was made only after U.S. concern shifted from the anticipated introduction of Mig–23s into Nicaragua to accusations of Sandinista interventionism in El Salvador.

Turning finally to the matter of alleged Sandinista subversion in El Salvador—which would shortly become the overriding concern of the United States, even before the inauguration of Ronald Reagan in January 1981—facts, issues, and interpretations became confused. There can be little doubt that the revolutionary government in Nicaragua strongly identified with the insurgent movement in El Salvador, and, indeed, political offices for the joint command of the Salvadoran guerrillas were allowed to be established in Managua. (It should be noted, in comparison, that Costa Rica had permitted Sandinista political activity in that country during the Nicaraguan insurrection, and that the former president of Costa Rica admitted to helping hand load material destined for the Nicaraguan insurgents.) That the revolutionary regime in Nicaragua should identify with the insurgents in El Salvador was to be expected: Salvadoran leftists had rendered direct financial assistance to the Sandinistas during their struggle, and it was perceived in Nicaragua that the Salvadoran guerrillas were attempting to depose a regime not entirely dissimilar to Somoza's. Still, these facts in themselves did not mean that the Sandinistas were "behind" the Salvadoran conflict.

The Reagan Hard Line

American concern with Nicaraguan involvement in the turmoil in El Salvador came to the fore with the election of Ronald Reagan to the U.S. presidency in November 1980. After taking office in January 1981, the Reagan administration's approach was extremely insensitive, demanding that the Sandinista government make a public promise to halt activities in which the Sandinista government still insisted it was not involved. And in any event, any such public submission to American demands would have severely injured the political prestige of the revolutionary government at home, meaning that the American demand was altogether unrealistic. Inevitably, then, U.S. economic aid was finally suspended in 1982 after the failure of lengthy private negotiations between both parties.

Even before the eventual suspension of U.S. assistance (most of which had already been disbursed anyway), the Reagan administration began to allude publicly to what it considered hard evidence of Nicaraguan subversion in El Salvador and stepped up the level of public attacks on Nicaragua by high-ranking officials. The evidence was of three basic types: Second- and thirdhand reports from individuals often located in third countries (such as Honduras), supposition and extrapolation leading to generalized conclusions based on fragmented intelligence, and forged documents.

An early example of the first type of evidence was an October 1980 U.S. intelligence field report stating that a 180-man "political agitation team" headed by Cubans had been dispatched from Nicaragua, through Honduras, to El Salvador. The report continued by noting that as many as six additional agitation teams were to have been infiltrated into El Salvador except that the first was liquidated by security forces. Unfortunately from the standpoint of the Reagan administration, which came under increasing pressure to document its allegations from the press and a skeptical world community, reports such as the above, of which there was an increasing number after Reagan's election, could not be verified with either physical evidence or direct observation.

An example of the second type of "evidence" involves the Reagan administration's estimates of the volume of weapons that had been shipped from Cuba through Nicaragua to El Salvador. The figure made public by Washington (over eighty tons of weapons and munitions) was based largely on two separate pieces of intelligence, which remain classified. In the first, a CIA informant in Havana reported that a cargo box being loaded onto a passenger aircraft destined for Nicaragua fell and broke open, revealing automatic weapons. This intelligence was then correlated with information provided by an informant at the airport in Managua that cargo boxes of the general description as the one reported to contain weapons in Havana were routinely off loaded from Cuban planes onto trucks. U.S. officials therefore proceeded to calculate how many such containers Cuban planes would be able to transport on any given flight, multiplied that figure times the number of Cuban flights, and arrived at an approximation of the amount of weapons being smuggled into El Salvador.

The best illustration of the third category of "evidence" is the extensive White Paper released by the U.S. State Department in February 1981, consisting primarily of translations of Salvadoran guerrilla documents pointing directly to Nicaraguan connections.[56] The so-called documents had reportedly been captured by Salvadoran security forces so that their precise origin could not be guaranteed by U.S. officials. Later, after retired U.S. intelligence officers commented that the documents were similar in nature to others which the CIA had manufactured during previous crises in Latin America, the State Department quietly downplayed them. In the final analysis, a large-scale, systematic Nicaraguan involvement in the internal affairs of El Salvador could not be convincingly demonstrated by the Reagan administration. This did not prevent official U.S. policy from continuing on the supposition that such involvement did indeed exist. In point of fact, Assistant Secretary of State Thomas Enders testified before a Senate Subcommittee on Western Hemisphere Affairs that Nicaragua "was the first link in a grand Cuban strategy to train and arm guerrilla groups with the end of toppling the existing governments in the region."[57] Statements such as these, nevertheless, revealed more about the institutionalized fears of U.S. foreign policymakers than actual developments in Central America itself. Since U.S. analysts had warned before the Sandinista victory that any change of government in Nicaragua could create a domino effect throughout the region, it was only natural afterward that they should see their own predictions as accurate. And, tragically, acting on prophecies can sometimes make them self-fulfilling.

A New Application of Old Remedies

By late 1981, the U.S. position toward Nicaragua was openly confrontal. The U.S. secretary of state led the attack. "Haig charged Nicaragua with providing training bases for Cuban military advisors who allegedly are aiding guerrillas in Guatemala and El Salvador. He also refused to rule out U.S. military action against Nicaragua."[58] The reasons behind this hard-line policy toward the Sandinista government, it must be emphasized, were rather complex. The Reagan administration's relations with revolutionary Nicaragua must be understood within the broader context of U.S. global policies.

> Reagan and his advisors came into office determined to alter significantly what they perceived to be the deleterious direction of the previous administration's policy . . . . This involved more than a shift in emphasis back toward a more traditional balance-of-power diplomacy of the Kissinger variety. National security was to be redefined as a militant anti-communism and the U.S. stance in Latin America and the world was to be one of strength, rejecting the "gun-shy" attitudes of the previous policy.[59]

In an era when American power, influence, and interests were perceived to be threatened nearly everywhere in the world, Central America presented itself as a seemingly low-risk area in which to begin to reassert U.S. greatness. To reverse the image of the United States (fostered and reinforced by events in Vietnam and Iran, respectively) as an impotent giant, the Reagan administration concentrated almost immediately on controlling the situation in Central America. In an effort to grasp intellectually the outlines of the "problem," revolutionary Nicaragua, in conjunction with Cuban-Soviet expansionism, was targeted as the source of instability throughout the region.

By early 1982, a three-point program to deal with the perceived communist threat emanating from Nicaragua was well on the way to implementation. The three components of the plan were: U.S. support for the development of a paramilitary threat to Nicaragua; the creation of a regional development assistance program to stimulate support for future U.S. actions in the area; and efforts to polarize the Nicaraguan population and undermine Sandinista popularity. At a minimum, the plan aimed at containing the Nicaraguan revolution and, at an optimum, bringing down the regime.

To implement the first point of the program, the United States permitted the training of anti-Sandinista paramilitary units in

Florida and elsewhere. More threateningly, Washington increased its military aid to the Honduran armed forces and, indirectly, to the ex–National Guard units still poised along Nicaragua's northern frontier. According to press reports, the Reagan administration had authorized $19 million for the CIA to create "action teams" for paramilitary and political operations and intelligence gathering in Nicaragua. The principal recipients were the counterrevolutionaries (contras) operating in Honduras along the border with Nicaragua. The CIA-trained forces took credit for blowing up two key bridges in northern Nicaragua in March 1982. By the end of 1983, the number of contras in Honduras was estimated at 8,000 to 10,000. According to the Nicaraguan government, during 1983 the contras were responsible for the death of over 600 Nicaraguans, mostly civilians and militia members. It is estimated that the contras had caused $50 million in economic damage by the end of 1983. The contras tried several times to establish liberated zones in Nicaragua but failed on each occasion.[60]

The second point of the program was the introduction of the Caribbean Basin Initiative. Just as the first point was reminiscent of the Bay of Pigs approach to the region, this second point was a resurrection of the Alliance for Progress strategy of providing economic assistance to render regional governments less susceptible to communist subversion. The Caribbean Basin Initiative (CBI) consisted of (1) free trade agreements to provide friendly regional governments greater access to the American market on which their exports are largely dependent; (2) economic inducements to American capital to invest in the development efforts of regional nations; and (3) an increased level of "concessional" assistance. Criticisms of the CBI were diverse, however. First, "relatively modest expenditures are being asked of the U.S. Congress to carry out the economic portions: a supplemental appropriation of $350 million in fiscal year 1982 to the $475 million already budgeted for the region, and a total of $664 million for fiscal year 1983."[61] Not only would such sums be inadequate to stimulate real development, but it was also argued that they were "aimed more at insuring the survival of the existing unsatisfactory social and economic status quo, than meeting basic human needs of poor majorities." Such objections to the CBI missed the other major point, however. The clientelistic provisions of the Caribbean Basin Initiative were designed to draw regional governments politically closer to the United States and create an environment within which the United States would have a freer hand in dealing with Nicaragua. Also, since between 14 and 19 percent of the assistance would be for the military needs of the region, Washington hoped to bolster the counterinsurgency capabilities of embattled allies like Guatemala and, of course, El Salvador.

The third leg of the Reagan administration's policy for dealing with Nicaragua involved efforts to encourage the private sector and middle and upper classes within the country to resist the revolutionary government. This, it was hoped, would both weaken the regime politically and create a foreign impression that the Sandinistas are totalitarian, thus legitimizing U.S. efforts to overthrow them. In this regard, the United States kept up a constant public condemnation of the actions of the Sandinista regime—actions which by mid–1982 had become somewhat repressive given the state of siege under which the regime was functioning, but actions which the United States traditionally overlooks when committed by allies. Such behavior against the middle and upper classes, U.S. officials said, justified American intervention in the country. Interestingly enough, even the Sandinistas' most implacable conservative and private-sector critics denounced this stance by the United States. Reacting to one of the earliest U.S. threats of military intervention in defense of the Nicaraguan bourgeoisie,

> The MDN [led by millionaire industrialist Alfonso Robelo] issued a communiqué labeling the charges a violation of Nicaragua's "self-determination and sovereignty," and called for Nicaraguans to "energetically reject and condemn all intervention, interference, or blockade that the hegemonic powers of the world might try to carry out against Nicaraguans."[62]

In addition, "the daily La Prensa, which Haig pointedly singled out as being victimized by repression, condemned his 'interventionist and threatening attitude' in an editorial."[63] Even Nicaragua's Superior Council of Private Enterprise (COSEP) denounced the aggressive attitude of the United States. In short, U.S. attacks on the legitimacy of the Sandinista government served to rally nationalistic support behind the regime from all social sectors. The policy line already having been decided upon, however, it was continued.

The Reagan administration hoped to undermine the legitimacy of the Sandinista government by creating economic difficulties for Nicaragua. In January 1982 the United States blocked a $16 million loan to Nicaragua. Since the renegotiation of the debt in 1980, Nicaragua paid $160 million interest on the $900 million owed to private banks but received only $11 million in new loans. U.S. pressure resulted in freezing $50 million at the World Bank and $182 million from the Inter-American Development Bank (IDB). Multinational funding dropped from $231 million in 1979 to $21.8 million in 1983. The lack of backing by the World Bank made private banks hesitant to loan money as well.[64]

Ostensibly, the constriction of loans occurred because Nicaragua had not clarified the "rules of the game" for the private sector. For instance, an IDB loan for a rural road in a coffee-growing district mainly serving private farmers was vetoed by the United States. The Reagan administration stated that Nicaragua's macroeconomic policy "was not conducive to the development of the country."[65] Similar arguments were made to block loans to Chile when Allende was in power.

James Conrow, Treasury Department official responsible for the IDB, said they would approve loans if the Nicaraguan government revitalized the private sector, improved the efficiency of the public sector, cut agricultural price subsidies, and permitted greater freedom to market forces. This would mean returning to an economic situation similar to the Somoza period, which clearly had disastrous effects for the majority of Nicaraguans. Presently, the state-controlled banking sector has the cheapest credit available in Central America. Even U.S. Embassy officials admitted privately that the banks have given generous support to the private sector.[66]

The closure of Nicaraguan consulates in early 1983 by the Reagan administration greatly complicated normal import operations. The threat of a naval quarantine by the United States necessitated the planning of a greater stockpile of goods when extraordinary economic hardship already existed due to natural disasters of floods and a drought. In May 1983, the Reagan administration cut the Nicaraguan sugar quota by 90 percent for fiscal year 1984. In 1982, this would have amounted to $15.6 million. The administration claimed this was done as a warning to Nicaragua to stop its "subversion and extremist violence." The quota was redistributed among the other Central American nations. It is somewhat ironic since Nicaragua initially received its quota after the Cuban revolution proved to be to the disliking of the U.S. government. Finally, in June 1983, the Civil Aeronautics Board, responding to a request by the State Department, revoked permission recently granted for the Nicaraguan national airlines to have charter flights between Managua and Miami.[67]

The administration's actions brought mixed political results for the United States. The Central American nations excluding Nicaragua were brought closer diplomatically to the United States, while most of Latin America remained vocally critical. The majority of Third World nations and European allies condemned U.S. actions. At home, more members of Congress became critical of escalating U.S. involvement. Public opinion, though fluctuating, increased in opposition to intervention in Central America.

The inability of the administration to convince the Congress and American public that more escalation was needed in Central America prompted it to announce the National Bipartisan Commission on Central America to be headed by Henry Kissinger.[68] Kissinger was a logical choice to head the committee because the values and parameters with which he viewed the Third World agreed with those of the administration. He took part in the decisions to bomb North Vietnam and the secret bombings of Laos and Cambodia. He helped engineer the economic blockade and the CIA's political sabotage against Allende's Chile.

After a much publicized tour of Central America, which included only six hours in Nicaragua, the report released in January 1984 claimed that:

> . . . The consolidation of a Marxist-Leninist regime in Managua would be seen by its neighbors as constituting a permanent security threat. Because of its secretive nature, the existence of a political order on the

Cuban model in Nicaragua would pose major difficulties in negotiating, implementing, and verifying any Sandinista commitment to refrain from supporting insurgency and subversion in other countries. In this sense, the development of an open political system in Nicaragua, with a free press and an active opposition, would provide an important security guarantee for other countries in the region and would be a key element in any negotiated settlement.[69]

In this context, the Commission recommended large increases in military aid to Nicaragua's neighbors to "contain the export of subversion" and the continued paramilitary and economic pressure on Nicaragua to induce "broadened" participation in the government.

Since the administration had not formally acknowledged U.S. covert activities in Nicaragua, the report backed the continuance of covert actions in characteristic diplomatic parlance: "As a broad generality, we do not believe that it would be wise to dismantle existing incentives and pressures on the Managua regime except in conjunction with demonstrable progress on the negotiating front."[70] Only committee members Henry Cisneros and Carlos Diaz-Alejandro filed dissenting notes on Nicaragua. They called for a cessation of covert aid to the contras because their actions were counterproductive in pressuring the Sandinista government toward "pluralism." Cisneros called for a one-year grace period to see if the promised elections would be held. Diaz-Alejandro claimed covert activity helps to push Nicaragua toward the Soviet Union.[71] This limited criticism indicates the extent of shared values on the "bipartisan" commission. Central America was placed within the East-West conflict by all members rather than recognizing the true nature of underdevelopment and the nationalist revolutionary movement it fosters.

The Kissinger Commission recommended $8 billion in economic and military aid for Central America by the end of the decade. The administration immediately endorsed the Commission's analysis and recommendation. By early February, the administration was requesting additional funding for its anti-Sandinista activities which are based in Honduras: For fiscal year 1984, $180 million on top of the $80 million already appropriated and $123 million for fiscal 1985.[72]

CONCLUSION

As of early 1984, U.S. relations with the postinsurrectionary government of Nicaragua were at a new low. In its pursuit of a low-risk, high-visibility demonstration of America's new toughness, the Reagan administration actually added to its foreign-policy problems. On the one hand, the logic of its own description of Nicaragua forced it to increase its commitments to Central American governments that claimed to be the victims of "subversion." Such commitments strained scarce resources and raised troublesome political issues for the president at home, and tied the United States more closely to governments whose political futures were becoming increasingly uncertain (as a result of their own internal policies). On the other hand, U.S. policy toward Nicaragua and the region as a whole strained America's relations not only with European allies, but also with Mexico. Interestingly enough, at the very heart of the Reagan administration's policies in Central America was the fear that if communist subversion was not contained there, it would eventually reach its real objective of fomenting revolution in Mexico—a concern not shared by Mexico itself. More significant than either of these considerations, however, was the fact that no tangible "victory" over alleged Soviet-Cuban-Nicaraguan subversion appeared within reach by 1984. This meant that administration policies in the area, which indeed were attracting the attention that the White House had anticipated, were merely taking on the appearance of another example of U.S. inability to shape events. This was precisely the image of U.S. foreign policy that the administration's actions toward Nicaragua were intended to reverse.

The history of U.S.-Nicaraguan relations raises a number of bothersome questions about American foreign policymaking. Among the more puzzling questions are:

Why are the assumptions underlying U.S. relations with Third World nations so simplistic?

Why does the United States consistently react to events rather than anticipate them?

Why does American foreign policy intellectually reject the existence of social revolution, preferring instead to explain developments in Third World nations as consequences of East-West rivalry?

Why are nationalism and populism in the Third World always defined as ultimately dangerous to American interests (which they eventually become when threatened by the United States)?

These may appear to be naive questions, and in practice they have been addressed from a variety of ideological perspectives already. But they have not necessarily been answered in an entirely satisfactory manner.

It is perplexing that American foreign policymakers constantly return to strategies that have previously failed, that they define situations in terms that make the United States appear the loser whenever social change occurs in the Third World, and that they systematically resist any attempt to seriously examine the internal political forces that give rise to revolutions like the one in Nicaragua. Part of the problem seems to be that foreign policymakers consistently confuse what is desirable (from their own unique perspective) with what is attainable. There can be no question that over the short run it is easier to conduct business with a foreign leader who is "strong," anticommunist, and a demonstrated "friend" of the United States. But to translate the advantages that accrue to the United States from this type of leader in Third World nations into a national interest that must be defended against every threat places the United States in the position of orienting its policies toward people and not nations. A sound policy toward a nation—which would necessitate an understanding of that nation's needs and an intelligent response to them—should be able to survive the overthrow of a single individual or even an entire political system. This does not mean that U.S. foreign policies should be altruistic, only self-enlightened. If the United States continues its policy of hostility toward virtually all revolutionary governments, it will gradually find the number of governments with which it has cordial relations in the Third World considerably restricted.

NOTES

1. The area is increasingly referred to as the Caribbean Basin, not only in response to President Ronald Reagan's Caribbean Basin Pro-

gram of economic and commercial assistance to counter a perceived communist threat, but also because the region as a whole is experiencing similar socio-economic problems that pose political challenges to U.S. foreign policy.

2. For a brief review of the history of U.S. interventions in Nicaragua, see Hubert Herring, *A History of Latin America* (New York: Alfred A. Knopf, 1968), pp. 490–492, and Eduardo Crawley, *Dictators Never Die: A Portrait of Nicaragua and the Somoza Dynasty* (New York: St. Martin's Press, 1979), pp. 49–79.

3. Thomas W. Walker, *Nicaragua: The Land of Sandino* (Boulder, Colo.: Westview Press, 1981), p. 20.

4. See Edwin Lieuwen, *U.S. Policy in Latin America* (New York: Praeger, 1967), pp. 11–126.

5. Crawley, *Dictators*, p. 99.

6. Walter LaFeber, *America, Russia, and the Cold War: 1945–1975* (New York: John Wiley and Sons, 1976), p. 67.

7. Lieuwen, *U.S. Policy*, p. 84.

8. LaFeber, *America, Russia, and the Cold War*, p. 179.

9. Crawley, *Dictators*, pp. 106–108.

10. Lieuwen, *U.S. Policy*, p. 114.

11. *Ibid.*, p. 134.

12. Paul E. Sigmund, "Latin America: Change or Continuity?" *Foreign Affairs*, 60, no. 3 (1982), p. 630.

13. Heliodoro Gonzales, "U.S. Arms Transfer Policy in Latin America: Failure of a Policy," *Inter-American Economic Affairs*, 32 (Autumn 1978), p. 68; and IDB, *Economic and Social Progress in Latin America* (Washington, D.C.: Inter-American Development Bank, 1981), p. 402.

14. Crawley, *Dictators*, pp. 149–151.

15. Richard Nixon, *U.S. Foreign Policy for the 1970s: Shaping a Durable Peace*, (Washington, D.C.: Government Printing Office, 1973).

16. *Ibid.*, p. 118, emphasis added.

17. Richard Millett, *Guardians of the Dynasty* (Maryknoll, N.Y.: Orbis Books, 1977).

18. *Ibid.*, p. 230.

19. Concerning the backward political approach of Anastasio Somoza Debayle, see Stephen M. Gorman, "Nicaragua: The Socioeconomic Foundations of Revolution," in Steve Ropp and James Morris, eds., *Central America: Crisis and Adaptation* (Albuquerque: University of New Mexico Press, 1984).

20. Millett, *Guardians*, p. 232.

21. On the corruption of the Guardia, see Crawley, *Dictators*, pp. 148–161; and Walker, *Nicaragua: The Land of Sandino*, pp. 57–58.

22. Millett, *Guardians*, p. 235.

23. Walker, *Nicaragua: The Land of Sandino*, p. 31.

24. Millett, *Guardians*, p. 237.

25. *Ibid.*, p. 238.

26. John Booth, "Revolutionary Theory and Nicaragua's Sandinista Revolution," paper presented at the Southwestern Council of Latin American Studies, Arlington, Texas, March 1981, p. 3.

27. *Congressional Record*, 94th Cong., 1st Sess., vol. 121, no. 136 (September 17, 1975), pp. 1–2.

28. *Ibid.*

29. Millett, *Guardians*, p. 243.

30. On the radicalization of the Nicaraguan church, see Michael Dodson and T. S. Montgomery, "The Church in the Nicaraguan Revolution," in Thomas W. Walker, ed., *Nicaragua in Revolution* (New York: Praeger, 1982), pp. 161–180.

31. The alienation of the middle-class intellectuals from the Somoza regime was reflected in the formation of the opposition group Los Doce, composed of twelve nationally respected leaders from different walks of life. This would be the first centrist group of any import to endorse the FSLN publicly.

32. For further details on the Sandinista ideology and its political appeal, see Harry E. Vanden, "The Ideology of the Insurrection," in Walker, ed., *Nicaragua in Revolution*, pp. 41–62.

33. See Vanden, "Ideology"; Crawley, *Dictators*, pp. 123–157; and Tomás Borge, *Carlos, el amanecer ya no es una tentación* (Managua: Departamento de Propaganda y Educación, 1979). Also see Stephen M. Gorman, "Power and Consolidation in the Nicaraguan Revolution," *Journal of Latin American Studies*, 13 (May 1981), pp. 139–149.

34. See Jaime Wheelock, *Deciembre victorioso* (Managua: Secretaria Nacional de Propaganda y Educación Politica, 1979).

35. Three tendencies emerged within the FSLN during this period. For a discussion of their political orientations and the ideological diversification within the Sandinista Front that this encouraged, see James Petras, "Whither the Nicaraguan Revolution," *Monthly Review*, 31 (October 1979); and "Sandinista Perspectives, Documents," *Latin American Perspectives*, 20 (Winter 1979), pp. 114–127.

36. On the question of U.S. aid to Nicaragua, see Carl Curtis, "Economic Aid to Nicaragua: Should It Be Continued?" in Belden Bell, ed., *Nicaragua: An Ally under Siege* (Washington, D.C.: Council on American Affairs, 1978), pp. 136–137.

37. Frei Betto, *Nicaragua Livre: O primeiro passo* (Rio de Janeiro: Civilizacao Brasileira, 1980), p. 19.

38. Mayo Antonio Sanchez, *Nicaragua: Año Cero, la caida de la dinastia Somoza* (Mexico City: Editorial Diana, 1979), p. 128.

39. *Ibid.*

40. Jeffrey St. John, "Human Rights and Revolution: A Case Study in Moral Confusion," in Bell, ed., *Nicaragua: An Ally under Siege*, p. 83.

41. Curtis, "Economic Aid to Nicaragua," p. 183.

42. Jeffrey B. Gayner, "Nicaragua and U.S. Latin American Policy," in Bell, ed., *Nicaragua: An Ally under Siege*, p. 25.

43. Grace M. Ferrara, ed., *Latin America 1978* (New York: Facts on File, 1978), pp. 123–124.

44. On the negotiations for a plebiscite, see Ferrara, ed., *Latin America 1978*, pp. 127–131; and on the U.S. mild sanctions, see *Latin America Political Report* (February 16, 1979).

45. Concerning the early Sandinista rejection of "Somocismo sin Somoza," see "Sandinista Perspectives," *Latin American Perspectives*.

46. The U.S. debate on possible military intervention is discussed in *Latin American Political Report* (June 29, 1979).

47. Juan Colindres, *Anastasio Somoza: Fin de una estripe de labrones y asesinos* (Tizapan, Mexico: Editorial Posada, 1979), pp. 133–134.

48. *Ibid.*, p. 136.

49. Crawley, *Dictators*, p. 164.

50. Washington's anger with Somoza's instructions to his replacement caused the United States to consider sending Somoza back to Nicaragua to be dealt with by the Sandinistas. This led Somoza to depart the United States and eventually take up residence in Paraguay, where he was assassinated, apparently on orders from Tomás Borge, a leading member of the Sandinista government.

51. See Susanne Jonas, "The Nicaraguan Revolution and the Reemerging Cold War," in Walker, ed., *Nicaragua in Revolution*.

52. *Ibid.*

53. The general outline of this information is available from a wide number of sources. Specific information on this point was obtained from classified State Department documents.

54. For details see *Los Angeles Times*, December 5, 1981.

55. For further information on the Sandinista Popular Army, see Stephen M. Gorman, "The Role of the Revolutionary Armed Forces," in Walker, ed., *Nicaragua in Revolution*.

56. See U.S. State Department, "Communist Interference in El Salvador: Documents Demonstrating Communist Support of the Salvadoran Insurgency," February 23, 1981.

57. *Washington Report on the Hemisphere* (January 12, 1982), p. 8.

58. *Ibid.*

59. Sigmund, "Latin America: Change or Continuity?"

60. *New York Times*, February 24, 1982; *Latin American Weekly Review* (September 16, 1983).

61. *Washington Report on the Hemisphere*, May 4, 1982, p. 4.
62. *Ibid.*, January 12, 1982, p. 8.
63. *Ibid.*
64. *Latin American Weekly Review*, July 29, 1983.
65. *Latin American Weekly*, July 29, 1983.
66. *Facts on File*, June 29 and 30, 1983.
67. *Ibid.*, May 9 and June 10, 1983.
68. Bipartisan Commission members were: Henry Kissinger, former secretary of state under Presidents Nixon and Ford; Nicholas Brady, board chairman of Purolator, Inc., a conglomerate, who helped found the CIA; Henry Cisneros, first Latino mayor of San Antonio, Texas; William Clements, Republican governor of Texas from 1979 to 1983, a multimillionaire oilman; Carlos Diaz-Alejandro, Cuban-born professor of economics at Yale University; Wilson Johnson, president, National Federation of Independent Business; Lane Kirkland, president of the AFL-CIO; Richard Scammon, political scientist and public opinion analyst; John Silber, president, Boston University; Potter Stewart, former Associate Justice of the Supreme Court; Robert Strauss, former chairman of the Democratic party and of former President Carter's reelection campaign; William Walsh, physician and founder of Project Hope (international medical relief).
69. *Report of the National Bipartisan Commission on Central America* (Washington, D.C.: U.S. Government Printing Office, 1984), p. 114.
70. *Ibid.*, p. 116.
71. *Ibid.*, pp. 128–130.
72. *Los Angeles Times*, February 4, 1984, Part 1, p. 1.

BIBLIOGRAPHY

Prior to the insurrections in Nicaragua led by the Sandinista Front of National Liberation, most English works on the country fell within the category of case studies in the tradition of liberal U.S. scholarship. In particular, most works limited themselves to either an uncritical review of Nicaraguan history or a more detailed examination of some facet of the contemporary political-economic setting within the country. A notable exception was Neill Macaulay's *The Sandino Affair* (Chicago: Quadrangle Books, 1967), which provided an excellent examination of Augusto Cesar Sandino's struggle against U.S. military intervention in Nicaragua between 1927 and 1933. The political writings of A. C. Sandino himself remained untranslated for the most part until the recent English language version of Gregorio Selser's 1958 two-volume study of the guerrilla leader which included some of Sandino's original writings: *Sandino* (New York: Monthly Review Press, 1980).

Three useful sources for beginning research on Nicaragua are: Ralph Lee Woodward, Jr., *Central America: A Nation Divided* (New York: Oxford University Press, 1976); Eduardo Crawley, *Dictators Never Die: A Portrait of Nicaragua and the Somoza Dynasty* (New York: St. Martin's Press, 1979); and Thomas W. Walker, *Nicaragua: The Land of Sandino* (Boulder, Colo.: Westview Press, 1981). Woodward provides a detailed and scholarly treatment of the political and economic development of Central America as a whole from colonization through the early 1970s. In the process, he helps explain Nicaraguan evolution in terms of both its internal dynamics and its regional environment. Crawley relies on a more journalistic style to present a brief history of the Somoza dynasty up to the year preceding the overthrow of the dictatorship. While easy to read and extremely interesting, Crawley's book has been criticized for lack of citation and some occasional factual errors. The picture it paints of the dictatorship's internal workings, however, is accurate. Walker's book, written shortly after the Sandinista victory, is extremely sympathetic to the revolution. It is a brief and somewhat topical treatment of the political and economic history of Nicaragua leading up to and following the Sandinista Revolution of July 1979, whose principal value is its clear identification of the stages of dependent capitalist development within the country. Another useful source for beginning research is Ralph Lee Woodward, Jr., *Nicaragua* (Oxford, England: Clio Press, 1983). It is an annotated bibliography covering the colonial period through the first years of the revolution. Works are divided into more than forty categories from flora and fauna to foreign relations and includes extensive cross referencing.

Two other important works focusing mainly on the Somoza dictatorship itself are the chapter on Nicaragua in Steve Ropp and James Morris, eds., *Central America: Crisis and Adaptation* (Albuquerque: University of New Mexico Press, 1984), and Richard Millett, *Guardians of the Dynasty* (Maryknoll, N.Y.: Orbis Books, 1977). The chapter on Nicaragua by Stephen M. Gorman in the Ropp and Morris volume explains the collapse of the Somoza dictatorship in terms of the increasing social, political, and economic mobilization of Nicaraguan society and the progressively backward, atavistic political style of Anastasio Somoza Debayle. The Millett work traces the history of the U.S.-created Guardia Nacional of Nicaragua which functioned between 1936 and 1979 as the power base of the dictatorship. As a form of follow-up to his study of Somoza's dependence on the Guardia Nacional, Millett has published a second work that examines the internal and external political relations of the dictatorship during its final years: *The Death of the Dynasty: The End of Somoza Rule in Nicaragua* (Maryknoll, N.Y.: Orbis Books, 1982).

A work available in English that provides an excellent account of the years of armed struggle against Somoza is George Black, *The Triumph of the People: The Sandinista Revolution in Nicaragua* (London: Zed Press, 1981). Also, it contains a brief overview of early twentieth-century Nicaragua, Sandino, and the rise to power of Somoza. The final part of the book examines the first year of revolutionary power and its handling of class questions. Two books by Margaret Randall, *Sandino's Daughters: Testimonies of Nicaraguan Women in Struggle* (Vancouver, Canada: New Star Books, 1981), and *Christians in the Nicaraguan Revolution* (Vancouver, Canada: New Star Books, 1983), use interviews to describe how the Nicaraguan people overthrew Somoza. The extent to which women and Christians were integrated into the civil war and the Sandinista government has been inadequately understood by the average observer of Central America.

By far the greatest volume of recent works on Nicaragua deal with some aspect of the new revolutionary order, its policies and programs, or its external relations. Two of the earliest English publications to provide information on the ideology, programs, and structures of the Sandinista regime that came to power in July 1979 were Pedro Camejo and Fred Murphy, eds., *The Nicaraguan Revolution* (New York: Pathfinder Press, 1979), and the Ecumenical Program for Inter-American Communications and Action (EPICA), *Nicaragua: A People's Revolution* (Washington, D.C.: EPICA, 1980). The Camejo and Murphy volume includes original speeches by members of the revolutionary government as well as two short essays assessing the Nicaraguan Revolution as a victory over U.S. imperialism (one of them written by Fidel Castro). The EPICA task force work documents U.S. ties with the Somoza dictatorship, chronicles the insurrection, and outlines the political and economic structures that began to take shape after the victory. Tomás Borge *et al.*, *The Sandinistas Speak: Speeches and Writings of Nicaragua's Leaders* (New York: Pathfinders Press, 1982) constitutes a companion volume for the Camejo and Murphy edition. It contains speeches by important Sandinista leaders on essential questions facing Nicaragua in areas such as the economy, human rights, religion, and foreign relations. Also, it contains an important interview with Defense Minister Humberto Ortega on the "strategy of victory" for the insurrection against Somoza. Another publication in the same style is John Vandermeer and Peter Rosset, *The Nicaragua Reader: Documents of a Revo-*

lution under Fire (New York: Grove Press, 1983). It contains sixty-one entries on a broad spectrum of topics including the state, the Atlantic coast, and education.

Without question, one of the most authoritative sources on the Sandinista insurrection and its aftermath is Thomas W. Walker, ed., *Nicaragua in Revolution* (New York: Praeger, 1982). This work includes original essays by more than twenty scholars who completed field research within Nicaragua. This lengthy volume covers a wide range of issues, including U.S. policies toward Nicaragua during the insurrection, the formation of the new revolutionary armed forces, and the direction of government policies in health, economics, and even sports. Much shorter treatments of the insurrection and the immediate post-insurrectionary government structures can be found in "Nicaragua's Revolution," *NACLA Report on the Americas*, 3 (May-June 1980); James Petras, "Whither the Nicaraguan Revolution?" *Monthly Review*, 31 (October 1979); and Stephen M. Gorman, "Power and Consolidation in the Nicaraguan Revolution," *Journal of Latin American Studies*, 13 (May 1981). The Petras article, in particular, examines the alliances within the country that helped bring about the insurrection and the distribution of power between moderates and radicals in the immediate aftermath of the revolution.

Two books by the Institute for Food and Development Policy provide very readable introductions to life in revolutionary Nicaragua. Frances Moore Lappé and Joseph Collins, *Now We Can Speak: A Journey through the New Nicaragua* (San Francisco: Food First, 1982), combines personal observations with interviews with people from all walks of life. It records their reactions and involvement with the new programs of the government. Joseph Collins, *What Difference Could a Revolution Make? Food and Farming in the New Nicaragua* (San Francisco: Food First, 1982) takes a closer look at the paradoxes and successes of Nicaragua's agrarian reform. Collins is an unpaid adviser to the Ministry of Agriculture and has made numerous trips to Nicaragua. It has enabled him to provide the reader with interviews and insights not offered by most works.

Many of the best sources of the overthrow of the Somoza dictatorship or studies of its socio-economic underpinnings are in Spanish. Fifty of these works have been reviewed in English in John Booth, "Celebrating the Demise of the Somocismo: Fifty Recent Spanish Sources on the Nicaraguan Revolution," *Latin American Research Review*, 17, no. 1 (1982). Many of the sources reviewed adopt specifically Marxist frameworks. Booth's *The End and the Beginning: The Nicaraguan Revolution*

(Boulder, Colo.: Westview Press, 1982), in contrast, provides a socio-political analysis of the revolutionary process from the perspective of mainstream liberal scholarship.

Publications on Reagan administration policy include National Bipartisan Commission on Central America, *Report of the National Bipartisan Commission on Central America* (Washington, D.C.: U.S. Government Printing Office, January 1984); Policy Alternatives for the Caribbean and Central America (PACCA), *Changing Course: A Blueprint for Peace in Central America and the Caribbean* (Berkeley, Calif.: PACCA, 1984); Robert Leiken, ed., *Central America: Anatomy of Conflict* (New York: Pergamon Press, 1984); *The Americas at the Crossroads: Report of the Inter-American Dialogue* (Washington, D.C.: Woodrow Wilson International Center for Scholars, April 1983). The Kissinger Report (Bipartisan Commission) emphasized a policy of military containment of Nicaragua. In contrast, the other works emphasized that Central American revolutions should not be cast in the East-West conflict. They are collections of essays by scholars and former government officials. PACCA calls for a cutoff of support for the anti-Sandinista guerrillas and recognition of Nicaragua's right to self-determination. Leiken edited the volume for the Carnegie Endowment and it is informally considered the Democratic party alternative. Leiken's essay calls for linking El Salvadoran negotiations and "broadening" participation in Nicaragua. The Wilson Center participants included numerous former Latin American government officials as well as big business representatives such as David Rockefeller. They recommended negotiation between the United States and Nicaragua as well as between the Sandinistas and opposition groups.

Four final sources of varying interest and utility are Amnesty International, *The Republic of Nicaragua: An Amnesty International Report Including the Findings of a Mission to Nicaragua, 10–15 May 1976* (London: Amnesty International Publications, 1977), which documents the brutality of the Somoza dictatorship; "Documents," *Latin American Perspectives*, 20 (Winter 1979), which includes three interviews with Sandinista guerrilla leaders and two communiqués issued by the FSLN outlining the ideology and objectives of the insurrection; Belden Bell, ed., *Nicaragua: An Ally under Siege* (Washington, D.C.: Council on American Affairs, 1978), which presents the clearest exposition of the U.S. conservative establishment's rationale for demanding continued support for the Somoza dictatorship; and Anastasio Somoza Debayle and Jack Cox, *Nicaragua Betrayed* (Belmont, Mass.: Western Islands, 1980), which, in the process of presenting Somoza's own understanding of the Nicaraguan insurrection, reveals the pivotal role of the United

States in supporting dictatorships to survive longer than might otherwise be the case.

For keeping up on current events in Nicaragua and Central America in general, as well as U.S. policy toward the area, three of the better English-language publications are *Latin America Political Report* (a weekly published in London), *Washington Report on the Hemisphere* (a biweekly publication put out by the Council on Hemispheric Affairs), and *MesoAmerica* (a monthly publication originating in San Jose, Costa Rica).

4

Vietnam

> He knew nothing about Asia, about poverty, about people, about American domestic politics, but he knew a great deal about production technology and about exercising bureaucratic power . . . . This man, whose only real experience had been in dealing with the second largest automotive empire in the world , . . . was the last man to understand and measure the problems of a people looking for their political freedom.
>
> —David Halberstam, *The Best and the Brightest*
> (discussing Secretary of Defense Robert S. McNamara)

The United States was actively involved in the fighting in Indochina—Vietnam, Cambodia (now Kampuchea), and Laos—for nearly a quarter century. At increasingly enormous cost, first to the land and peoples of Southeast Asia and eventually to its own society, six U.S. administrations doggedly pursued the goal of an anticommunist victory. Today, the consequences of their collective failure are still apparent—in the absence of normalized relations between the United States and Vietnam; in the occupation of Kampuchea by Vietnam, amidst continuing guerrilla warfare; in sporadic violence between Vietnam and China, now a quasi-ally of the United States; in the desperate economic conditions of the Vietnamese people; and, at home, in the U.S. leadership's efforts to overcome our alleged "Vietnam syndrome" with a massive buildup of conventional and nuclear arms. Vietnam's "lesson"—that intervention against revolutionary nationalism in the Third World is at the least futile

Table 8
Cost and Consequences of the Vietnam War

UNITED STATES	INDOCHINA (OR VIETNAM ALONE)
(1) Casualties	
--About 57,000 dead and 300,000 wounded.	--About 1.7 million soldiers dead (2 million soldiers and civilians in Vietnam alone); about 3.2 million total wounded.
--Returned veterans experienced high rates of suicide, psychological problems (some, like delayed stress syndrome, emerged well after combat), unemployment, drug addiction, and health damage (often from herbicides such as Agent Orange).	--About 12 million refugees; 800,000 children orphaned.
(2) Bombing	
--Total U.S. munitions exploded in Indochina (1965-1971), in the air and on the ground, has been estimated at 13 million tons, the equivalent of 450 Hiroshima atomic bombs.	--80 percent of U.S. explosives dropped on or used in Indochina was expended in South Vietnam (1965-1971).
	--On average, 142 pounds of U.S. explosives per acre and 584 pounds per person were used. An estimated 26 million bomb and shell craters were created.
(3) Social and Economic Consequences	
--Veterans: 790,000 veterans with less-than-honorable discharges; tens of thousands of draft resisters and deserters.	--Widespread disintegration of urban and rural society: displacement of populations; drug use and prostitution; disease; destruction of transportation, housing, agricultural animals, irrigation systems, and farm tools; broken families.
--Military spending's effects on the economy: high inflation and accelerated decline of the dollar, decline of the U.S. international trade position (balance of payments), and increase in budget deficits; further drain of scientific knowhow into military research, contributing to declines in U.S. productivity and international competitiveness. (Chief beneficiaries: arms sellers and multinational corporate investors abroad.)	--Major, in some cases irreversible, damage to the ecosystem and to people's health due to massive bombing and use of herbicides.
--Politics: Congressional challenges to Executive power, culminating in the War Powers Bill (1973) and other restrictions on the President's use of force abroad; widespread social division, culminating in the shootings of students at Kent State and Jackson State Universities; and Nixon's paranoia over resistance to the war and the Pentagon Papers, culminating in the Watergate "affair" and his resignation.	--Lasting effects on national economies, delaying recovery for decades, promoting dependence on foreign help, helping ensure highly centralized and authoritarian politics, and (according to some writers) compelling Vietnam to occupy Cambodia and repress overseas Chinese merchants in north and south Vietnam.

and unacceptably costly, and at the most, immoral, inhumane, and arrogant—has been lost in the higher circles of government. Instead, the war seems to have taught that the use of force abroad must be better managed, that the key issues concern public relations and command and control rather than political goals and values.

Our examination of U.S. intervention in Vietnam from 1950 to 1975 will seek to explain its origins and its expansion in terms of our framework of ideas, institutions, and instruments. Rather than attempt to chronicle the war's entire history, we focus on persistent themes and behavioral patterns across time and personalities. We see the Vietnam War as a multidimensional defeat for U.S. policy and policymakers—at the level of ideas, a defeat of the politics of deception, intervention, and escalation; at the level of institutions, a defeat of "guns and butter" economics, closed-circle decision making, and presidential hubris; and at the level of instruments, a defeat of strategies for winning "hearts and minds" by coercion and infusions of more and more money.

Before discussing U.S. policy at each of these levels, we should take note of some painful facts. America's intervention in Indochina was its longest and costliest war. No bland accounting with words and figures can appropriately impress upon readers the enormity of the catastrophe for all those whose lives were, and in many cases still are, affected by the war. To say, for example, that the war "cost" the "United States" $150 billion between 1965 and 1975 does not even begin to convey the full scope of costs or which people paid them. Table 8, therefore, is a very brief resume of costs to the governments, societies, and peoples of the United States and Indochina from the mid-sixties to the end of the war. (The figures are taken from numerous public and private sources; inevitably, some of them shall always remain only crude approximations.)

THE IDEA OF VIETNAM

They were, as David Halberstam said, "the best and the brightest." Although they had diverse origins, the architects of America's Vietnam policy—not only in the Kennedy-Johnson years when the Eastern establishment "whiz kids" took over, but in every administration—had much in common. They were tough minded, thoroughly professional, intellectually certain to the point of arrogance, ambitious, zealous, patriotic, cool under fire, and supremely loyal to their chief. In a word, these were the men (for there were no women) who had climbed the ladder of corporate success and, in the Vietnam conflict, found the ideal arena for testing America's power and their own. They called themselves "crisis managers" in Kennedy's time—properly so, since they considered their special gift to be the ability to "orchestrate" U.S. military power and diplomacy so adroitly that communism could be contained anywhere with minimal costs to American society. To these officials, underdeveloped Third World societies such as Vietnam had chiefly symbolic, not historical or cultural, significance. They were pawns on the chessboard of international political struggle between East and West, to be won or lost depending on which superpower proved to have the most "will."

In assessing why Vietnam came to be the crucible of containment, a careful reading of the Pentagon Papers and other documents leads to the conclusion that the war was not an accident, a series of mistakes or blunders, or a conspiratorial design. Rather, Vietnam was the logical culmination of ideological suppositions, values, and models that had long predominated in U.S. foreign-policy thinking and behavior, especially with respect to the Third World. "The best and the brightest" presided over a modern-day empire, and revolutions in faraway places threatened it. United by a common sense of purpose, they decided, not once but numerous times, that Vietnam was the place to make a stand. They did not want so large a war; but they believed it was, or had become, so important to "the national interest" that it had to be fought to the finish.

To maintain (and in a moment to demonstrate) that the key Vietnam decision makers operated from shared beliefs and values is not to argue that there was unanimity and uniformity on particular policy choices. Politics, and therefore debate, bargaining, and disagreement, were very much at work throughout the war years. To cite only a few examples: Some high officials favored direct U.S. intervention in Vietnam on behalf of French colonialism in 1954, while others (notably, President Eisenhower) did not. Officials and bureaucracies differed in their estimate of which, and how many, "dominoes" would fall if Vietnam went communist. The strategy for bombing North Vietnam produced many views on its timing, its targets, its purposes, and its probable results. Estimates of the communist forces (the Viet Minh from 1945 to 1954, the National Liberation Front [NLF] or Viet Cong thereafter)—their sources of strength and weakness, their morale, and their support inside and outside the country—varied considerably. So did assessments of the U.S.-supported leadership in Saigon, especially its stability, its staying power, its potential to reform in accordance with U.S. desires, and ultimately its susceptibility to U.S. pressure to accept a peace agreement with Hanoi.

Yet despite divergent opinions on issues such as these, the war went on. Different priorities, tactics, and perceptions were debated but not premises, objectives, or basic interests. At every critical decision stage of the war—to support the French in 1950; to replace them in 1954 and 1955; covertly to introduce U.S. military advisers in 1961; to assassinate the South Vietnamese leader, Ngo Dinh Diem, in the coup of 1963; to carry the air war to the North in 1964; to send in large numbers of ground combat forces in 1965; to begin negotiations with North Vietnam in 1968; to invade Cambodia in 1970; and to bomb the North heavily in 1972 to induce a final settlement—debate was circumscribed by general agreement on America's larger purposes. Where they arose, disagreements concerned predicted costs versus benefits. The key question typically was, "what will work?" and not "should we be there?"

Paul Joseph, in a valuable work on the war called *Cracks in the Empire*, has characterized U.S. policymaking this way: There were three distinct "policy currents" within the state leadership—left, right, and center—which, although united by a dedication to capitalist class interests and values, differed in the lessons they drew from U.S. foreign-policy history. They also differed in their responses to the pressures put on them by business leaders, the antiwar movement, and the political and military successes of the Vietnamese communists. These differences, which were reflected in the kinds of debates mentioned above, were essentially pragmatic: Questions of how much, when, and for how long; they did not concern foreign-policy principles. "Ideological bridges" connected these three currents, Joseph maintains, since "the supporters of each current argue that their approach will, in the long run, best stabilize world capitalism and the position of the U.S. within it."[1]

Joseph's contribution is to go beyond a dogmatically radical understanding of U.S. policy that would simply explain it in terms of the determination of "the ruling class" to quash a communist threat. His analysis is sensitive to the domestic and international policy environments that complicate U.S. decision making in any crisis. And his juxtaposition of policy currents with ideological bridges enables us to understand why, even when some U.S. leaders began to acknowledge that their cause was losing, they persisted in (and even expanded) the war effort, always believing the cause itself justified more shedding of blood. Joseph's book seeks to explain how a capitalist system failed in a faraway war, but his concepts can be applied as well to explain the behavior of any social system that is based on expansionist values and that denies a people the right of self-determination.

We can now turn to the ideological precepts that framed U.S. policy discussions throughout the war. The three axioms of national interest introduced in Chapter 1 should be kept in mind, for the precepts that guided the best and the brightest derive from those axioms.

American leaders believed, first of all, that the nation's own security was in some substantial sense tied to the outcome of the war. Vietnam was not a marginal struggle to them: As early as 1950, Truman's National Security Council had determined that "Indochina is a key area of Southeast Asia and is under immediate threat."[2] Two years later the Council added that the "loss of any of the countries of Southeast Asia to communist control . . . would have critical psychological, political and economic consequences" for the United States.[3] All of Southeast Asia would be imperilled by a communist victory anywhere. Thus was the "domino principle" (the words were first used by Eisenhower in 1954) embraced as a shorthand summation of the war's essence. Every administration thereafter repeated the formula: As Vietnam went, so went the rest of Southeast Asia. Several officials extended the falling dominoes to the Middle East and Latin America. Take President Kennedy: Shortly before his death he reiterated his belief in the domino theory because "if South Viet-Nam went , . . . the wave of the future in Southeast Asia [would be] China and the Communists."[4] Vice President Lyndon Johnson returned from a tour of the war zone in 1961 to warn that the loss of Vietnam would mean the "United States, inevitably, must surrender the Pacific and take up our defense on our own shores."[5] As U.S. involvement deepened in Vietnam, the perceived stakes in terms of national security increased, and therefore so did the commitment to victory. It was a vicious circle that was constantly in motion.

Success in Vietnam was deemed so crucial because it became, during the early 1960s and afterwards, a "test case" of U.S. power and will. To the Joint Chiefs of Staff in 1964, Vietnam was "the first real test of our determination to defeat the communist wars of national liberation formula."[6] Secretary of State Dean Rusk frequently justified the U.S. intervention by asserting that the NLF's "indirect aggression" in South Vietnam was similar to the communist "formula" tried in Greece, Malaya, and the Philippines in the 1940s and 1950s. "The militant Asian Communists have themselves proclaimed the attack on South Vietnam to be a critical test of this technique," Rusk said on one occasion in 1966. "And beyond South Viet-Nam and Laos they have openly designated Thailand as the next target."[7] The flawed assumption here was that the Vietnamese revolution did not have independent origins, that it was part of a global pattern of aggression instigated by and even manufactured in Moscow and Peking. That being the case, President Johnson said in a July 1966 speech, the United States should make "Communist aggression unprofitable" and thereby "demonstrate that guerrilla warfare . . . can never succeed. Once that lesson is learned, a shadow that hangs over all of Asia tonight will begin, I think, to recede."[8]

The conviction that "aggression must not pay" had importance for many U.S. policymakers well beyond the matter of defeating an Asian insurgency. To them, fighting in Vietnam was the continuation of the essential struggles against aggression in the two world wars and in Korea. Secretary Rusk wrote in January 1967:

Behind the words and the commitment of the [Southeast Asia Collective Defense] Treaty lies the lesson learned in the tragic half century since the First World War. After that war our country withdrew from effective world responsibility. When aggressors challenged the peace in Manchuria, Ethiopia, and then Central Europe during the 1930s, the world community did not act to prevent their success. The result was a Second World War—which could have been prevented.[9]

Vietnam, Rusk continued, is the consequence of having learned "from painful experience . . . that aggression must not be permitted to succeed." Historical "lessons" such as these, as Ernest R. May has shown, are powerful influences on decision makers.[10] But in equating the revolutionary nationalist struggle of the Vietnamese with fascist aggressions of another era, U.S. leaders revealed how "lessons" can be intellectually and emotionally crippling rather than be useful reference points.

Finally, Vietnam also was considered a test of America's free-world leadership—its integrity as an ally, its reliability when the next domino began to waver. "To leave Viet-Nam to its fate," said Johnson in 1965, "would shake the confidence of all these people [in Southeast Asia] in the value of an American commitment and in the value of America's word."[11] Indeed, by early 1965, as the Johnson administration prepared to send in U.S. ground combat troops, all else in U.S. war aims had paled beside the importance of maintaining U.S. "credibility." Nowhere did such thinking stand out more clearly than in a draft memorandum by Secretary of Defense Robert McNamara's chief aide, John T. McNaughton. He listed 70 percent of U.S. aims as being "to avoid a humiliating U.S. defeat (to our reputation as a guarantor)," and he elaborated:

It is essential—however badly [Southeast Asia] may go over the next 1–3 years—that U.S. emerge as a "good doctor." We must have kept promises, been tough, taken risks, gotten bloodied, and hurt the enemy very badly. We must avoid harmful appearances which will affect judgments by, and provide pretexts to, other nations regarding how the U.S. will behave in future cases of particular interest to those nations—regarding U.S. policy, power, resolve and competence to deal with their problems.[12]

Such overwhelming emphasis on national reputation fed into the traditional American sense of mission as the free world's champion. A major U.S. commitment in Vietnam was axiomatic in light of the widely shared assumption that the nation had a historic responsibility there, regardless of the character of the regime it wished to rescue. "History and our own achievements have thrust upon us the principal responsibility for the protection of freedom on earth," President Johnson declared in 1965.[13] Such euphoria was commonplace in the Kennedy-Johnson years; but the missionary element, in more subdued form, remained in every subsequent administration that fought in Vietnam. When, for example, President Nixon announced the invasion of Cambodia on April 30, 1970, one of his chief justifications for it was that the United States had to prove itself worthy of world leadership and not become a second-rate power. Even in the wake of defeat in Indochina, Henry Kissinger said (in April 1975): "Our nation is uniquely endowed to play a creative and decisive role in the new order which is taking form around us. In an era of turbulence, uncertainty, and conflict, the world still looks to us for a protecting hand, a mediating influence, a path to follow."[14]

The belief in Southeast Asian falling dominoes and an American mission to save Vietnam for the free world had the combined effect of delegitimizing the Vietnamese revolution. The struggle over Indochina was a symbol in the minds of U.S. leaders of the global competition between capitalism and communism and not a human drama that grew out of the colonialist era and the Vietnamese quest for independence. As such, Ho Chi Minh, with whom the OSS, the CIA's forerunner during World War II, had cooperated in fighting the Japanese after the war was ignored by Washington when he attempted to enlist American support for Vietnam's independence from France. Ho rapidly emerged in the American perception as a tool of international communism; the possibility that he (or Mao in China at that same time) could be both a communist and an independent nationalist was dismissed.[15] Denying the revolution any historical or political legitimacy, U.S. policymakers could then presume a right of intervention to subdue it.

The ideological precept that nationalism and revolution cannot coexist, and therefore that U.S. intervention to "restore" national independence to a society is justifiable, had profound implications for U.S. policy in Vietnam beyond intervention itself. The precept led U.S. policymakers consistently to underestimate the resiliency and ignore the reasons for popular support of the National Liberation Front of South Vietnam. Predictably, the NLF was portrayed instead as a mere puppet of the North, without whose military and political support it would cease to exist. Hence, the U.S. government's characterization of the southern revolution in the 1960s as aggression from the North instead of as a continuing struggle for national unification; its belief that bombing the supply lines between North and South Vietnam would strangle the southern revolution; and its inability to understand why, despite one of the most ferocious military efforts in modern history against it, the NLF maintained its morale and cohesion and in fact grew steadily in size. American puzzlement was not better displayed than in late 1964 when Ambassador (and General) Maxwell Taylor said: "The ability of the Vietcong continuously to rebuild their units and to make good their losses is one of the mysteries of this guerrilla war." Their units, he said in this secret briefing of other officials, "have the recuperative powers of the phoenix."[16] The possibility that popular support, often at risk of death, lay behind the NLF's resiliency never seems to have crossed his mind.

Since, moreover, Southeast Asian societies were merely dominoes, and the U.S. war effort was (as Walt Rostow, a top national security adviser to Kennedy and Johnson, put it) an "exercise" in the global ideological contest, even the American partner in the war lacked authenticity. The Saigon regime was often privately disparaged by U.S. officials. Its leaders were considered corrupt and inefficient; it could neither be persuaded nor coerced into reforming itself in ways that would make it more appealing to peasants (and eventually the Americans stopped trying); and its military officers often failed to act in accordance with American wishes. By the early 1960s the Americans had already concluded, therefore, that the war and not the Vietnamese should be the object of American efforts. In Kennedy's words at one of his last news conferences, "What helps to win the war, we support; what interferes with the war effort, we oppose."[17] Thus was "nation-building," Kennedy's favored concept for Third World development along U.S. lines, summarily dropped. Thus also was Diem's demise signalled, for he had outlived his usefulness. But stability rarely lasted, and the next year, 1964, found Ambassador Lodge hoping forlornly that yet another military junta would not "bungle and stumble" like the others.[18] It did, causing William Bundy, Assistant Secretary of State for East Asian and Pacific Affairs, to suggest: "The best we can expect is that he [General Khanh] and the [Saigon government] will be able to maintain order, keep the pacification program ticking over (but not progressing markedly) and give the appearance of a valid government."[19]

The long-standing U.S. goal of an independent, noncommunist Vietnam was therefore a contradiction in terms of actual American policy from 1963 on. Vietnam was no longer treated as an independent state; it was an instrument of U.S. policy and a symbol of U.S. commitment. (The crowning demonstration of that fact came in the last stages of negotiations with Hanoi that led to the January 1973 Paris Accords: The Saigon government of Nguyen Van Thieu was deliberately misled about the final terms and felt betrayed when it was informed of them.) What Washington and Saigon had in common was nothing more or less than the desire to defeat the communists militarily. Such a marriage of convenience was inevitably fraught with peril, for while it led to agreement on what the two partners were against—such as a coalition government with the NLF and Hanoi or the neutralization of South Vietnam (as the French suggested in the mid–1960s)—it created constant suspicion and friction about what they were fighting for and especially how to get it.

The Americans themselves were, by the mid–1960s, far from clear in their own expectations about how much could be accomplished. Every key decision maker wanted victory; but some were willing to settle for less—not losing or even losing but only after having inflicted and endured terrible pain (in line with McNaughton's "good doctor" concept). Regardless, the key axiom was always that the role of the United States in world politics is central and must be protected. As Walt Rostow wrote in 1965:

> I know well the anxieties and complications on our side of the line. But there may be a tendency to underestimate both the anxieties and

complications on the other side and also to underestimate that limited but real margin of influence on the outcome which flows from the simple fact that at this stage of history we are the greatest power in the world—if we behave like it.[20]

BUREAUCRATIC BREAKDOWN

Bureaucracies and their leaders, we have generally observed, often operate independently in accordance with their narrow self-interest rather than the precise game plan of an executive board. Indeed, a chief executive has his own interests, as do other institutions such as the press, the military, and big business. Because, in the American system of government, these institutions divide and subdivide into seemingly endless numbers of bureaus, agencies, and loose associations, they give the appearance of being separate entities with few overarching commitments. The Vietnam experience, however, convincingly demonstrates the political reality behind this pluralism: Namely, that while bureaucratic and institutional behavior consistently displayed a certain diversity and autonomy, it was limited to the boundaries set by the national leadership's dominant values and ideology. We can most clearly see the impact of values and ideology on bureaucracies and institutions by noticing how political choices and priorities conformed closely with those defined or implied by the leaders' shared axioms.

We look first at the activities of the national-security establishment. For Presidents dealing with Vietnam, Daniel Ellsberg has observed, the first rule of thumb was not to "lose" the South before the next election.[21] Getting re-elected is a new President's first task, as his closest advisers will always remind him. And no President, whether facing re-election or not, wants to be the first to lose a war. Johnson said soon after taking office: "I am not going to be the President who saw Southeast Asia go the way China went."[22] But in 1968 he was forced to bow out of a re-election bid. It is reasonable to suppose that to the North Vietnamese, he was then no less dangerous than when he was a candidate for re-election—which may explain why they accepted the offer of negotiations he made in the same March 1968 speech in which he said he would not run.

Particularly in war, presidential ego—his claim to a special place in history—is very much on the line. It is sometimes indistinguishable from the national interest. Sensing that, some bureaucratic leaders play on it, as when Walt Rostow urged Johnson to show the same "kind of Presidential commitment and staying power" that Kennedy had displayed during "the long test on Berlin and the short test on the Cuba missiles."[23] Likewise, when Nixon decided to send U.S. troops into Cambodia, he spoke of avoiding "humiliation" and not being "the first President to preside over an American defeat."[24] Like his predecessors, Nixon was always looking over his shoulder at the far right, conscious of the political consequences of failing to act tough with the communists. But his concern over a personal humiliation was just as real.

Bureaucratic games in the high echelons were also influential on policymaking. One, which fit particularly well with presidential political needs, was the formulation of options and contingency plans in ways that ensured outcomes desired by key advisers. Options were "loaded" to give the appearance of a range of choices while actually stacking the deck in favor of only one. Contingency plans were drawn up not merely to anticipate possible presidential need, but also to influence their implementation. In both cases, two things stand out. First, the choices emphasized by bureaucratic leaders were dressed up to give the appearance of being moderate alternatives to either the ultra-right's desire for all-out escalation or the left's desire for a "precipitate" withdrawal. These middle-range options enabled the President to present any new escalation to the public and key allies as a responsible, modest alternative to other more "extreme" measures. Secondly, the choices were invariably to step up the U.S. commitment and use of force.

Some examples may be useful here.[25] In August 1963 most of the top U.S. officials gathered at the State Department to consider alternatives to continued support of Diem and his brother, who headed the Vietnamese equivalent of a secret service. Only one official, a middle-level State Department specialist, argued for withdrawal. This alternative was immediately ruled out; everyone concurred that any option should be based on the assumption of continued U.S. involvement. Similarly, in 1964, 1965, 1968, 1970, and 1972, when alternatives for dealing with North Vietnam in increasingly unfavorable military circumstances were considered, withdrawal was never more than a token option. The choices invariably came down to how much additional effort the United States should make. Choices in the direction of deescalation were not likely to be taken seriously in a decision-making group stacked with the very people who had developed the bombing strategy in the first place.

These same officials also followed bureaucratic form by having plans for escalation ready for the President's approval months before he asked for them. The Gulf of Tonkin Resolution of 1964 was prepared three months before any naval "incidents" ever occurred there; all that was missing was a few dates and money figures. Similarly, the strategy of "graduated escalation"—the air attacks on North Vietnam under the code name ROLLING THUNDER—was worked out well before it ever saw the light of day. Throughout Nixon's presidency, Seymour M. Hersh clearly establishes in *The Price of Power*, the surest way to win his favor was to develop or support options for escalating the military pressure on Hanoi. Bureaucrats are, of course, paid to anticipate the President's needs; but in these cases, they successfully maneuvered to make his choice certain.

The team nature of decision making on Vietnam also accounts for the escalations of force. Although there were exceptions—such as Eisenhower's decision in the spring of 1954 not to authorize Operation VULTURE to save the French from defeat at their Dien Bien Phu garrison—in general the key decisions were made by "in" groups whose world views coincided. They shared ideological premises about America's leadership role in the world; they shared illusions of invincibility and invulnerability; and they shared a supreme optimism (until 1968) about final victory—all features of "groupthink."[26] The dangers of optimism had been clearly evident in the 1950s, when French assurances of imminent victory time and again proved groundless. But the lesson was never learned. General Taylor assured Kennedy in 1961 that a U.S. military advisory presence in South Vietnam posed few risks, since Hanoi would be deterred from retaliating by the U.S. threat to bomb the North. In the same period the Joint Chiefs of Staff estimated "that 40,000

U.S. troops will be needed to clean up the Vietcong threat."[27] The bombing campaign was undertaken in confidence the North could not withstand continuous punishment and in the expectation that its and the Southern revolutionaries' morale would be depressed by the losses suffered. None of these predictions proved accurate, but that did not lead the various administration teams to question their assumptions or the values behind them.

As for the occasional "dove" who did question existing policy, access to the inner circle of the President's men suddenly was closed off. Nixon and Kissinger had an extensive "back-channel" communication system whose purpose (and effect) was to exclude from the policy process those high officials, such as Secretary of State William P. Rogers, whose views on the war were considered too "soft." James C. Thomson, Jr., refers to the "domestication of dissenters," a process that allowed people who urged deescalation to speak their piece so they could believe they were being heard while their listeners could assert they were open to alternative viewpoints.[28] These dissenters believed they were being effective—more so than if they had resigned in protest—when in fact they were being coopted. The inner circle only had room for those people who were anxious to get on with the job of winning the war.

Martial language, values, and attitudes were common coin in these closed deliberations. The gun was typically conceived as the ultimate peacemaker, and Vietnam was *High Noon*.[29] Decision makers spoke easily of "turning up" the level of Hanoi's pain, playing "hardball" with the enemy, "taking out" targets, employing a "slow squeeze," and establishing a good "kill ratio." Detached bureaucratic language had audacious implications: "Free-fire zones" provided license for indiscriminate bombing of peasant villages; "graduated escalation" and "sustained reprisals" stood for increasingly devastating air attacks on the North; and "protective reaction" was a Nixon-era phrase intended to make ongoing air raids seem defensively motivated.

James C. Thomson, Jr., who served in the East Asia division of the State Department in the early 1960s, concluded that "crypto-racism" compounded the bureaucratic detachment.

Vietnamese, like all Asians, were widely presumed to be barbaric and uncaring about the loss of life—which made them easy to blow up in great numbers. Thomson asks: "Would we have pursued quite such policies—and quite such military tactics—if the Vietnamese were white?"[30] Racism is always difficult to prove; yet the ferocity of the American involvement, which reached new heights of barbarism in places like My Lai, makes an answer to Thomson's question in purely administrative terms seem very incomplete. For far too many Americans from top to bottom in the chain of command, the Vietnamese were "gooks" and "slants." And hadn't President Johnson told GIs to "nail the coonskin to the wall"?

If racism was built into U.S. policymaking, it ought to figure in American relations with their Vietnamese allies as well as their enemies. Such seems to be the case. As was noted earlier, Saigon officials were often treated with contempt, like necessary evils in a war that unfortunately required their cooperation. One of the many examples from the Pentagon Papers occurred in December 1964, as Ambassador Taylor lectured a group of South Vietnamese military officers for having defied U.S. wishes: "Do all of you understand English?" Taylor began. "I told you all clearly at General Westmoreland's dinner we Americans were tired of coups. Now, you have made a real mess. We cannot carry on forever if you do things like this." After discussing the proper way to stage manage a coup, Taylor ended matters by saying: "You people have broken a lot of dishes and now we have to see how we can straighten out this mess."[31]

Senior U.S. officials operated with few legal or moral restraints in waging war in Indochina. The Pentagon Papers collection and research by scholars and journalists reveal numerous instances of deliberate executive deception of Congress and the public. Every President from Eisenhower to Ford approved U.S. activities which they knew violated international and domestic law. Among the most notable examples are: The clandestine raids into North Vietnam, under the command of Colonel (later Major General) Edward J. Lansdale, to disrupt its economy and society shortly after the Geneva Accords were reached in mid–1954; the secret dispatch by Kennedy in spring 1961 of 400 Special Forces personnel and 100 additional military advisers, in clear violation of the Geneva agreements; the "green light" given South Vietnamese generals in November 1963 to stage a coup against Diem and his brother, which resulted in the slaying of both; the provocative DE SOTO patrols of the North Vietnamese coast and U.S.-sponsored clandestine South Vietnamese raids into North Vietnam (called Operation Plan 34A), which began in February 1964 and evidently had much to do with the later Tonkin Gulf incidents (the second of which may never have occurred); and the array of additional and more "sophisticated" covert operations (all undertaken without consultation with or approval from Congress) such as YANKEE TEAM overflights of neutral Laos, RANCHHAND herbicide operations, and SIDESHOW, the fourteen-month-long secret bombing campaign in neutral Cambodia prior to the 1970 invasion.

The bureaucratic environment in which these actions were authorized was one dominated above all by arrogant self-confidence: First, that raw military power would defeat the Vietnamese revolution; second, that such power could be "orchestrated" so as to bend Hanoi's will to the United States; and third, that military power could be exploited without damaging the administration's domestic programs or alienating public and international support. Groupthink, sheer bureaucratic inertia, and a lack of Vietnam expertise—the last largely the consequence of the purge of the State Department in the early 1950s after the fall of China to Mao's forces—all contributed to the insulation of the decision-making group from reality. Plans for a negotiated settlement invariably took a back seat to plans for continued fighting.

To be sure, bureaucratic in-fighting was commonplace; but to repeat an earlier point, it occurred within a consensus over desirable outcomes and values. In the early 1950s, for instance, the State Department's European desk consistently was at odds with other elements of the bureaucracy because of its partiality to the French and its reluctance, therefore, to see U.S. pressure put on them to grant the Indochinese states unequivocal independence. In later years, the CIA was divided in its evaluation of the NLF's strength and resiliency; the team in the State Department that was responsible for negotiating strategy was consistently outflanked by the much larger and more powerful staffs dedicated to winning the war; the Army and the CIA clashed over counterinsurgency jurisdictions; ambassadors often had a hard time exercising authority over CIA operations in the field; and the military and civilian agencies as a whole, as Nixon took office, offered sharply conflicting assessments of basic war issues such as the value of the bombing program, the capacity of the South Vietnamese military forces, and the ability of the North Vietnamese leadership to continue absorbing punishment without caving in. Inevitably, those assessments that lacked appropriate optimism and hubris were given short shrift.

The American conduct of the war in Vietnam not only exemplified what Richard J. Barnet calls "bureaucratic homicide," it also showed the appalling human consequences when an enormously powerful military machine is set in motion to preserve the "national interest."[32] The Vietnamese revolution challenged traditional American concepts of warfare, and the U.S. military responded in accordance with standard operating procedures: It sought to overwhelm the opposition with brute force.

The military leadership faced extremely difficult problems in Vietnam, the most important of which had led to the French defeat in 1954. It faced an opponent that had increasing popular support in the countryside, an extraordinary network of agents and tunnels in the cities (as the Americans belatedly discovered in the last days of the war), an ingenious supply and defense system both above and underground, and a tightly knit but decentralized political organization that was able to sustain troop morale under unprecedented military attack. The U.S. military also had to deal with difficult, unfamiliar jungle terrain; an allied military organization that was corrupt, suffered severe morale problems, and was not used to the clumsy, heavy equipment given it by the United States; and a population so alien to itself as to create the belief in every GI's mind that any man, woman, or child might be a Viet Cong agent.

To these problems were added others internal to the American military itself. Every soldier was aware that the justification for this remote war was being widely challenged back home and that service in it favored white middle- and upper-class students at the expense of all others. Morale problems and racial conflicts were frequent in U.S. units. These took forms such as drug abuse, "fragging" incidents, intra-unit tension, and gratuitous violence directed at innocent civilians. For the military brass, the war was a golden opportunity to advance in rank and test out new tactics and weapons. But for the ordinary soldier, the war was simply hell.[33]

Faced with obstacles such as these, the military often moved blindly forward. Technology was increasingly relied on for ultimate solutions. The cratering of Indochina described earlier made sense, in a perverse way, given the near-total irrelevance of the American way of warfare to the Vietnamese situation. By the mid–1960s Kennedy's favored counterinsurgency program had to be abandoned: The notion that communist guerrillas could be outwitted and outgunned on their home turf by Green Berets, who would be in the vanguard of the "pacification" and "nation building" programs, failed to cut off the NLF's sources of support. A more purely military alternative, centered on bombing and large numbers of ground forces, took over.

U.S. military leaders led the way in such planning.[34] As optimistic and self-certain as their civilian counterparts who made the policy decisions, the military chiefs ran ahead of them in urging (and largely getting) an all-out commitment of U.S. power. The ground and air wars became more electronic and impersonal; the killing became more indiscriminate and disproportionate to the announced policy goals; and both the actual and the projected results were inflated to "prove" that the brute-force solution was working. Only later was it gradually revealed that such figures were mostly the product of creative imaginations incited by bureaucratic need.

Remote warfare was logical for a military establishment in a hostile environment of "faceless masses." That circumstance made it natural for a Marine captain to say: "I don't think anyone here thinks about blowing in and dropping bombs and killing a person. It's all very impersonal. You don't hear the bombs. It's all very abstract." Or for an Army captain to say, in a classic summary of the American effort in Vietnam: "We had to destroy the village in order to save it."[35] As the Cornell University study of the air war (*The Air War in Indochina*) observed, remote-control warfare helped dehumanize the mass destruction, insulated the war from moral and public-opinion restraints, decreased the perceived need for human judgment in military decisions, and created future incentives for further scientific investment in automatic, long-range weapons systems.

To the military, as post-Vietnam appraisals by several American generals attest, the war was lost at home, not on the battlefield or in the air.[36] The predictable pointing of fingers at weak-kneed civilian leaders and antiwar protesters made any critical self-searching largely unnecessary. If only the military had been given freer rein, so the argument goes, the war would have been won, and quickly. It was General Douglas A. MacArthur in Korea all over again. So much for lessons learned. Like the civilians who supposedly shackled them, the military chiefs regarded Vietnam as an unfortunate aberration, an experience the nation would do well to put behind it. They left open the possibility of new Vietnams to come, perhaps employing weapons and tactics more appropriate to a people that doesn't like long and costly wars.

INSTITUTIONS: THE COLLAPSE OF THE WAR CONSENSUS

"Lyndon Johnson's greatest fault as a political leader was that *he chose* not to choose between the Great Society and the war in Vietnam," wrote Larry Berman in *Planning a Tragedy*.[37] Unlike Eisenhower, who quailed before the prospect of a half-million Americans fighting in Vietnam, and Kennedy, who tried to get by with far fewer military advisers than his key aides recommended, Johnson plunged into the war convinced the nation could afford both guns and butter. Johnson's remedy was to make the war palatable by keeping its full dimensions secret and rejecting measures that would have put the country on a war footing: Raising taxes, calling up the reserves, and mobilizing the military for an all-out effort. But by 1968 the Great Society's programs were overwhelmed by public disillusionment with the war.

In this section we will take brief looks at the breakdown of public, press, business, and congressional support of U.S. intervention in Vietnam. In each case, not coincidentally in our view, two characteristics stand out. The first is that the impetus for the breakdown was the practical calculation that the war's costs had begun to outweigh its benefits. The second is that the framework of debate within each sector mirrored the narrow limits of the debate in the highest circles of government.

Public opinion, as distinct from clear expressions of dissent such as were found in the antiwar movement, is an extremely elusive thing. The polls that report it are never as scientific as they purport to be. They measure opinion of the moment, we must remember, and not political behavior. They convey the false impression that every person's opinion is equally influential politically. Even "opinion" is quite ambiguous since, especially as it appears in polls, it is in direct response to the poller's question and therefore does not reflect the priorities or range of alternatives in the mind of the person polled. In the late sixties and early seventies, for example, a majority of Americans both thought the war a tragic error and did not approve of immediate withdrawal from it. Public opinion, the Vietnam experience would clearly show, is a highly manipulable commodity.[38]

The impact of public opinion on foreign policymaking is largely indirect: It places limits to what the public will probably tolerate rather than establishes a policy preference. The antiwar movement that began in earnest in the sixties of course went further than mere opinion: It spoke to the specific desires for ending the bombing and for an immediate U.S. withdrawal from Vietnam. But the movement never represented the mainstream of public opinion, which generally supported—or did not actively oppose—U.S. policy until about mid–1967. Even then, immediate withdrawal was not the option most favored by the general public. For while, after mid–1967, a clear majority of the public disapproved of Johnson's work as President and his handling of the war, it did not therefore endorse unilateral withdrawal. In fact, in the next few years the favored alternative for U.S. policy was a cease-fire, with escalation (beyond that already carried out) in second place and a pull-out in third.[39] And since each of these alternatives contained several possible variations that would further subdivide opinion, any administration was left with plenty of room within which to maneuver for public support or manipulate public disagreement.

With all these qualifications, it remains true that public opinion influenced U.S. policymaking throughout the war. Specifically, it established a ceiling in the minds of the top political leaders—particularly those responsible for protecting the President's political image and ensuring his re-election—beyond which U.S. war actions could not go without potentially disastrous domestic political consequences. Official perceptions of adverse public reactions influenced Eisenhower's decision in May 1954 not to intervene directly in Vietnam. Time and again similar high-level perceptions persuaded Kennedy, Johnson, and Nixon to rule out full-fledged escalation in favor of relatively more cautious interventionary options. Lyndon Johnson's guns and butter approach—"graduated escalation" plus no additional taxation—was explicitly geared to the public's level of tolerance, although there was no way he could hide the casualty figures. His March 1968 decision proposing negotiations and removing himself from the presidential race was certainly a consequence of the public's embrace of his two top Democratic rivals, Robert F. Kennedy and Eugene McCarthy, both of whom stood for deescalation of the war. And Richard Nixon's "Vietnamization" program, which boiled down to maintaining and even expanding the total war effort while diminishing U.S. casualties, was as oriented to public perceptions of the war as it was to the need for a new strategy to win. Nixon could hardly divulge that his secret plan to end the war was to bomb Hanoi into submission.

Perhaps the best single indicator of public opinion's impact on Vietnam policy was the government's consistent resort to secrecy and duplicity in its conduct of the war. Fear of adverse public reaction explains why so many critical military operations, many of which were illegal, became covert. On the domestic front, such fear frequently surfaced in presidential defensiveness about criticism of U.S. policy (Johnson would often say, "if you knew what I know" about the war, you wouldn't be protesting; and Nixon simply referred to the protestors as "bums") and, especially under Nixon, in paranoid reactions to dissent. Nixon authorized Project CHAOS, a program of CIA surveillance and infiltration of antiwar groups to break the back of resistance to war policies. He and Kissinger also approved extensive wiretapping of their aides' telephones to prevent leaks and ensure absolute loyalty. Vietnam became the most visible of all American wars thanks to television, but it was also the most covered up.

It is not coincidental that the Johnson and Nixon administrations began with great residues of public and press support but ended amid a torrent of disapproval. In both cases the war came home to haunt them—and a once-sympathetic and unquestioning press had a critical part in making that happen. The turn of the nation's major newspapers against the war occurred at about the same time as the shift of public opinion: Roughly, between mid–1967 and early 1968. Escalation of the war and rising casualties—and then, in 1971, the Pentagon Papers revelations—overstepped the bounds of tolerability so far as editorial boards were concerned. But with the press as with the public, disapproval of war policies had its own limits.

In understanding the change of attitude among newspaper editors and publishers, it should be borne in mind that until 1967 the major newspapers had been highly supportive of U.S. policy in Indochina. This was not merely a matter of editorials. Newspaper support was also reflected in a lack of investigative journalism concerning the war's origins; a failure of reporters to ask penetrating questions at news conferences; a srong tendency for them to accept official figures, analyses, and language; and, notably in the early years of the war (1955–1963), active cooperation by some reporters in Vietnam with official U.S. agencies (such as the CIA) at the same time that the few journalists who had begun to raise critical questions about U.S. policy were finding their editors under government pressure to reassign them. Only when, in the late sixties, it became abundantly clear that U.S. policy was failing did newspapers react with critical, independent judgment. They had been "had," sold a bill of goods on the war's progress and its causes.

Still, the kind of response fell far short of endorsement of the antiwar movement's demands. Newspaper criticism, like public opinion, eschewed calls for immediate withdrawal and concentrated instead on deescalation alternatives such as a cease-fire or limitations on the bombing of North Vietnam. As Paul Joseph observes in *Cracks in the Empire*, "the press remained within the limits of loyal criticism."[40] Many major dailies supported the Johnson and Nixon programs without any reservations, or limited them to questions about spending, enemy casualties, and other figures. The press was therefore quite restrained even when it realized it had been deceived. Yet its criticisms did make their mark on policymakers. Their eyes were constantly on media reactions to policy (Johnson for one would typically watch several television news programs simultaneously to note their responses to the day's events) and they sensed by the late sixties that an important source of support had seriously eroded.

That erosion eventually seeped into the business community and a majority in the Congress. For a number of major business leaders the war by the late sixties had ceased to be cost effective, and they so told the President. What had once loomed as a war that would secure and expand markets, or prevent them from falling into enemy hands, had turned into an inflationary monster that was overfueling the economy and hurting productivity. Big business wanted guns and butter, too; but as a community it realized, sooner than the government leadership, that such was not possible and that given a choice, butter was preferable to endless fighting.

The congressional response to the war was no different from that of the other institutions. It moved very slowly from sycophancy to restrained hostility. When the Gulf of Tonkin Resolution passed in the Senate in August 1964, only two Senators dissented. But the same body pushed through a War Powers Bill in 1973, over a President's veto, that at least theoretically restricted his ability to involve the country in new Vietnams.[41] In the first case, Johnson rode the crest of flag-waving determination to protect the national honor in the face of alleged North Vietnamese attacks at sea. But in the second, Nixon, already mortally wounded by Watergate, succumbed to a different tide: Widespread dissatisfaction with Vietnamization, the bombing, and the lack of progress in the peace talks. Earlier in the 1970s, Congress had voted legislation to restrict or to cut off funds for U.S. military deployments and aid in Indochina.

But the administration had found ways around these restrictions. The War Powers Bill followed; and although its weaknesses were revealed in its first test (President Ford's dispatch of marines to Cambodian waters, without consulting the Congress, to rescue the *Mayaguez* in May 1975, after the U.S. pullout from South Vietnam) it set the tone of congressional opposition to a further surrender of authority in foreign affairs. Over the years Congress, like the press, had, in several instances enthusiastically, supported expanded powers for the executive branch in foreign policy. Now the chickens had come home to roost, and a majority in Congress did not like the consequences either for the nation or for their own authority.

Taken together, the breakdown of institutional consensus over the Vietnam War showed the limits of pluralism in the making of U.S. foreign policy. The range of alternatives given the most respectability and treated most seriously was limited to important but narrow departures from existing policy. Neither extraordinary escalation, on the right, or extraordinary deescalation, on the "left" (or so it was perceived to be), was sanctioned in public opinion, in the press, in the business community, and in the Congress. What had happened was not the stirring of a true Great Debate on foreign policy, but a shifting of the center to accommodate the reality of defeat. The war had come to cost too much.

The constraints on policymaking imposed by these institutions left important issues of foreign policy unresolved. In this war at that time the government had been judged to have gone too far. But in the next? From a pluralist political perspective, the system worked in the end: Extremist policy alternatives had been rejected by those institutions responsible for checking and balancing official policy. But with rare exceptions, ethical, legal, and philosophical (or ideological) issues regarding U.S. intervention in Third World societies had not been seriously considered or debated by national leaders. The system may have "worked," but only at a terrible price. And while many individuals were deeply affected for the first time by the politics of a foreign adventure, interventionism as a phenomenon of the American system and as foreign-policy doctrine remained largely intact.

NOTES

1. Paul Joseph, *Cracks in the Empire: State Politics in the Vietnam War* (Boston: South End Press, 1981), pp. 304–305.

2. National Security Council (NSC) paper 64 (February 1950), in *The Senator Gravel Edition, The Pentagon Papers: The Defense Department History of United States Decisionmaking on Vietnam*, 5 vols. (Boston: Beacon Press, 1972), 1, p. 83. Hereafter cited as *PP (Gravel)*.

3. NSC paper 124/2 (June 1952) in *ibid.*, pp. 83–84.

4. NBC interview of September 9, 1963 in *ibid.*, 2, p. 828.

5. In Neil Sheehan et al., *The Pentagon Papers* (New York: Bantam, 1971), p. 128. Hereafter cited as *PP (Bantam)*.

6. *Ibid.*, p. 275.

7. *PP (Gravel)*, 4, p. 660.

8. *Ibid.*, p. 667.

9. *Ibid.*, p. 661.

10. Ernest R. May, *"Lessons" of the Past: The Use and Misuse of History in American Foreign Policy* (London: Oxford University Press, 1973).

11. Speech by Lyndon Johnson at Johns Hopkins University, April 17, 1965; in U.S. Senate, Committee on Foreign Relations, *Background Information Relating to Southeast Asia and Vietnam*, 3d rev. ed. (Washington, D.C.: U.S. Government Printing Office, 1967), p. 149.

12. Memorandum by John T. McNaughton, March 24, 1965 to McNamara; in *PP (Bantam)*, pp. 432–438.

13. Lyndon Johnson, quoted in Richard J. Barnet, *Intervention and Revolution: The United States in the Third World* (Cleveland: World, 1968), p. 12.

14. Speech by Richard Nixon, April 17, 1975 to the American Society of Newspaper Editors; Department of State transcript.

15. On the American reaction to the emergence of Ho Chi Minh, see *PP (Gravel)*, 1, pp. 20–50.

16. *Ibid.*, 3, p. 668.

17. John Kennedy, September 12, 1963 in *ibid.*, 2, p. 828.

18. *PP (Bantam)*, p. 218.

19. *PP (Gravel)*, 3, p. 560.

20. Cited in *PP (Bantam)*, p. 422.

21. See Ellsberg's essay, "The Quagmire Myth and the Stalemate Machine," in his *Papers on the War* (New York: Simon and Schuster, 1972), pp. 42–135.

22. Quoted in Tom Wicker, *JFK and LBJ: The Influence of Personality Upon Politics* (New York: Morrow, 1968), p. 244.

23. *PP (Bantam)*, p. 421.

24. Nixon's speech of April 30, 1970; text in *Los Angeles Times*, May 1, 1970, p. 1. And see Joseph Alsop, "The President on Vietnam," *Newsweek*, October 13, 1969, p. 33.

25. These are mostly taken from Gurtov, *The United States against the Third World*, pp. 146–150.

26. See the Vietnam study (ch. 5) of Irving L. Janis, *Victims of Groupthink* (Boston: Houghton Mifflin, 1972).

27. *PP (Bantam)*, pp. 97, 141–143.

28. James C. Thomson, "How Could Vietnam Happen? An Autopsy," *The Atlantic*, April 1968, pp. 50–55.

29. See the quotations in Richard J. Barnet, *Roots of War* (New York: Atheneum, 1972), p. 69.

30. "How Could Vietnam Happen? An Autopsy," *The Atlantic*, April 1968, p. 51.

31. *PP (Bantam)*, p. 379.

32. Barnet, *Roots of War*, pp. 23–47.

33. There is a growing literature on the ordinary soldier's experiences in Vietnam. Among the best is A. D. Horne, ed., *The Wounded Generation: America after Vietnam* (Englewood Cliffs, N.J.: Prentice-Hall, 1981).

34. "In the final analysis the U.S. military simply would not fight a war that was not as total as they could make it. For all their talk about commitment to more limited and politically sophisticated uses of military power, the American high command never really gave up its belief that the only way to fight a war is to bring about the destruction of the enemy's armed forces and of his ability to wage war." David S. McLellan and Robert Hange, "The Joint Chiefs and the Expanded War," *Worldview*, vol 17, no. 4 (April 1974), p. 44.

35. Cited in *Harpers*, June 1972, p. 55.

36. For a critical review of these writings, see Frank A. Burdick, "Vietnam Revisioned: The Military Campaign against Civilian Control," *Democracy*, vol. 2, no. 1 (January 1982), pp. 36–52.

37. Larry Berman, *Planning A Tragedy: The Americanization of the War in Vietnam* (New York: W. W. Norton, 1982), p. 150.

38. For a similarly critical perspective on public opinion and foreign policy, see Charles W. Kegley, Jr., and Eugene R. Wittkopf, *American Foreign Policy: Pattern and Process*, 2d ed. (New York: St. Martin's, 1982), pp. 270–293.

39. Joseph, *Cracks in the Empire*, pp. 170–172.

40. See table 5.4 in Joseph, *Cracks in the Empire*, p. 171.

41. The War Powers Bill requires that the President, in the absence of a formal declaration of war, report to congressional leaders within

forty-eight hours of a decision to introduce U.S. forces into combat situations abroad. Unless Congress acts to uphold the President's action, it must be terminated within sixty days. Although this legislation was designed to inhibit the unfettered exercise of executive authority in using force abroad, several of its proponents found that the wording left unfortunate loopholes and might even have *expanded* presidential war-making power. Their point was amply demonstrated by the Reagan administration's maneuverings to maintain U.S. marines in Lebanon in 1983–1984 and its invasion of Grenada in late 1983.

BIBLIOGRAPHY

American scholarship turned to Vietnam only after the war heated up in the 1960s. With a few exceptions, it focused narrowly on U.S. policy, ignoring the larger cultural and social roots of the revolution in favor of close examination of strategy and tactics. For today's student, it is indispensable to start with these exceptions, which include: Frances FitzGerald, *Fire in the Lake: The Vietnamese and the Americans in Vietnam* (Boston: Atlantic–Little, Brown, 1972); John T. McAlister, Jr., and Paul Mus, *The Vietnamese and Their Revolution* (New York: Harper and Row, 1970); Gerald C. Hickey, *Village in Vietnam* (New Haven, Conn.: Yale University Press, 1964); and, in a larger regional historical perspective, David Joel Steinberg, ed., *In Search of Southeast Asia: A Modern History* (New York: Praeger, 1971). Needless to say, the writings of Ho Chi Minh should be consulted, for example, in the compilation edited by Bernard B. Fall, *Ho Chi Minh on Revolution: Selected Writings, 1920–66* (New York: Praeger, 1967). Prior to the 1960s the major histories, sociologies, and cultural studies are in French with the notable exception of Ellen J. Hammer's *The Struggle for Indochina* (Stanford, Calif.: Stanford University Press, 1954).

There are now several good general histories of U.S. policy in the war. Three worth noting are: Peter A. Poole, *The United States and Indochina from FDR to Nixon* (Hinsdale, Ill.: Dryden, 1973); George C. Herring, *America's Longest War: the United States and Vietnam, 1950–1975* (New York: Wiley, 1979); and Stanley Karnow, *Vietnam: A History* (New York: Viking, 1983).

For the 1945–1954 period, that of the "first Indochina war," the work of Bernard B. Fall is always a good starting point: *The Two Viet-Nams: A Political and Military Analysis*, 2d rev. ed. (New York: Praeger, 1967); *Street without Joy: Insurgency in Indochina, 1946–1963*, 3d rev. ed. (Harrisburg, Pa.: Stackpole, 1963); and *Hell in a Very Small Place: The Siege of Dien Bien Phu* (New York: Vintage, 1966). U.S. policy is the main concern of Melvin Gurtov's *The First Vietnam Crisis: Chinese Communist Strategy and United States Involvement, 1953–1954* (New York: Columbia University Press, 1967) and Robert F. Randle, *Geneva 1954: The Settlement of the Indochinese War* (Princeton, N.J.: Princeton University Press, 1969).

Concerning the post-1954 years, the literature becomes voluminous and sometimes highly specialized. There are several studies each, for instance, of Vietnam and international law, government and politics in Vietnam, battlefield developments and tactics, the nature of the NLF, public opinion, the press, U.S. domestic politics, the war's effects on the ordinary soldier, and the personalities of the key decision makers. Students should also keep in mind that many of the last have published memoirs that deal entirely or in significant part with their first-hand experiences of the war, including Presidents Eisenhower, Johnson, and Nixon, and Dean Acheson, Henry Kissinger, George Ball, Roger Hilsman, and Arthur M. Schlesinger, Jr.

Here it seems best to cite particularly valuable analytical studies that attempt to come to grips with the essence of American interest, strategy, and politics in the 1960s and 1970s. These are: Chester L. Cooper, *The Lost Crusade: America in Vietnam* (New York: Dodd, Mead, 1970); Richard J. Barnet, *Roots of War* (New York: Atheneum, 1972); Daniel Ellsberg, *Papers on the War* (New York: Simon & Schuster, 1972); David Halberstam, *The Best and the Brightest* (New York: Fawcett Crest, 1972); Leslie H. Gelb with Richard K. Betts, *The Irony of Vietnam: The System Worked* (Washington, D.C.: Brookings Institution, 1979); Earl C. Ravenal, *Never Again: Learning from America's Foreign Policy Failures* (Philadelphia: Temple University Press, 1978); Paul Joseph, *Cracks in the Empire: State Politics in the Vietnam War* (Boston: South End Press, 1981); Raphael Littauer and Norman Uphoff, eds., *The Air War in Indochina*, rev. ed. (Boston: Beacon/Cornell University, 1972); Ralph Stavins, Richard J. Barnet, and Marcus G. Raskin, *Washington Plans an Aggressive War* (New York: Vintage, 1971); William Shawcross, *Sideshow: Kissinger, Nixon and the Destruction of Cambodia* (New York: Simon & Schuster, 1979); Larry Berman, *Planning a Tragedy: The Americanization of the War in Vietnam* (New York: Norton, 1982); and Seymour M. Hersh, *The Price of Power: Kissinger in the Nixon White House* (New York: Summit Books, 1983).

We leave for last the major documents. There are three separate compilations of the Pentagon Papers, which form the basis of this chapter. None of these versions is complete, including the largest of them, published by the House Committee on Armed Services in forty-seven typescript volumes. The other two collections are much more accessible and readable. *The Senator Gravel Edition, The Pentagon Papers: The Defense Department History of United States Decisionmaking on Vietnam* (Boston: Beacon Press, 1972) consists of four volumes of once-classified documents and public statements and a fifth volume of scholarly analyses. The papers published in the *New York Times,* and issued under the editorship of Neil Sheehan et al. *The Pentagon Papers* (New York: Bantam, 1971), have far fewer documents than the Gravel edition, but do contain useful introductions to each period of the war that they cover, from 1945 to 1968.

5

National Security and the Third World: Revising the Agenda

> I refuse to express myself with [political people's] words, their labels, their slogans, left and right, socialism and communism, capitalism and Luxemburgism. I express myself with my words: good, bad, better and worse. And I say: If it serves the people, it is good. If it doesn't serve the people, it is bad.
>
> —Lech Walesa, March 1981

ROOTS OF FAILURE

What can one say of a world in which 1 billion people in the Third World are chronically malnourished; in which over 2 billion people do not have access to clean water; in which 60 percent of all scientists are engaged in research on weapons; in which about 500 million people are jobless, double-digit inflation is the rule in most countries, and average personal income for a quarter of the world's population is below $200 annually; in which, at present rates of depletion, by the year 2000 forests in the Third World will be reduced by one-half, up to 1 million plant and animal species will be eradicated, and one-third less topsoil will be available for food production, all at a time when there are expected to be 50 percent more people in the world? These figures, and their implications for the quality of life on the planet less than twenty years from now, are staggering. All the more so when, as was noted in the first chapter, the arms race annually reaches new heights of frenzy in destructive power and costliness.

Insofar as world politics is concerned, the most obvious thing that can be said about such figures is that even if the arms race were to be brought under control, the planet's survival would still be imperiled. It is by now commonplace to say that all societies are interdependent, with no nation—least of all a superpower—capable of insulating itself from the monumental economic, social, and ecological disruptions of our time. When we consider, moreover, that these disruptions are especially acute in the Third World, which is home to about three-quarters of the globe's population, we may better understand just how widespread and immediate these problems are.

A second conclusion to be drawn from the state of the planet is that the First World's elaborate theories, models, and technologies have largely failed to alleviate poverty, spur economic or political development, or create real security in the underdeveloped countries. In fact, the opposite has, with some exceptions, occurred. Trickle-down economic theories, whether "supply side" or "demand side," have basically reinforced the power of entrenched elites, further marginalized the powerless, and largely ignored environmental consequences. Both "left" and "right" models of economic growth and political development have revealed enormous gaps when put into practice: On the left, the subordination of civil liberties and personal freedom and the overcentralization of economic and political power; on the right, the neglect of social and economic justice, the accountability of institutions to the collective and the community, and the redistribution of economic and political power. Finally, advances in weaponry and in strategic theory have not only failed to deter wars, they have heightened sensitivity to threats and made possession of nuclear weapons a mark of prestige.

The final set of conclusions about global insecurity is most immediately relevant to the present study. Its basic premise is that global interdependence has discredited the national interest as an appropriate standard of U.S. foreign policy. In the remainder of this section, we want to elaborate, against the background of our case studies, the two ways in which the national interest has run afoul of the global interest. Both are rooted in the axioms of national interest that, we suggested in the first chapter, dictate U.S. foreign-policy ideology. Both legitimize intervention in the Third World: In one case, by asserting that Third World development may require U.S. support of authoritarian rule to ensure "stability"; in the other case, by denigrating Third World nationalism and failing to appreciate its roots and its universal appeal. The chief consequence of this national-interest perspective is a strong and persistent American preference for military, or militant, responses to what are essentially social and economic problems.[1]

Ever since the Marshall Plan for Western Europe, U.S. foreign policy has rested on the assumption that political stability—which, to U.S. leaders, has always meant strong central-government leadership and the absence of radical political opposition to it—will emerge out of capitalist economic growth. As Secretary of State George C. Marshall said when he introduced the plan on June 5, 1947:

> It is logical that the United States should do whatever it is able to do to assist in the return of normal economic health in the world, without which there can be no political stability, and no assured peace. Our policy is directed not against any country or doctrine but against hunger, poverty, desperation, and chaos. Its purpose should be the revival of a working economy in the world so as to permit the emergence of political and social conditions in which free institutions can exist.

Of course the plan *was* directed against a country and a doctrine; and its success was predicated on the integration of regional (West European) economies with a U.S.-dominated world economy. As the cold war shifted from Europe to the Third World, these same assumptions were carried along. They were integrated with U.S. military as well as strictly economic assistance programs (such as Point Four in the 1940s, the Alliance for Progress and the "Green Revolution" in the 1960s, and the Caribbean Basin proposal in the 1980s) in the conviction that political stability requires not only capitalist development but also the guns to protect it from advocates of socialist and nonsocialist national development.

Throughout the postwar period, poverty, hunger, and disease have been considered not so much as symptoms of global underdevelopment, but even more as potential breeding grounds for communism, and hence as threats to U.S. national security. For if local communist or radical nationalist groups should take power in the Third World, American access to their economies for trade and investment would be limited or cut off, corporate property would be nationalized, and military basing rights would be eliminated and possibly transferred to a hostile power. Development along capitalist and (in the distant future) liberal-democratic lines would be abandoned. Instead of opportunities for profit and political advantage, the United States would be faced with a possibly successful showcase of noncapitalist development, such as China and Cuba have become and such as Allende's Chile was feared would become. A radical nationalist regime then might be emulated by other Third World governments. The dominoes would begin falling. So the stakes have always been considered very high indeed. Political instability in countries such as Iran, Nicaragua, and Vietnam has been important to U.S. policymakers regardless of the dollar value of U.S. economic ties to them, precisely because U.S. national security is a global political-economic matter. What happens in small countries is literally big business, which is the meaning behind the contention of U.S. policymakers that "peace is indivisible."

In this light, U.S. policy toward the Third World has been to protect and to strengthen regimes having common economic and strategic interests and professing adherence to common values. The political character of such regimes, which is usually authoritarian, has mattered far less to U.S. policymakers than has their commitment to law and order, gradual reforms, and private property. In fact, as we have seen, authoritarianism in friendly Third World governments has typically been excused by U.S. policymakers on the basis that, first, economic development must precede the evolution of democratic institutions and, second, that underdeveloped societies cannot be expected quickly to implement Western-style civil liberties. Such assumptions, although reasonable in themselves, have cleared the way for making alliances with the most unsavory leaders—people like Somoza, Diem, Shah, and their cohorts—on the basis that, unfortunately, the United States really cannot export democracy. But toward socialist Third World governments, these same two guidelines have been abandoned in favor of coercive policies, as in U.S. policy toward Nicaragua today.

Such discrimination has proven to be an ideological trap. It leads U.S. policymakers to give stability top priority and incorrectly to equate it with the effectiveness of a friendly regime's law-and-order policies. Lip service is paid to democratic ideals, and friendly leaders quickly learn that to the extent the Americans are concerned about democratic politics, promises of free elections, broad-based coalition governments, and new constitutions will satisfy them. U.S. policymakers lend legitimacy to Third World governments on the basis of their cooperation with U.S. strategic and corporate interests, of which a stable (that is, nonunionized) work force and closed political system are key parts, rather than because of their accomplishments in building a humane, accountable political-economic order.

The ominous and obvious consequence of these American concerns has been to make the United States a full partner with authoritarian regimes in maintaining internal order in their countries. Supplying the means of repression, including military and police training, has long been a standard U.S. role in the Third World, one the United States has preferred to direct intervention. For how else could U.S. assets there, including client elites in the military, political, and economic leaderships, be adequately protected at low cost against "subversives"? In the same manner as their counterparts in the Soviet Union, U.S. leaders have framed their Third World policies around the export of the national-security state. And when such exports have been closed off by revolution, CIA funding of counterrevolutionary armies and political parties has taken their place.

We find, then, not merely that U.S. policymakers have created an artificial and self-serving distinction between acceptable authoritarianism in friendly regimes and unacceptable totalitarianism in unfriendly ones. Beyond that, it would seem that authoritarianism is a natural ally and necessary condition of U.S. policy: It is actively supported, not merely tolerated. Authoritarian regimes are considered best equipped to fight external and internal threats, to command and to channel a society's resources, and to provide stable conditions for foreign investors. As the case studies show, U.S. officials have supported authoritarian regimes with perfect awareness of their limitations and fallibilities. They have recognized that such support is always a calculated risk; but it is a risk they have believed is worth taking, since the projected benefits are considered global in scale. But implementation of such a model, in our view, does more than simply delay steps to create political and economic justice for the overwhelming majority of an underdeveloped country's citizens; it makes justice almost impossible to realize.

The American model in fact creates precisely the opposite conditions of real development, by which we mean the mobilization of a society's human and material resources to create and to sustain not only political, social, and economic justice, but also environmental balance and contributions to world peace. Each case study, and numerous other cases (such as Brazil, Argentina, El Salvador, and Chile in recent years), shows the actual consequences of authoritarian rule: The centralization of political and police power, leading to increasingly widespread repression of all opposition including in the end even members of the inner elite; the development of sham political institutions (parties, constitutions, courts, parliaments) that provide nothing more than the appearance of dispersed power; the alienation of nonpolitical institutions, such as the church and small business, along with the elevation of the military as a dominant political force; the integration of local with international big business, agricultural and industrial, creating a largely dependent economy that is heavily in debt and skewed toward foreign markets; the shifting of national resources, not to mention most foreign aid, from employment and production for human needs to satisfying the military's needs and those of international capital markets. As many writers have observed, U.S. policy in the Third World frequently helps deepen underdevelopment and undermines regime legitimacy, thereby promoting the very conditions that favor political instability.

The need for imposed order, and the conditions of repression, keep recreating themselves. For as economic growth fails to trickle down, and political liberalization is replaced on the regime's agenda by police coercion, opposition to authority becomes more extreme and acquires new support. The politicization of the church in Latin America around a liberation theology illustrates this phenomenon, as does the authoritarian regime's response to it, which is to authorize or to condone the murder of archbishops and priests. (Such has been the situation in El Salvador since the murder of Archbishop Romero in 1979). All pretense of partnership with the United States for democratic purposes is then dropped in the name of national security. The role of the United States becomes more direct, although intervention may range from Marines to the manipulation of aid programs and the staging of "free" elections. The military may assume power and suspend an already bloodstained constitution. An all-out struggle for power is at hand, with radical organizations—not necessarily Marxist, as Khomeini's following shows—in the vanguard of the opposition.

This often rapid evolution to armed confrontation, in which the United States has been embroiled so often in the recent past, faces its leaders with unpalatable choices. Unwilling to deal with the radicals, who are considered illegitimate, yet forced finally to dissociate themselves from the dictator they have long supported, the Americans, as was the case in all three studies here, make a last-ditch effort to salvage the situation. They comb the friendly ranks for a "moderate" to replace the tyrant who has now become a liability: Somocista without Somoza. Sometimes, as in Vietnam, they find one; other times, as in Iran and Nicaragua, they cannot. In most cases the results are only important in the short run; in the longer run, such eleventh-hour machinations poison relations with the revolutionaries for years to come. Seizure of the U.S. embassy in Tehran; conflict with the Sandinista government of Nicaragua over El Salvador and other issues; and deadlock with Vietnam over a host of issues left over from the war, including its control of Kampuchea—confrontations such as these were predictable given U.S. support and intervention before the revolutions occurred and, in the Nicaragua case, efforts to destabilize the new government after it had taken power.

Why, given the consistency with which such outcomes occur, does U.S. policy continue to support authoritarian regimes and resist revolutionary movements? America's anticommunist impulse does not provide a complete answer, since noncommunist nationalism and religious fundamentalism have also been targets of U.S. policy. Ideologically, social-change movements in general are the things most feared in Washington, whether communist or not. Support of authoritarian allies is support of that which is predictable, penetrable, and controllable: An objective of state bureaucracies everywhere.[2] Over the short run, it is easier to conduct business with a foreign elite that is strong, friendly, accessible, and oriented to the status quo than to deal with social radicals who seek to transform the foundations of politics, economics, and even culture. Radicals threaten those values that American leaders most cherish, and even though compromises are possible—for even the most ardent Marxists need capital and technology to keep their economies running—they are seldom sought, much less obtained. U.S. policymakers consistently confuse what is desirable, from their own unique perspective, with what is attainable.

National self-determination, like humane economic and political development, is also a victim of thinking in the groove of the national interest. Analyzing events abroad from a national-interest perspective, as U.S. officials invariably do, puts emphasis on costs and benefits to U.S. society alone, focuses on the threatening aspect of social change, identifies forces and actors outside the United States as those responsible for upsetting the status quo, pushes coercive measures to the forefront of U.S. options, and especially neglects the deep historical and social roots of national turmoil. In fact, social division and political turmoil in Nicaragua, Iran, and Vietnam did not begin with the appearance of revolutionary movements, any more than those issues entirely disappeared with those movements' victories. Nationalism, land reform, underdevelopment, foreign control, and authoritarian politics were the common denominators in the three countries; overwhelming poverty, class and ethnic inequalities, and the abrogation of civil liberties were among their severe human rights problems. The revolutionary movements represented the coming together of these historical legacies, but Washington chose to view them as conspiracies that threatened long-held positions of advantage. From there it was a relatively small leap of logic to presume that these movements could not be worked with and should instead be resisted, whether by intrigue or more direct forms of intervention.

The ultimate danger of foreign policy formulated on the basis of the national interest is that turmoil in any one place is globalized; every society is a potential domino. Such a narrow vision sharply limits opportunities for a more creative diplomacy that would, first, take account of the role of the United States in having contributed to and intensified revolutionary nationalist violence and, second, see such violence in its proper global context, as the logical culmination of many years, and perhaps centuries, of exploitation.

Beyond those factors of self-determination, which is perhaps the strongest force that defines an otherwise extremely diverse Third World, lie considerations of longer-term U.S. self-interest. Even though the United States relies increasingly on Third World countries for resources, jobs, and export markets, does intervention make good business sense? We do not think so. Strictly from a business point of view, a confrontative policy toward the Third World undermines American economic growth. Precisely because so many jobs, trade opportunities, and vital resources depend on sound relations between the United States and the Third World, wars and interventions are bad for business. The arms trade will flourish, but it doesn't create new markets or jobs to anywhere near the extent created by expanded trade in manufactured goods.

Excessive, wasteful U.S. military spending in support of a globalist foreign policy adds to the problem. It accounts in great part for the huge federal deficit, which helps drive up interest rates, strengthen the dollar, and thus make U.S. exports too expensive. The resulting U.S. trade deficit promotes protectionism which limits imports and further complicates the ability of Third World governments to increase their exports and to pay back loans. Lost trade opportunities are reckoned by the U.S. government to mean about 30,000 jobs directly eliminated for every $1 billion of deficit—a total loss of nearly 2 million jobs at the end of 1983, when the trade merchandise deficit went over $65 billion. Direct private investments by U.S.-based multinational corporations have dramatically increased over the years in response to the decline in the U.S. trade position. But investments are no substitute for trade, since they amount to the export of capital and jobs under tax arrangements that limit what the U.S. government ultimately collects. U.S. interventions, furthermore, may be prompted by the need to protect investments abroad, whereas trade relations are best promoted by a dynamic world economy centered on stable currencies and reasonably balanced exchanges of consumer goods and services.

Intervention alienates new leaderships and often, as in the cases of revolutionary Cuba, China, and now Vietnam, drives them into dependent economic as well as political relationships with the Soviet Union. The official U.S. prophecy that the revolutionary leaders will be anti-American or Soviet proxies becomes largely self-fulfilling to the detriment of U.S. business. In reality, these are independent revolutionaries, who, having come to power on the wings of national self-determination, are anxious to preserve their national and socialist independence. U.S. policy often gives them little choice but to accept aid from whoever proffers it—typically, along with compromising political strings. Consider then, the different opportunities that might have become available to the United States, and the healthier relationship that would undoubtedly have resulted, had these observations been incorporated in U.S. policy as the revolution in each of the three countries studied achieved success.[3]

In Iran, what if U.S. officials had accepted the legitimacy of Khomeini's revolution and not attempted to find a last-minute replacement for the departed Shah? What if they had acknowledged the CIA's role in returning the Shah to power in 1953, offered an apology as Khomeini was demanding, and rejected pressure from the Shah's powerful American friends (such as former Secretary of State Henry Kissinger and David Rockefeller, head of the Chase Manhattan Bank, which held billions of dollars in Iranian assets) to allow him to enter the United States for medical treatment? For one thing, the subsequent seizure of the U.S. embassy and its occupants, which embassy officials had warned was a distinct possibility if the Shah were allowed to enter the United States, would probably not have happened. No "hostage crisis" would have resulted, Iranian-American relations could have been put on a new footing, and official U.S. fear mongering about a Persian Gulf crisis and Soviet intervention in Iran would have gotten nowhere with the public or Congress. Possibly the Khomeini regime's subsequent gross violations of human rights could have been ameliorated due to its lower level of insecurity.[4]

In Nicaragua, what if the U.S. government, instead of attempting to undermine, to derail, and then to sabotage the Sandinista revolution, had viewed it as an understandable alternative to decades of oppression under the Somozas? What if U.S. officials had seen the revolution, not as a tool of Soviet or Cuban interests, but as the outcome of events specific to Nicaragua? The Sandinistan program of social change would have been given a chance to work, Cuban nonmilitary assistance to Nicaragua would not have been considered threatening to U.S. interests, and U.S. economic aid, instead of being held out and then cancelled, would have been tendered in good faith. Nicaragua, which today is treated as another Cuba and therefore as a Central American domino (along with El Salvador and Guatemala), could have been dealt with more rationally on its own terms.

In Vietnam, what if the United States had early normalized relations with a unified Vietnam, made good on some part of the $3.25 billion in reparations promised the Vietnamese by President Nixon, and become involved in an international economic aid program to help in the country's reconstruction? It seems doubtful that Vietnam's dominant influence over the rest of Indochina could have been avoided. But friendly U.S.-Vietnam relations might well have affected Hanoi's decision late in 1978 to invade Kampuchea, as well as China's decision shortly afterwards to invade Vietnam with apparent U.S. acquiescence. Vietnamese dependence on the USSR for economic help would have been substantially lessened; instead, the Vietnamese would have had more incentive to work cooperatively with its Southeast Asian neighbors, one of which (Thailand) has competing interests with Vietnam in Kampuchea.

The question of alternative policies ought properly to lend itself to analysis of the roles of Congress, the media, and public opinion. But the three cases point up the very severe limits placed by presidential decision making on the roles of outsiders. After several years of giving various administrations *carte blanche* on Vietnam policy, Congress did constrain the Nixon administration in the early 1970s by cutting funds for certain bombing and military assistance programs in Indochina and by prohibiting allocations for U.S.-backed movements fighting for control of Angola in 1975. The lessons of Vietnam clearly have influenced congressional initiatives to hold down military aid to U.S. allies in Central America, to prevent the CIA-backed destabilization of Nicaragua, and (in 1983–1984) to limit the length of stay of U.S. troops in Lebanon. But the truth of the matter is that, with the exception of Angola, Congress could do no more than nibble at the edges of presidential policy. It could not prevent the bombing of Cambodia, which was carried out in secret; nor the provision of military aid and training in Indochina under different program titles; nor the surreptitious assistance to the favored factions in Angola; nor the private deals with the Shah; nor about $1 billion in military aid to El Salvador (as of 1984); nor CIA operations in and around Nicaragua (which are direct violations of U.S. treaty commitments); nor the unprecedented U.S. military buildup throughout Central America and the Caribbean in the 1980s. Policymaking is from the top down in the United States as elsewhere; and Congress, while having the power of the purse and the power to resolve, can only infrequently muster either one in ways that cut directly into a President's formidable arsenal of constitutional and extra-constitutional prerogatives of war making.

Still less has the press, in any concerted fashion, proved willing or able to cut through the thick layers of bureaucratic jargon and policymaking machinery in order effectively to challenge official policy. Not that the press was immobile or ineffective during the last years of the Vietnam war or in recent times concerning the fighting in Central America. Credit the press with lending legitimacy (or respectability) to criticisms of U.S. policy that had been building for some time, and in some cases (for example, the My Lai massacre in South Vietnam, the Pentagon Papers, and the right-wing death squads in El Salvador) with exposing abuses of power. As we have shown, however, the media, like the Congress, has been limited by both political will and human and technical resources from acting as a formidable check on presidential power, especially in the decisive early stages of U.S. interventions. And in the later stages, when significant parts of the mass media have turned a critical eye on U.S. policy, it has done so without questioning the basic assumptions and objectives on which policy has turned.

The overall effect of what the Congress and the media did and did not do when dealing with interventions was, it appears, to restrict an administration's range of acceptable alternatives. But neither institution had—nor is it likely to have—either the authority or the machinery to mold a different set of foreign-policy premises around which an informed public might rally. And Presidents, who have both the authority and the machinery, seem to want to use them in defense against perceived congressional inroads into decision making and the media's constant quest for a story. Post–Vietnam and post–Pentagon Papers, we see less presidential accountability and more manipulation: Witness, for example, with respect to Congress, the stretching of the War Powers Act, starting with the *Mayaguez* incident and continuing, most recently, with a generous eighteen-month timetable given President Reagan for keeping Marines in Lebanon; and, with respect to the media, the prohibition of press coverage of the invasion of Grenada. James Madison's statement, quoted in the introduction, that liberty (including democracy) at home is often sacrificed to real or imagined dangers abroad continues to have meaning nearly 200 years later.

A GLOBAL-HUMANIST ALTERNATIVE

For alternative courses of action even to be put on the decision makers' agendas and debated as "live options" requires radical alterations of their ideology, values, and attitudes. It also requires major changes in the way foreign-policy bureaucrats perceive and act upon problems. For ultimately, as we have argued, threats and crises become such only when officials, based on their prior philosophical conditioning and (secondarily) their bureaucratic position, so choose. Making choices that benefit popular majorities rather than entrenched elites comes from asking questions that reflect a human-interest, global-community perspective on the world.

We contend there is urgent need for a new globalism to become the conceptual basis of U.S. (and other nations') foreign policy. The core values of a new globalism have already been laid out in a number of places: Peace, civil and political liberties, social and economic justice, ecological balance.[5] Specific steps at the national level that would seek to implement these values, moreover, have been incorporated in several UN documents that have received the endorsement of most of the world's governments.[6] Significantly, the United States has not ratified the human-rights covenants. Over the years members of Congress have stalled ratification because of the perceived impact of international human-rights codes on national sovereignty and the behavior of U.S.-based multinational corporations.

A humanistic globalism would be a sharp departure from the standard of "enlightened self-interest" that has traditionally guided U.S. foreign policymaking. It would also depart significantly from the kind of globalism touted by the Carter administration under the rubric of "interdependence." Both kinds of globalism spring from justifiable alarm about the human community's rapidly declining quality of life and from the failure of nation states and international organizations to acknowledge, much less come to grips with, the global crisis. But the old globalists, while attuned to the negative aspects of nationalism, offer solutions that speak mainly to the interests of multinational corporations in a stable and unregulated world market. The hallmark of their preferred world is the Open Door—a global marketplace in which the giant conglomerates of the Trilateral states (the United States, Western Europe, and Japan) will freely wheel and deal, ultimately penetrating even the most closed economies to create a new global culture. Like their Realist colleagues, these globalists view world social and economic upheavals, and efforts by Third World countries to redress inequities, as threats to national security, to be countered with increased trade, loans, private investments, military sales, and other profitable "partnerships" with the Third World. In contrast, a new globalism would seek to get beyond national self-interest by resetting the conditions and content of international exchange, reversing and ultimately ending the arms race, and putting teeth into national and international human-rights legislation—changes that could only be meaningful with the active cooperation of the United States. "Global interdependence" amounts to deceptive rhetoric when, as has been the case for a decade, it means continuing to treat the Third World as rival.

The specific policy implications of a new globalism run in two different but complementary directions: Support for international regimes and mechanisms to deal with global problems and changes in U.S. policy toward the Third World. In both cases, U.S. foreign policy would need to be guided by the realization that past behavior, based on selective interventionism and the open market, has not really enhanced world order, the self-determination of peoples, or even U.S. national security; that, in any case, new forces in international political economy threaten to overwhelm rich and poor nations alike; and that policies to promote a truly cooperative approach with the Third World on underdevelopment and human rights may actually produce more long-term benefit for all than policies designed for short-run and one-sided economic or political advantage.

Listed below are the kinds of changes in international institutions and in U.S. policy that the authors believe would promote movement toward a new global vision.[7] Clearly, these would not be sufficient in and of themselves to implement such a vision, for among other things they neglect the necessity of changed values and attitudes among public officials and citizens generally and of new rules in bureaucratic games. But the constraints and new directions imposed on the foreign-policy establishment by policy or legislative changes may, as we witnessed in Congress's response to Vietnam in the 1970s, exert considerable influence on attitudes and behavior.

With respect, first of all, to international organizations, there are five areas in which active U.S. support could substantially contribute to a more positive relationship with the Third World:

1. Through support of *international regimes* that would have independent powers to monitor, to assess, and to take action on issues affecting global security. These issues include peacekeeping opera-

tions, disarmament (adherence to treaties and surveillance of weapons tests and troop movements by satellite), environmental pollution, weather forecasting, the behavior of multinational corporations, and equitable access to resources of the commons (such as in the Law of the Sea Treaty which is currently opposed by the Reagan administration).

2. Through support of *international law* in settlement of disputes, including not only full use of the International Court of Justice, but also increased reliance on nongovernmental mediators and negotiators, and support of standing international machinery for conciliation and arbitration.
3. Through contributions to *international stockpiles* of crucial agricultural commodities, essential drugs, and possible other items.
4. Through increased *aid to international organizations* for economic development. The U.S. contribution of development assistance as a percentage of GNP has been falling since 1960; it stood at 0.27 percent in 1980, or fifteenth among seventeen Western aid donors. As the Brandt Commission's study emphasizes, even a minute shift of funds by the world's governments from weapons to human needs could dramatically alter the prospects for survival of impoverished Third World people.[8] But neither bilateral aid nor aid administered by U.S.-dominated institutions such as the International Monetary Fund and the World Bank promotes equitable resource distribution in the Third World countries to which aid is given. Hence the need to channel far more funds than the United States typically does through organs of the United Nations or, as suggested below, through nongovernmental people-to-people programs.
5. Through *ratification of UN covenants* on human rights. Ratification obviously does not, by itself, ensure adherence to the covenants' terms. But through U.S. adherence and actual use by U.S. citizens of the appeal process established under the covenants, their political force could be greatly strengthened. The United States would set an example that would at least put moral pressure on other signatories to act likewise.

In the second area of proposed change, we offer the following principles and practices for U.S. policy in the Third World:

1. Strict adherence to *nonintervention and noninterference* in the internal affairs of other peoples—the only exception being multilateral action by a significant part of the world community to prevent genocide or other such outrages. Implementing this principle would

mean, for example, disbanding expeditionary outfits such as the Rapid Deployment Force, proscribing CIA covert operations (while increasing congressional or other surveillance of CIA intelligence-gathering operations), terminating all forms of aid (and especially military sales and grants) to regimes that engage in systematic human-rights violations, vigorously enforcing U.S. laws to prevent the use of U.S. territory by foreign exiles for military or political activities against another state, and prohibiting all forms of bribes by U.S.-based transnational corporations to foreign governments or political officials. Agreements with the Soviet Union and other states should be sought to gain reciprocity on each of these points, perhaps starting with a bilateral undertaking to prevent deployment of military forces to specific regions.

2. Take concrete steps to *freeze and to reverse the arms race*—specifically, by reaching agreement (initially, with the USSR; later with other nuclear-weapons states) to halt the production, testing, and deployment of nuclear weapons; by completing negotiation of a Comprehensive Test Ban; by supporting and expanding the number of nuclear-free zones (especially, by creating such a zone in the Middle East and the Indian Ocean); by enacting legislation to prohibit the sale and shipment abroad of nuclear weapons plants, technology, and materials; by creating and carrying out a step-by-step agenda to reduce arms stockpiles, both nuclear and conventional; and, in similar fashion, by drawing up a comprehensive multilateral agreement to eliminate at least the most dangerous (and expensive) weapons systems from among those sold to Third World governments.
3. Adopt policies and programs that promote *a new international economic order and address the basic needs* of underdeveloped societies. Such steps could include emphasizing people-to-people development programs; increasing total development assistance to 1 percent of GNP annually; replacing existing tax and investment privileges for multinational corporations with tax credits for those which promote use of small-scale technology, production (especially in agriculture) for self-reliant development, expansion of human services, and indigenous ownership and management of enterprises; removing trade barriers on Third World–manufactured goods and working to stabilize prices on primary products the Third World exports; and reaching agreement on a debt moratorium.

Of special urgency is the need to create a more *self-reliant domestic energy base* in the United States by shifting from oil imports and nuclear energy to extensive reliance on renewable resources and conservation. That shift would force down the price of petroleum to Third World users but, more importantly, it would strengthen their incentive to develop and to use less energy-intensive, locally controllable technology.

The implications of sweeping changes such as these are frankly enormous, not only because of what would be immediately accomplished, but also because of what these changes would portend for the future of world politics. For instance, they would substantially strengthen the authority of global institutions over global problems yet without seriously compromising the power of nation states. They would begin to introduce balance and equity in North-South relations, as well as link changes in the international economic order with progress in satisfying basic needs such as food. They would impose responsibility on transnational corporations to operate both for profit and for people. They would encourage economic development, North and South, that is much more attuned than presently to planetary sustainability—and, probably, that entails a major increase in exchanges between underdeveloped countries. The pattern of U.S. transactions with the Third World would shift away from overconsumption of food, fuel, and raw materials and from overreliance on sales of weapons, grains, and sophisticated technology to pay for imports. U.S. production and employment would be much more centered than at any time since World War II on the home market. Such changes in U.S. international political economy would be necessarily accompanied by an erosion of the rationale for interventions in the Third World. For with reduced needs and dependencies abroad must surely come reduced military budgets, alliances, forces in being, official aid programs, bank loans and services, and other fixtures of the old globalism.

A foreign policy that accords with principles such as human rights, basic needs, and nonintervention may provide the key to strengthening real national security. Such a policy may not only offer an irresistible power of example, affecting friend and foe alike in their internal as well as their external behavior; it may also lessen international insecurity, and thus the instability and disorder that have occasioned great-power interventions in others' affairs. The year 2000 may then represent the start of a new era in global cooperation rather than, as it presently does, the year of humanity's final hours.

NOTES

1. The persistence of the military approach to problems of underdevelopment is currently being illustrated in U.S. policy toward El Salvador. A study released in 1982 by the Center for International Policy in Washington, D.C., examined the U.S. aid program and its recipients and concluded: "The El Salvador aid program is a gigantic mismatch between means and ends, and like the Vietnam war itself, will stand as a monument to the futility of trying to solve deep social and political problems through military means." The study pointed out that only 14 percent of U.S. aid would go to the needy; that most of the remainder was being funneled into the Salvadoran Army; and that the major causes of death in El Salvador were "malnutrition and gastrointestinal diseases caused by poor sanitation," and not fighting in the civil war.

2. Richard Barnet makes the same point in *Roots of War* (New York: Atheneum, 1972), p. 74, when he writes that the "real enemies [of the national security manager] are chaos and disorder," especially in the form of a revolution. "For the number one nation any disturbance of existing power relations (even in the enemy's domain) holds certain risks," making a stable, authoritarian government "infinitely preferable to an experimental government, whatever its ideology."

3. Obviously, the best of worlds would have seen U.S. officials implement these two points as soon as the popularity of each revolution became apparent. We offer the speculations merely to illustrate alternative outcomes at only one stage (the last) of each relationship.

4. According to Amnesty International, about 4,500 executions by the Khomeini regime took place between February 1979 and July 1982.

5. See, for example, the works of Falk and Johansen in the bibliography.

6. These documents include the Universal Declaration of Human Rights (1948); the Convention on the Prevention and Punishment of the Crime of Genocide (1948); the International Convention on the Elimination of All Forms of Racial Discrimination (1965); the International Covenant on Economic, Social, and Cultural Rights (1966); and the International Covenant on Civil and Political Rights (1966). The U.S. Senate has not ratified the last four covenants, but they have been ratified by the overwhelming majority of the UN's member states.

7. Most of these proposals are drawn from the document "A Transformation Platform: The Dialogue Begins" of the New World Alliance (Washington, D.C.: 1981), which one of the authors, Melvin Gurtov, helped to draft. Readers should also consult the bibliography at the end of this chapter, especially the works of Falk, Mische, and Brown.

8. One example from the Brandt Commission report: "One-half of one percent of one year's world military expenditure [in 1982, roughly $2.75 billion] would pay for all the farm equipment needed to increase food production and approach self-sufficiency in food-deficit low-income countries by 1980." See Willy Brandt et al., *North-South: A Programme for Survival* (Cambridge: MIT Press, 1980), p. 14.

BIBLIOGRAPHY

Whether writing in defense or in criticism of U.S. foreign policy, students and analysts need to confront their own values and moral principles. They rarely do, and even more rarely do they set them out for their readers. As one stimulus to intellectual honesty, we recommend an article by Professor Glenn D. Paige, "On Values and Science: *The Korean Decision* Reconsidered," *American Political Science Review*, vol. 71 (December 1977), pp. 1603–1609. The article is a self-criticism of the author's book published nine years earlier. From there the reader might wish to pursue one value—nonviolence—in its application to foreign policy by consulting, for example, Gene Sharp, *The Politics of Nonviolent Action* (Boston: Porter Sargent, 1973), and Severyn T. Bruyn and Paula M. Rayman, eds., *Nonviolent Action and Social Change* (New York: Irvington, 1979). Extending outward from these sources is a distinguished literature on morality and politics, beginning with the writings of Reinhold Niebuhr in the 1930s. A more recent stimulating effort is John C. Bennett and Harvey Seifert, *U.S. Foreign Policy and Christian Ethics* (Philadelphia: Westminster, 1977).

Putting morality and human values back into foreign-policy thinking is the mark of recent world-order and globalist-humanist scholarship. See, for instance, Gerald and Patricia Mische, *Toward a Human World Order: Beyond the National Security Straitjacket* (New York: Paulist Press, 1977); Richard A. Falk, *A Study of Future Worlds* (New York: Free Press, 1975); Falk, Samuel S. Kim, and Saul H. Mendlovitz, eds., *Toward a Just World Order*, vol. 1 (Boulder, Colo.: Westview, 1982); Samuel S. Kim, *The Quest for a Just World Order* (Boulder, Colo.: Westview, 1984); Robert C. Johansen, *The National Interest and the Human Interest* (Princeton, N.J.: Princeton University Press, 1980); Harold and Margaret Sprout, *Toward a Politics of the Planet Earth* (New York: D. Van

Nostrand, 1971); Robert A. Isaak, *Individuals and World Politics* (North Scituate, Mass.: Duxbury, 1975); Gustavo Lagos and Horacio H. Godoy, *Revolution of Being: A Latin American View of the Future* (New York: Free Press, 1977); Saul H. Mendlovitz, ed., *On the Creation of a Just World Order: Preferred Worlds for the 1990's* (New York: Free Press, 1975); and Johan Galtung, *The True Worlds: A Transnational Perspective* (New York: Free Press, 1980). Most of these titles are products of the Institute for World Order in New York City, which also publishes *World Policy*, a quarterly magazine on international issues from a world-order values perspective.

Concern about the global consequences of U.S., and other developed states', policies is also reflected in recent writings on the coming crises in food, environmental pollution, population growth, and related areas. The work of Lester R. Brown of the Worldwatch Institute in Washington, D.C., is especially important. His most recent book is *Building a Sustainable Society* (New York: W. W. Norton, 1981). It should be consulted along with the Brandt Commission report (North-South) and the *Global 2000 Report to the President* (Middlesex, England: Penguin Books, 1982) and Richard J. Barnet, *The Lean Years: World Resources and the Politics of Security* (New York: Simon and Schuster, 1980). Each of the problem areas just mentioned also has its more specialized literature. On food politics, for instance, see Susan George, *How the Other Half Dies: The Real Reasons for World Hunger* (Montclair, N.J.: Allanheld, Osmun, 1977); Frances Moore Lappé and Joseph Collins, *Food First: Beyond the Myth of Scarcity* (Boston: Houghton Mifflin, 1977); Dan Morgan, *Merchants of Grain* (New York: Viking, 1979); and the publications of the Institute for Food and Development Policy in San Francisco. Students should also be aware of many recent efforts to explain the global economic and social crisis within a comprehensive theory of underdevelopment, such as dependency, imperialism, and world system. Andre Gunder Frank's *Crisis: In the World Economy* (New York: Holmes & Meier, 1980) is a particularly valuable treatment. The underdevelopment of Latin America has received by far the most scholarly attention in this regard. References to the literature are conveniently available in Ronald H. Chilcote, *Theories of Comparative Politics: The Search for a Paradigm* (Boulder, Colo.: Westview, 1981).

Lastly, due largely to the stress on human rights in the Carter administration, there is a considerable amount of literature concerning U.S. human-rights policy as well as the relationship of human rights to international law. On U.S. policy, see Sandy Vogelgesang, *American Dream, Global Nightmare* (New York: W. W. Norton, 1980); Peter G. Brown and Douglas MacLean, eds., *Human Rights and U.S. Foreign Pol-*

icy (Lexington, Mass.: Lexington, 1979); Donald P. Kommers and Gilburt D. Loescher, eds., *Human Rights and American Foreign Policy* (Notre Dame, Ind.: University of Notre Dame, 1979); and Lars Schoultz, *Human Rights and United States Policy toward Latin America* (Princeton, N.J.: Princeton University Press, 1982). From the standpoint of international law, see Myres S. McDougal, Harold D. Lasswell, and Lung-Chu Chen, *Human Rights and World Public Order* (New Haven, Conn.: Yale University Press, 1980) and Richard A. Falk, Samuel S. Kim, and Saul H. Mendlovitz, eds., *International Law and a Just World Order* (Boulder, Colo.: Westview, 1984).

Index

About the Authors

MELVIN GURTOV is Professor of Political Science at the University of California, Riverside. He is the author of *China under Threat, Southeast Asia in Transition,* and *Southeast Asia under the New Balance of Power,* among others. His articles have appeared in numerous periodicals.

RAY MAGHROORI is Lecturer in Political Science at the University of California, Riverside. He is the author of *Globalism Versus Realism: International Relations' Third Debate* and *The Yom Kippur War: A Case Study in Crisis Decision-Making in American Foreign Policy.*